KU-319-364

LIST OF PLATES

ACKNOWLEDGEMENTS

Our thanks are due as follows for permission to reproduce the plates in this book: Plates 1C, 2A, 5A, 16A, 16B, 17A, 17B, 19A, 19B, 22A, 23B, 24B: Antikvarisk-Topografiska Arkivet, Stockholm; Plates 7A, 8, 9, 10, 11, 12, 20A, 21, 22B: Universitets Oldsaksamling, Oslo; Plates 3A, 3B, 20B: Sophus Bengtsson; Plate 6D: Lennart Larsen, Nationalmuseet, Copenhagen.

CONTENTS

CHAPTER I

BEFORE THE VIKINGS

FROM the convents of northern France in the ninth century rose a prayer which was abundantly justified: 'Save us, O God, from the violence of the Normans.' These Normans (Northmen) were the Vikings from the north, whose ravages included not only private acts of piracy and coastal raids, but also full-scale invasions in quest of new colonies. Their depredations, which began shortly before A.D. 800 and persisted for more than two centuries, spread as far south as the Mediterranean, between Gibraltar and Asia Minor. At the same time they were penetrating eastern Europe and colonizing what is now western Russia. What causes lay behind this Viking expansion? Why were these comparatively small, and hitherto not very powerful, Nordic peoples able to achieve a domination which brought great tracts of England, France, and Ireland under the sway of Danes and Norwegians and extensive areas of western Russia under that of the Swedes? The numerous factors involved in this speculation can be summarized in two main inquiries. First, why was the rest of Europe so relatively weak at the beginning of the ninth century, while its northern peoples were so strong? And, secondly what were the motives and pressures which impelled the northerners to embark upon the long series of far-reaching invasions which historians call the Viking raids?

To answer the first of these fundamental questions we must look at the social, political, and mercantile development of Europe during the centuries preceding the rise of the Vikings. The most notable historian of this period is the late Henri Pirenne, the great Belgian scholar, one of whose basic contentions was that the real dividing-line between Ancient Europe and the Middle Ages does not fall in the period of the Gothic migration (*c.* 500) but three centuries later, in the time of Charlemagne. The break with the past, he maintained, went much deeper in 800 than in 500. Let us examine this argument.

The Late Roman Empire – all the states and countries conquered by Rome up to the fourth century A.D., the whole vast unity called in Late Latin 'Romania' – constituted a unit based upon the Mediterranean, the great Roman sea, that did not separate the lands and peoples but, on the contrary, linked them together. It provided the route 'along which travelled religion, philosophy, and trade'. The cults of Egypt and the Orient were diffused through the Mediterranean; so were the religions of Mithras and of Christ and, eventually, the great monastic orders. From the East it carried cargoes of ivory, silk, spices, papyrus, wine, and oil; and from the West a reciprocal traffic in many commodities, especially slaves. Throughout this immense Empire there was a common currency – the Constantinian gold *solidus* – and its commerce was handled in the main by Syrians and Jews. What happened to this vast and complicated empire when the Gothic invasions of the fourth and fifth centuries occurred? Its political power disintegrated in the western countries, including Italy, which were overrun by Germanic tribes. Though this was a catastrophe in a way, yet these political conquests by no means involved the destruction of the ancient culture of the western half of the Empire.

The invaders were numerically a small minority in the Roman territories which they conquered. It is impossible, of course, to provide exact figures, but historians have offered the following estimates: in Italy the Eastern Goths may have numbered 100,000, and in Spain and southern France there were possibly 100,000 Western Goths. The number of Burgundians in south-east France may have been about

25,000; while the Vandal people who crossed the Straits of Gibraltar to Africa did not in all likelihood exceed 80,000 individuals, or one per cent of the population of that fertile North African province of the Roman Empire which absorbed them. It is not believed that such totals as these were to any extent augmented by reinforcements from the Gothic homelands; on the contrary, they may have been somewhat reduced, especially in Africa, by the trials of the unfamiliar climate. The Germanizing of the conquered territories must have been slight and superficial. It can be said to have been accomplished more deeply only in those regions where Germanic languages have survived, that is to say, along a narrow northern border of the Roman Empire. Elsewhere there are vestigial survivals of a slight Germanic influence to be noted in, for example, the 300 or so Germanic words borrowed in the French, but there is no evidence of any Germanic influence upon the syntax or the phonetics of the Romance languages. What evidently occurred in western Europe and Italy soon after these Gothic migrations was that the invaders were rapidly absorbed, virtually without trace, into the populations they had overrun. Germanic 'types' are difficult to find among the present inhabitants of Italy.

'Romania' survived the Germanic occupation of its western part; the Roman traditions endured, somewhat weakened, and Goths, Vandals, and Burgundians governed their newly acquired territories on the patterns of Late Roman practice. So did the Franks. In the new States the king possessed all power and authority exactly as the Roman emperor had done formerly. Far from obliterating antique customs and practices, the Germans in fact followed exactly the opposite course and confirmed the traditions which the Romans had so long established. It is not difficult to see why. For centuries the Germans had been neighbours of the Roman Empire, and had learned to respect its forms of government and social order. Inheritors now, by force of arms, of the Roman provinces, they sought to copy and perpetuate the Roman procedures of social and political organization. Nevertheless, intellectual life and refinement declined. The only spiritual power to keep its influence was the Church in spite of its being subject, as in the Roman Empire, to the secular authority. The civil servants were still recruited from the laity, not from the clergy. So the new Germanic territories remained under absolutist governments, as the Roman Empire had remained; they were supported by the laity and financed by taxes and duties collected mostly in coined gold. But they were not national states as such, and they continued the pattern of the former Roman satellites and provinces. That pattern was, indeed, renewed when in the sixth century the Byzantine emperor Justinian reconquered large areas of the old West Roman Empire; under him the Mediterranean again became a Roman lake. Later came the Germanic reaction: the Lombards, who were pure Germans, crossed the Alps and descended upon northern Italy where they too were assimilated and Romanized. The Roman pattern was tenacious. Antique forms continued. Corn trade and money currency were still the same throughout the whole of 'Romania'. Life was not fundamentally altered. As before, the Syrians and Jews were the main importers of luxury wares from the Orient. The Mediterranean countries maintained their close contacts with each other – so that, for example, African camels were imported as beasts of burden into Spain and France. Many races lived side by side, as in Narbonne, where, in the year 589, were to be found Goths, Romans, Jews, Syrians, and Greeks. The Germanic rulers in western Europe governed their territories with the aid of administrators trained in the political traditions of Rome, and Roman learning, though somewhat diminished, still survived and left its mark.

It was not until the seventh century that the catastrophe occurred which was really to transform the face of Europe.

This was the Arab invasion which began in 634, two years after the death of Mohammed. The attack was entirely unexpected. The Byzantine Empire seemed to be firmly established in the eastern Mediterranean, and its emperor Heraclius had lately won, at Nineveh (in 627), a decisive victory over its hereditary enemy, Persia. Nothing now seemed to threaten the Eastern Roman Empire, and the Arab Bedouin were certainly not regarded as a danger to Byzantine security. Yet the small fanatical Arab armies, aflame to subjugate the world to Allah, were now to achieve one of the most spectacular conquests in history. In 634 they crossed the Jordan, won Damascus, Jerusalem, and Syria, and within seven years had overrun Egypt and despoiled the Byzantine Empire of its most precious provinces. After these victories by land they ventured upon seaborne invasions, and were checked only by the Byzantine 'secret weapon' known as 'Greek fire' – a species of flame-thrower.

In the next sixty or seventy years the Arabs pushed on from Egypt along the northern shores of Africa until, in 711, they crossed the Straits of Gibraltar and penetrated Spain. Within a year they had mastered the whole peninsula, and pressing farther north into France were finally stopped twenty years later by Charles Martel at Poitiers and thrust back to the Pyrenees. By now the Arab domination extended over Sicily and southern Italy; and there was no fleet in the western Mediterranean to prevent Arab ravages of the coasts of southern France and northern Italy. The western Mediterranean had become an Arab sea.

There are some significant differences between this Arab conquest and the Germanic invasions of two centuries before. Unlike the Germans, the Arabs were not assimilated by the people they conquered; and for this there is one obvious reason. The Arab war was a religious war; Mohammedan monotheism was irreconcilable with other religions, not least with Christianity. The Germanic tribes, on the other hand, had either been Christians themselves, or had practised one of those polytheistic faiths which are tolerant of other religions. The Germans, again, were peoples culturally inferior to those they vanquished, and willing enough to adopt the cultures they encountered in the lands they conquered. But the Arabs were fanatically confident of their faith and their culture, and despised those of the nations they overran. Wherever they went Greek and Latin were displaced by Arabic. If the subjugated peoples wished to survive they had to accept progressively the religion and the language of their Arab rulers.

The country which finally stopped the Arab invasion of Europe was France, and the centre of gravity of western Europe now shifted to France from the Mediterranean countries of the south. The first reason for this transference was the destruction of the former commercial unity of the Mediterranean, which was now split in two. In the eastern half, where the Byzantine Empire still survived, guarded by a powerful fleet, the old mercantile trade could still flourish; but in the western half the Arabs had wiped it out. Thus by the eighth century the goods which used to be imported into Gaul by Syrian and other traders had vanished – papyrus, silk, oil, gold, and spices. In this process of decline the native Gaulish merchant-class also suffered, and its place began to be taken by Jews who possessed an aptitude for acting as commercial intermediaries between the Christian and the Arab worlds. Such were the basic reasons for the political and social eclipse of the Merovingian rulers of France in the seventh century. The distribution of the country's commerce had catastrophic results upon the king's revenues, and the royal power became steadily undermined by that of the landed nobility. These transformations affected southern France rather than the northern provinces. In the south the towns, based on commerce, decayed; whereas in the north, where communities were based on landed property, they were relatively unaffected. And it was in the north of France, accordingly, that there rose the Carolingian dynasty which was to exert so wide a sway in Europe. The son of Charles Martel who had stopped the Arabs at Poitiers was Pepin, and the grandson who began to reign in 768 was the famous Charlemagne. (The Pepins, incidentally, sprang from Belgian stock in the neighbourhood of Liège, and the surname Pepinster still survives in those parts.)

Profound differences are to be observed in the condition of France if we compare the Carolingian rule of the eighth and ninth centuries with the preceding rule of the Merovingians in the sixth and seventh. An agricultural economy has superseded the former mercantile trade; silver has replaced gold currency; the power of the Church is in the ascendant. Latin as a language of daily use is now dead, displaced by peasant dialects, and pure Latin survives only within the Church, as the language of ritual or as the speech of the learned, clerical classes (this, oddly enough, as a result of missionary activities from Anglo-Saxon England). The cursive penmanship which used to be the fashion has been replaced by an elegant modish minuscule which was to become the basis for the writing of Europe in the Middle Ages. The so-called Carolingian Renaissance with its concentration on the language and literature of Greece and Rome was limited to scholars and did not penetrate to any popular level.

This analysis of the impact of the Arabs upon the Merovingian and Carolingian dynasties is set out by Henri Pirenne in his posthumous work *Mohammed and Charlemagne,* and it is still vigorously discussed by historians. Not everything he claims can be accepted as, for instance, when he dates the beginning of the decline of the Merovingians at a time, around 640, when the first Arabic disruption of Mediterranean trade had hardly begun. But on the whole his interpretation is sound. His principal contention is that there could have been 'no Charlemagne without Mohammed'; that the development of the Carolingian empire emerged essentially from the preceding expansion of the Arabs in western Europe. It was the impulse of the Arab drive which, after all, produced an agrarian and militarily-powerful France oriented, now, towards the north.

These circumstances, it may be said, could hardly favour Viking attacks from the north at the beginning of the ninth century. Nor indeed did they. Warned of a danger from that quarter by sporadic attacks which took place around 790 on England, Scotland, Ireland, and, to some small extent France, Charlemagne fortified his northern coasts with a chain of watch-towers, beacons, and garrisons. The result was that during his reign, despite very strained relations between France and Denmark, his country was preserved from Viking devastation. The Danish king Godfred was an aggressive character, and when Charlemagne subdued north-west Germany and overran the Saxons as far as the Elbe, the territories of the two kings came perilously close to each other; so close indeed that Godfred was preparing for war against Charlemagne. But he died in 810; peace was maintained, and the Nordic pirates continued to respect the well-defended shores of the redoubtable Gaulish emperor.

When, however, in 814 Charlemagne died, and was succeeded by his son, Louis the Pious, the vast empire began to disintegrate. The strength of France declined, its coastal defences in the north were neglected, and the Vikings seized their opportunity. Shortly after 830 France became the scene, for the rest of the century, of violent and destructive assaults, always from the sea and nearly always launched from Denmark.

We must now consider another relevant factor in the rise of the Vikings – the condition of England in the eighth century. The country was divided into many minor kingdoms: Mercia, Wessex, Essex, Kent, East Anglia, North-

umbria. The most powerful of the English kings was Offa
– *rex Anglorum* – who ruled Mercia, and by the time of his
death in 796 dominated directly or indirectly the whole of
southern England. He was, indeed, the first English ruler to
carry any political weight abroad. He was on comparatively
good terms with Charlemagne, and was a man of such strong
character and personality that, had he lived longer, he might
well have proved a bulwark against the Viking assaults on
England. For a generation after Offa's death, southern England
was torn by dissensions until Egbert of Wessex in 825 established a very considerable sway over Mercia and south-east
England. But his son and successor Ethelwulf proved by no
means adequate to keep the Vikings out. Elsewhere, too, in
Northumbria and Scotland, there was no power sufficient to
cope with the Nordic attacks.

Ireland, a primitive and divided country, was another easy
victim, as the Norwegian invasion proved shortly after 800.
The Irish certainly resisted, and their annals from 807 onwards
are full of battles with the Norwegians – battles, indeed,
which, if we are to believe the story-tellers, the Irish frequently won! For all that, the Irish failed to keep the Vikings
out, and after a generation of battles the Norwegians were
firmly settled in many places in the west and the east of the
island.

Before this sketch of the background of the Viking invasions is concluded one factor must be emphasized which sub-
stantially accounts for their success. The Viking assaults on
Europe were always sea-borne. The Vikings were skilful
navigators, more confident on the sea than the Anglo-Saxons
and the French, and they had better vessels. They were not
exceptionally redoubtable warriors: they were, indeed, often
defeated in actual battle. But as marine architects they were
outstanding. They built fleets of fast, roomy, and sea-worthy
ships, and handled them supremely well. It was this mastery
of ships, unexcelled over most of Europe, which gave them

such decisive advantages in their descents upon so many coasts. The development of these Nordic ships can be traced a good way back. Some of the earliest archaeological discoveries show a large open rowing-boat, without mast or sail, and with a very rudimentary keel – such as the boat found at Nydam in south Jutland, Denmark. Archaeological finds are, of course, fortuitous, and a solitary boat does not prove that such vessels were the rule. But other finds, such as the carved and painted tombstones in Gotland, illustrate the evolution of the sail during the sixth and eighth centuries – from a bit of rag to the swelling sails of the Viking vessels – and the corresponding development of the keel.

It is strange that the sail should have taken so long to appear in the north, for it had been known from time immemorial by the Romans and Greeks in the Mediterranean. From literary sources we know also that it appeared in Holland in the first century A.D., for Tacitus tells of the Batavian chief, Civilis, who during a review of his fleet in the year 70 copied the Roman custom by letting his men use their coloured cloaks as sails. Caesar, indeed, records that the Veneti, the seafaring tribe of the French Atlantic coast, used sails of heavy leather. Sidonius Apollinaris, bishop of Clermont in 470, describes the Saxons returning home 'with swelling sails'. It seems strange, then, that sails took so long to reach the Viking countries; stranger still that they took so long to reach England. As late as 560 the Byzantine author Procopius writes of the English: 'These barbarians do not use the sail either, but depend wholly on oars' – a fact proved by the royal ship discovered at Sutton Hoo in East Anglia, dating from the mid seventh century, which had neither mast nor sail.

It can, then, truly be said that the Anglo-Saxons, the French, and the Irish could not compete with the Nordics in their management of ships, and there is no record of nautical counter-attacks upon the Viking fleets. This supremacy at sea adequately explains why the Vikings were able to harry and conquer such large areas of western Europe. But how can one account for their corresponding penetration of eastern Europe, which was wholly a land operation affording them no scope whatever for their mastery of ships and the sea?

In the eighth century the difference between Denmark and Norway on the one hand and Sweden on the other was that the latter was already an organized and unified country, strong enough to engage in colonial expansion beyond its frontiers. These extensions of its territory were partly into Latvia and Estonia and partly farther eastwards, towards the southern shores of Lake Ladoga, and the bases for these operations were Uppland (Svealand) and the island of Gotland in the middle of the Baltic. If such drives as these are to be regarded as Viking raids, then clearly the Swedish Vikings were making their mark on Europe well before the Danish and Norwegian Vikings. Here is one piece of evidence. Shortly before the Second World War there were discovered near the little town of Grobin (not far from Liepaja or Libau) on the Latvian coast, some prehistoric graves containing objects from Gotland which were ascribed to an older period than that of the Vikings. Swedish and Latvian archaeologists, continuing excavations on the site, unearthed an extensive burial-place containing at least one thousand graves, whose shape and contents unquestionably pointed to eighth-century Gotland. Soon afterwards another graveyard was found, almost as big as the first, but this time the contents undeniably indicated a central Swedish and not a Gotlandic origin. Both places had cremation graves, but there were two conclusive differences: in the second graveyard each grave was covered with a mound; and this second one, moreover, was a strictly military one, whereas in the first there were found many graves of women and more jewellery than weapons, factors suggesting that this was a civil cemetery established in peaceable conditions. These discoveries appeared to confirm existing suppositions about political conditions in Sweden in the period before the Viking raids: the Gotlanders were peaceful traders; the Swedes were men of war. The Grobin discoveries suggest that a Swedish military garrison was stationed there and that the Gotlanders on the other hand were settled in Grobin as peaceful traders.

If we turn now from archaeological to literary evidence we find in Ansgar's biography, written in 870 by Rimbert, Ansgar's disciple and his successor as Archbishop of Bremen, a reference to the fact that the people of Courland, which we now know as Latvia, had been attacked by both the Swedes and the Danes, and that the Swedish king Olaf at the head of a large army attacked and burned a town called Seeburg defended by no less than seven thousand warriors. On this evidence the Swedish archaeologist, Birger Nerman, who conducted the excavations at Grobin, has posed the question whether the two cemeteries could in fact have belonged to this old Seeburg, or perhaps more likely, to the site of a new garrison town built by the Swedes after the destruction of Seeburg. Even if we cannot in this case reconcile the literary and the archaeological clues, there is no lack of evidence that Swedish expansion to the east had begun well before the time of the Vikings proper. We shall resume our examination of the significance of these movements towards Russia later: meanwhile, let us take a look at what was happening in south-east Europe and in western Asia.

In these areas two powers were established in the eighth century, both so strong and both so remote from Scandinavia as to exclude any likelihood of clashes with the Vikings. The first of these, based on Constantinople, was the Byzantine Empire, the inheritor of the old eastern Roman Empire; the second, relatively new one, was the Arab Caliphate with its capital at Baghdad. The Byzantine sphere of interest was northerly, along the shores of the Black Sea and into the plains of the Ukraine. The Arabs, who had already subdued Persia in the seventh century, were pressing, also in a northerly direction, towards the south and west Siberian steppes (the ancient Scythia). During the eighth century these regions were peopled by Turkish nomads, and between them and the Byzantines there extended north of the Caspian the vast independent khaganate of the Khazars with its capital Itil in the Volga delta (their ruler bore the Avar-Turkish title 'khagan'). These Khazars closed the broad gap between the southern slope of the Urals and the north coast of the Caspian and they sealed off the Turkish nomads from spreading west, providing a peaceful frontier with the Byzantines from the Caucasus to the Crimea. The Khazars also checked the movement northwards into Russia of the Turkish Bulgars, who thereupon forked in two separate directions – one moving into the Balkans, the other settling on the Volga bend in their own khaganate with its capital at Bulgar. As time went on these two khaganates, that of the Khazars in the south and that of the Bulgars in the north, dominated and organized the great trade along the Volga. Little is known of the condition of central and western Russia at this time; the probability is that, as in the other Slav territories right up to the Elbe, these regions were divided among loosely related tribes lacking any political homogeneity, while the vast impenetrable forests blocked any significant movement of peoples or cultures.

Such, then, in general terms, is the layout of Europe and western Asia in the period preceding the Viking advance. Of the three great powers of the time, France was strong enough to keep off the fierce Northmen; while the Byzantines and the Arabs were too remote to become involved with them. But beyond the dominions of these three powers there was widespread weakness. For the condition of the three northern countries in this same pre-Viking period of the seventh and eight centuries literary evidence is lacking, and we must therefore look to archaeology to provide or suggest the facts.

Sweden must be reckoned the most advanced of the three northern countries at this time, as is attested by many splendid finds in Uppland and Gotland. The style and taste of these objects is impressive and bears the marks of the influence of southern Germany, whence there must have been a cultural penetration via the Baltic, unhindered apparently by the Slav-occupied regions of northern Germany. This coincides with the Nordic myths telling us about an ancient and powerful kingdom in Uppland. Of the northern monarchies the Swedish is certainly the oldest. The eighth-century expansion, already mentioned, from central Sweden to the Baltic border countries and Lake Ladoga also suggests a strong ruling power in Sweden at that time. From Uppland there can be traced clear links both to Finland and to Norway. Archaeological finds, for example, reveal Swedish-Norwegian cross-connexions along a trade route through Jæmtland to Trøndelag; and, apart from that, there was in the eighth century a direct route by sea from Norway to Merovingian France. Norway in general gives the impression of having a virile and adventurous population at that time, although doubtless divided into many tribes and lacking a unified leadership.

For Denmark the archaeological evidence is scanty. There are traces of a cultural unity in its eastward parts – Zeeland, Scania, Bornholm – through weapons and arts. One must observe caution, however, in these matters. It is of course reasonable to base positive conclusions upon copious archaeological material; but it is unwise to reach negative conclusions merely upon the absence of such material. Finds are sometimes lacking not because the country or region concerned was poor or weak or primitive, but simply because of local burial laws which forbade the placing of objects or presents in graves; or there was such peace and prosperity as to obviate any need to hide possessions in the earth. Another reason for the lack of archaeological finds is, of course, that modern villages and towns may be built over ancient settlements. In short, scarcity of archaeological evidence is not in itself a proof of backwardness or poverty. Indeed, when the first gleams of light fall upon Denmark's history (*c*. 800), the figure we encounter is that of King Godfred, a warrior powerful enough to be about to take up arms against the redoubtable emperor Charlemagne. This suggests a strong Denmark; and although we do not know which districts of the country Godfred governed, a monarchy was evidently already in being at that time.

So far we have been considering the relative strengths and weaknesses within Europe which provided the external and political incentives of the Viking raids. We now pass to an examination of the internal causes and pressures which drove the Nordic peoples forth on their innumerable and widespread Viking raids for more than 200 years. Many such internal pressures have been suggested or identified by historians and archaeologists:

Over-population. This was the thesis developed by Johannes Steenstrup. It is given colour, to some extent, by the terms in which the Viking armies were described in contemporary writings – where they are compared to swarms of grasshoppers, masses of storm-clouds, endless ocean waves, and so on, and when all allowance is made for poetic licence there seems to be more than a grain of truth in these comparisons. The old narratives, again, refer to the thousands lost in battle by the Vikings. The reason advanced for this over-population of the northern countries is the existence of widespread polygamy. The Northmen were virile creatures who prided themselves on the number of sons they could produce, and it was customary among them to have concubines as well as wives. Steenstrup also cites as evidence of over-population the northern practice, among the lower classes especially, of killing off unwanted infants by exposure. Another tradition asserts that it was their custom to ordain, from time to time, the compulsory exile of large groups of young men. This is doubtful evidence, but on the other hand the fact that the inheritance passed to the eldest son of a family would certainly produce a surplus of young men disposed to seek their fortunes elsewhere. On the whole it is reasonable to conclude that the Viking countries were indeed over-populated, and that this condition was at least a contributory factor to their invasions of Europe.

Internal Dissensions. The Nordic laws of inheritance were such that whenever an earl or other chieftain secured the succession there were liable to be discontented 'pretenders' to the title. These might well decide to leave the country temporarily and seek in raids abroad the resources to return and press their claims. But although such episodes were doubtless common enough, they cannot be regarded as a serious factor in touching-off these widespread Viking invasions.

Emigrations have frequently occurred in history because of the pressure of social or religious differences. There is no sign of such antagonisms having influenced the Viking break-out.

Foreign Pressure. This too, is a factor which has no application in this case. Mass migrations in history have often been the result of the hostility displayed by neighbouring countries, but no such danger threatened the northern peoples at this time.

Climatic Disasters. A frequent cause of migration in human history has been the failure of crops, and consequent famine, caused by a deterioration in climatic conditions. This was the compulsion which instigated the frequent and sustained attacks of Asiatic nomads against their neighbours; it was probably a factor, too, in the similar migrations of the Huns in Europe, and in the Cimbric raid from Jutland in the time of the Roman Republic (close of second century B.C.). Scandinavian geologists have been able to trace, through their researches in the peat-bogs, the traces of many variations of climate, but no such discoveries relate to the early ninth century. At this point, indeed, we may accept the fact that the Viking raids were in no sense whatever migratory movements. The Vikings had every intention of coming back home from their depredations laden with loot and glory.

The Quest for Trade. Here, undoubtedly, is a major factor in accounting for the Viking raids, perhaps the crucial one. As we noted earlier in this chapter, when the Arab invasion disrupted the trade of the western Mediterranean and southern France there was a corresponding growth of the mercantile operations of northern France. The Rhine became a great thoroughfare and new trading opportunities developed on the shores of the North Sea, especially for the commercially-minded Frisians who lived mainly in what is now Holland. As early as the eighth century Frisian commerce was well developed, and when Charles Martel acquired Friesland in 734 he also acquired the commercial skill and experience of the Frisians to give a new lease of life to French commercial expansion in the North Sea.

So far it had not been easy for Denmark, especially southern Denmark, to participate in North Sea commerce. The Elbe was not a Nordic river, and there was a dearth of good harbours on the east coast of Jutland; to get from the North Sea to the Baltic vessels had to round the dangerous northerly point of Jutland, Skagen. But soon after 800 the situation changed. The French emperor by subduing the Saxons had extended his northern frontier as far as the Elbe, and to resist any further expansion the Danish king Godfred built a powerful earthwork, the 'Danevirke' (Dane's work). This barrier not only served to protect his kingdom from attacks from the south, but also to shelter a new overland trade route, across the south of Jutland from the Eider in the west to the Schlei in the east, as a substitute for the long and perilous sea passage round Skagen mentioned above. This new commercial highway from the North Sea to the Baltic, thus protected by the Danevirke, offered attractive prospects of wealth and power for the Danes. Such opportunities for getting command of trade routes, ardently exploited as they were by the northern countries, also stimulated, incidentally, an activity which, in ancient times, invariably accompanied the development of trade – that is to say, piracy; and wherever seas and coasts were not defended, the Viking pirates preyed upon commerce. The expansion of trade and the lure of piracy were undoubtedly two of the most considerable factors behind the Viking raids.

But in appraising these factors there is one which lies outside mercantile considerations, and that is the characteristic Nordic way of life. This was a compound of daring, adventurousness, and belligerence. The Vikings were possessed by a desire to excel in battle, by a thirst for glory and a scorn for death. These qualities of heroism and virility, combined with their mercantile skills, made them a powerful and dangerous race. The early monastic historians emphasized in their records of the Vikings the cunning and cruelty of this warlike people; the Sagas, on the other hand, added other attributes to the picture, such as the generosity, the straightforwardness, and the discipline of these famous warriors. But the Vikings were not all alike, and every picture of them is different, according to which of these contrasting characteristics is emphasized. One thing, however, most of them had: a daring resoluteness. And the epoch of the Vikings was the greatest period in the history of the north.

CHAPTER 2

THE VIKING RAIDS

THE raids of the Vikings were committed on a massive and extensive scale, and embraced the whole of Europe: in the east they thrust down the great rivers of Russia to the Caspian and the Black Sea, and in the west along the Atlantic coasts, past Arab Spain, through the Straits of Gibraltar and on into the distant Mediterranean. They reached out across the wild Atlantic to the Faroe Islands, Iceland, Greenland, and even to America. The three Scandinavian countries from which the invasions were made differed from each other in their geography and consequently in their political spheres of interest.

The very names of the three countries are clues to their ancient history. The name Sweden is in Swedish 'Sverige', a derivation from 'Svearike' meaning the kingdom of the Svees. The word *rike* meant the territory ruled by a king, and the name is a reminder of the point made in the last chapter (p. 22) that the monarchy in Sweden was already an institution long before the Viking period. Denmark means the *marc* of the Danes, *marc* being a word for an uninhabited frontier region. The *marc* in this case must have been the Jutish peninsula, the waste land south of the Danevirke which separated the Danes from the Saxons and the Slavs. Gradually the name of this particular locality, *Danernes Mark,* or Denmark, came to be applied to the whole country, and this must have occurred before the year 900, for in one of King Alfred's writings, the foreword to Orosius's *History of the World*, there is found for the first time a reference to Denmark (Denemearcan). That the name of a region or province should eventually be applied to a whole country is nothing singular:

the French name for Germany, 'Allemagne', is taken from the name of a province (that of the Alemans) on the Upper Rhine. And when we remember how much of Danish history is bound up, through the centuries, with the disputed frontier territory of south Slesvig, the origin of the name Denmark has an obvious significance.

The name Norway – 'Norge' in Norwegian – has a mercantile meaning: it is 'the North Way', the long maritime route along its extensive coasts, described in the ninth century foreword of King Alfred mentioned above, which ranged as far as the White Sea to handle the trade in skins, furs, and walrus teeth. The name of this important trade route became that of the country along whose shores it ran. In Viking times the country was sometimes called Nordmannaland, the land of the Normans or Northmen, but the name which prevailed was the one which signified the country's position as a great trade route in the north.

An important geographical factor determined the part each of the three Scandinavian countries played in the Viking raids. Right down the middle of the Scandinavian peninsula there stretches a great mountain range, Kolen (the Keel), the structural spine of the country, a rough and barren region which divides the peninsula in two. The face of Norway looks west, towards the oceans and islands. The Norwegians were the people who took the lead in venturing upon the vast and stormy Atlantic with no knowledge of what they might find in its waters. Norway's sphere of interest beyond its own shores was a double one. The first part comprised the islands north of Scotland (which were inhabited by Norwegians when the Viking period began) and stretched on to the Isle of Man and Ireland and, indeed, to the English coastal areas bordering the Irish Sea – which could well at that time have been called the Norwegian Sea. From the north-west of England their raids penetrated deep, and indeed rivalled those of the Danes; and both Norwegians and Danes thrust farther south into France and to the Mediterranean. The second direction in which Norway's sphere of interest developed was to the north – to the Faroe Islands, Iceland, and Greenland – and the initiative in this development came from King Harald Fairhair, who at the end of the ninth century brought most of Norway within his domains and so forced many Norwegian free peasants to emigrate. Their raids into the Atlantic were not undertaken in search of plunder, but must be regarded as deliberate and daring endeavours in colonization.

Sweden faces east. Its eastward expansion across the Baltic was well advanced in the early eighth century, and in a later chapter we shall see how its mercantile pressure continued in a great penetration through Russia to the south. As far as the Baltic was concerned, however, the Swedes and the Danes had an equal interest.

South of the Scandinavian peninsula lies Denmark, a land made up of Jutland and numerous islands. Jutland, of course, is physically joined to the central European continent, but in the Viking period the barren lands of south Slesvig separated Denmark proper from its southerly neighbours – the Saxons towards the south-west and the Slavs to the south-east. Apart from this natural barrier there was another determining factor, namely, that the Vikings everywhere preferred sea-borne journeys to land operations. For that reason above all the expansion of the Danes did not occur in the southerly landward direction, but towards the south-west, along the Frisian and French coasts, and due west to England. This penetration was succeeded by raids farther still to the south-west which brought them finally, along with the Norwegians and Swedes, into the Mediterranean itself.

The Viking raids were inspired by several motives. On that account a mere chronological account of them would produce an obscure and contradictory pattern, and an attempt must therefore be made to classify them according to their varying motives and objectives. The Swedish scholar, Fritz Askeberg, has proposed a fourfold classification:

    (1) Pirate raids conducted by individuals
    (2) Political expeditions
    (3) Colonizing ventures
    (4) Commercial penetration

Such a division, as Askeberg himself points out, cannot be universally applicable, and many of the raids doubtless proceeded from mixed motives. But so long as it is remembered that this classification is in no sense a chronological one it serves to put the Viking period into perspective.

PIRATE RAIDS CONDUCTED BY INDIVIDUALS

The first category, that of private-enterprise piracy, is the least interesting, although it is probably the one which first comes to mind in remembering the more popular and conventional tales about the Vikings. One Norwegian historian has claimed that the pirate raids were in part genuine feats of exploration as well, and that the plunder acquired was no more than legitimate foraging, but this view comes very near to the naïve. Private raids were abundant throughout the Viking period, and a few typical ones deserve mention.

The oldest of those which can be authenticated is the descent, in 793, upon Lindisfarne, the Holy Island, which lies off the northerly shore of Northumbria, not far from the Scottish border. It was a sister-foundation of Iona in the Hebrides, and was widely celebrated in England as a place of pilgrimage. The *Anglo-Saxon Chronicle* tells how terrifying omens had been witnessed in 793 – tempests and fiery dragons among them – succeeded by a famine; and shortly after these dolorous events, in June of that year, the heathen band had fallen upon the island community and had pillaged God's house there. These plunderers were Norwegians and they slaughtered the monks and nuns and laid the place waste. Alcuin, the famous Northumbrian priest and scholar who was at the time in the service of Charlemagne in France, wrote a letter to King Ethelred of Northumbria declaring that the murderous raid was God's punishment for the sins of Northumbria. He found further ominous portents in the rumour that drops of blood had been seen to fall from the roof of St Peter's Church in York. He lamented that one of Christianity's noblest shrines in England should have been desecrated by the heathen and implored God to save his fatherland. Such was the resounding and bloody deed which served as a prelude to Viking aggression in the west.

While working on the restoration of Lindisfarne monastery, English archaeologists found a curious carved stone dating, apparently, from soon after the sack of the monastery, and illustrating the melancholy event. On one side of the stone were carved various symbols of Christianity – the Cross, the sun and the moon, God's hands, and worshippers at prayer. On the other hand were depicted the violators of the shrine dressed outlandishly in rough jerkins and narrow trousers, swinging their swords and battle-axes as they advanced to destruction. This Lindisfarne stone is a poignant monument, fashioned perhaps by some Anglo-Saxon monk who witnessed this early example of Viking pillage.

Towards the end of the eighth century and during the early years of the ninth, many similar Norwegian robber raids took place in northern England, Scotland, and Ireland. Some of these forays known from literary sources seem indeed to have been launched from what is now Scottish soil – from Caithness and the Shetlands, the Orkneys, and the Hebrides. There is archaeological evidence for the belief that, when the Viking raids began, these islands were already, to some extent, occupied by Norwegians who had found them virtually uninhabited. They were conveniently situated as bases for raids down either side of Scotland, and records of several such assaults exist in the chronicles. In 794, for example, there was an attack on the Wearmouth monastery (Sunderland) where, incidentally, the Vikings ran into a disastrous storm which cost them a heavy loss of life. In 795 there were descents upon St Columba's monastery at Iona and upon the little Irish island of Reerhu (Lambay). During the same year the Norwegians fell upon the coast of Wales; in 797 they plundered Kintyre in Scotland and the shrine of St Patrick on the Isle of Man. In 802 and 806 they revisited Iona and laid it waste again. Such were the first pirate raids, which reached their peak in the ninth century. They were mainly carried out by lesser chieftains rather than kings and earls, who had bigger objectives in mind. The Norwegians began them, but the Danes and Swedes followed suit, and these minor pirate raids continued throughout the whole Viking period.

POLITICAL EXPEDITIONS

Perhaps the most significant of the second category of Viking raids, those inspired by political motives, were those made by the expeditionary forces which King Godfred of Denmark conducted in the beginning of the ninth century. These were directed south-eastwards against the Slavs of the Baltic (the Wends and the Obotrites). He simply moved a Slavic town (Reric) from its site, presumably in Mecklenburg, to the Danish province of Slesvig and turned south-west against the Frisian territories at that time ruled by Charlemagne. Shortly before his death in 810, he launched a violent attack on Friesland from a fleet of 200 vessels, smashed the coastal defence forces, and occupied the country, imposing upon it a tribute of 200 pounds of silver. This was no pirate raid; it was calculated and sudden warfare aimed at the conquest of territories which were politically and commercially valuable to King Godfred. If it was not a pirate foray it was equally not a colonizing venture, although the boundary between conquest and colonization is not an easy one to determine.

COLONIZING VENTURES

The biggest Viking raids upon the west were, however, undoubtedly motivated by a colonizing impulse. They occurred in the latter half of the ninth century and the beginning of the tenth, and were resumed again in the early part of the eleventh. Although they were predominantly Danish and Norwegian, the Swedes also participated, and large parts of northern France, England, and Ireland were occupied. The invasions were led not by heads of states but by men of high rank, and these leaders often held equal powers, with no one supreme commander. The Vikings insisted on this equality; when the Franks on the river Eure asked the Vikings who was their leader they answered in the famous words 'We are all equals'. Nevertheless, they managed to maintain strict discipline among their forces, especially during the later years of the Viking period. It was invasions of this kind which penetrated to Hamburg and to Paris; which, under the sons of Lodbrog, attacked England and, under Rollo, northern France, while Norwegian Vikings attacked Ireland. The usual method followed in these invasions was for the armies to build themselves up on the beaches during the winter, and to march inland when spring arrived. In the end they succeeded in colonization and in forming new states. Within this category of colonizing ventures must be included the Norwegian expeditions, already mentioned, into the Atlantic to such places as the Faroes, Iceland, and Greenland which were so little inhabited as to call for no force of arms in their settlement by the colonizers.

COMMERCIAL PENETRATION

The fourth and final category of Viking expansion comprises journeys in search of new trading opportunities. These occurred most extensively in the east, where the Swedes energetically pursued commercial aims. The mercantile drive thus maintained by the Vikings through three hundred years, and the political significance of their activities during the same period, will be considered more closely in a later chapter.

ORIGIN OF THE WORD 'VIKING'

This is a convenient point at which to inquire into the meaning of the name 'Viking'. It is reasonable to suppose – although the evidence is not conclusive – that the word is Nordic in origin. In non-Nordic chronicles of the period it is rarely found; the Frankish chronicles used the word *Normanin*, the Anglo-Saxons called them *Dani* (Danes), and from their contexts it is clear that these two words were often employed for all Northmen, whether Danes or Norwegians. In German chronicles they are called *Ascomanni*, that is to say 'Ashmen', presumably because their ships were made from the ash-tree. In Irish sources they appear as *Gall* or *Lochlannach*, words which mean, respectively, 'stranger' and 'northerner'. To the latter there was sometimes added 'white' (for Norwegians) and 'black' for Danes, adjectives which may signify the predominant colours of their shields. In Byzantine and Arabic narratives the Swedish Viking is called *rus*, a word borrowed from the Slavs, who in turn had taken it from the Finns, whose name for Sweden was *Ruotsi*. According to Stender-Petersen *Ruotsi* originally meant 'rowers'. The same authority declares that the word *væring* or *vareg* given to Nordic warriors in Greek sources originally bore the meaning of 'trading agent'. In Spain the Vikings were known by the Arabic name of *Madjus* or barbarian wizards.

34

As to 'Viking' itself, Adam of Bremen, the German monk historian, writing about 1075, testifies that the word was used by the Danes. He speaks of 'the pirates whom the Danes call Vikings but we Germans call Ashmen'. But where did it originate? Is it Nordic or non-Nordic? If the former, then it may spring either from *vig,* which means battle, or *vik,* which means 'creek', 'inlet', 'fiord', or 'bay'. The first is plausible enough so far as associations are concerned, but scholars are inclined to reject it, on phonetic grounds. The derivation from *vik* (creek), on the other hand, has found much support. A Viking, on this basis, was a pirate who lay hidden in a fiord, creek, or bay, waiting to pounce upon passing vessels. We shall return later to this suggested derivation. Another suggestion is that the word is derived from the Norwegian *Viken,* meaning men from Vik, the region round Oslo. But this theory is unacceptable, for in the chronicles the inhabitants of this area are called *Vikverjar* or *Vestfalding* (the latter term, meaning people from Vestfold, is used in the French narrative of the Viking attack on Nantes in 843).

If, on the other hand, the word Viking is non-Nordic, it could obviously be related to the Anglo-Saxon word for a camp – *wic* (cf. Latin *vicus*). The Vikings, on this basis, were 'the campfolk' to the Anglo-Saxons. This derivation found support from the celebrated Norwegian etymologist, Sophus Bugge, and it is a fact that the word existed in Anglo-Saxon long before the time of the Vikings. The Swedish scholar, Wadstein, suggests a variant. According to him the word does in fact come from the Latin *vicus,* but in the sense of 'town' or 'settlement' rather than 'camp'. The Vikings, on this interpretation, were the 'town-dwellers', and as the inhabitants of the oldest towns were mostly seaborne traders who bargained with weapons as readily as with money, the appellation 'town-dweller' carried the ironical connotation of 'pirate'. Wadstein considered that the town of Slesvig provided an example and, indeed, perhaps the origin of this meaning: a 'Sles-viking', he suggested, would be a typical Baltic pirate from that town.

The Danish authority, Johannes Steenstrup, differed sharply from both Bugge and Wadstein. He claimed that the word is too seldom used in the Anglo-Saxon chronicles for it to have an Anglo-Saxon origin. It must be Nordic, he concluded. He rebutted Wadstein, incidentally, by pointing out that, despite the Slesvig example, the inhabitants of many towns elsewhere whose names ended in *vic* were never known as Vikings. There are other speculations on the question. It has been suggested that the word is related to *vige*, meaning 'to escape' and therefore connotating a pirate who escapes with his loot; or that it has some association with the noun *vikan*, a seal, and that Vikings were so called because they were dexterous seal-hunters. But these notions have found little support.

A theory which has won considerable acceptance – as, for example, from the scholar Elias Wessén of Sweden – is the one previously mentioned, which derives the word from *vik*, a creek or inlet, the natural lurking-place for nautical raiders. A viking was a vik-man, as sometimes a fiord-man was called a fiording. Fritz Askeberg, on the other hand, points out that all sailors spend much time hanging about in bays and estuaries, waiting for a wind, whereas Viking expeditions were usually launched from islands. Thus the island of Jeufosse, in the river Seine, was for years the headquarters of Viking attacks upon Paris – as were, a little later, a couple of islands near Rouen, nowadays a part of the mainland but still called Le Houlme (the islet). At the mouth of the Loire lies the island of Noirmoutier, famous for wine and salt: here the Vikings in 834 installed themselves so solidly that the islanders left and the Vikings settled down and made it a base for their excursions into the hinterland of the Loire. (These Vikings, by the way, were the '*Vestfalding*' mentioned above.) Askeberg gives other examples to show that the Vikings launched their attacks from islands rather than estuaries: the island of Île de Croix, off southern Brittany, where the remains of a Viking Norwegian ship were found; the island of Camargue where the Vikings had a permanent camp in 860; the island of Walcheren in the mouth of the Schelde, occupied by the Danish chieftains Harald and Rorik; Thanet and Sheppey in the Thames, which served as winter quarters in the year 850 during the Danish invasion of England. If the Nordic pirates, says Askeberg, were called after the terrain they favoured in mounting their attacks, they would be called *Øinger* (islanders) and not Vikings.

Askeberg's own hypothesis is an interesting one. According to him the male noun 'viking' was used only in western Scandinavia. (In eastern Scandinavia the word was *væring*.) It was not used only to denote northerners, but had a general application and meant 'sea-warriors who go on a long journey from their homestead'. The female noun, incidentally, 'viking', signified 'a nautical raid to distant shores'. Both these nouns, it will be observed, can refer only to those Viking raids which fall into the first two categories mentioned on p. 35.

If the *vik* in 'Viking' does not derive from *vik*, a creek or bay, then Askeberg says that it comes from the verb *vikja*, 'to turn aside, to deviate', and its basic meaning is 'a receding area', a corner or nook. *Land vikr*, for example, means 'the land recedes' or 'curves back'. The female noun 'viking', therefore, signifies a deviation or a detour or an absence; the male noun 'viking' denotes 'he who makes a detour, who absents himself from home'. This shrewd derivation, which fits so well the conception of Vikings as men who made long journeys from home, has not met with wide approval, but it nevertheless seems to me to merit consideration.

EARLY RECORDS

There is comparatively little mention, in the old literature, of the northern peoples of the Viking period. But three of these scant references are important. The first is Alfred the Great's account, at the end of the ninth century, of trade-routes and sailing-courses in the North Sea and the Baltic. The second is an account of a visit to the town of Hedeby, in the middle of the tenth century, by an Arab traveller, Al-Tartûshî. The third is a description, by the monk-historian Adam of Bremen, of the geography and people of the Nordic countries around 1075 and, especially, of the town of Birka, and the shrine of Gamla Uppsala. These three sources of information deserve some scrutiny.

Alfred the Great, king of Wessex, the main adversary of the Vikings in England, was a cultivated man who earnestly desired to enlighten his people. He took it upon himself to translate into Anglo-Saxon the ancient history of the world written about 400 by the Spanish monk, Orosius, and to supplement this by an account of contemporary knowledge about the lands and people of northern and central Europe. For this account he employed some primary sources – that is to say, he drew upon the experiences and opinions of travellers in those lands. As far as the north was concerned, he set down conversations he had had, for instance with the Norwegian Ottar from Helgeland, about north Norwegian trade and manufacture and about the trade-routes south to Skiringsal (on the west of the Oslo fiord) and to Hedeby. He recorded, too, what he heard from the Anglo-Saxon Wulfstan of a journey he had made eastward from Hedeby into the Baltic to the town of Truso at the mouth of the Vistula river. Such contemporary narratives are evidently of great importance.

Ottar tells King Alfred of his home in the remote north, of his reindeer herds, of the tribute he gathers from the Finns – walrus-teeth, bearskins, and birds' feathers – of the long journey he has made round the North Cape to the White Sea. The walrus, Ottar says, has fine strong teeth, and from its skin excellent rope can be made. He tells of the 'North

Way', the great trade route, and particularly its southern stretch, which he knows so well, from Helgeland to Skiringsal, a passage taking more than a month, even with a favourable wind. Ottar's description of the terrain is remarkable; he gives a magnificent picture of the special character of northern Norway, the broad wastes to the east and the narrow strip along the coast to the west; and he throws light on many matters – such as the favourable markets for trading which brought him south from his Nordic home to towns like Skiringsal and Hedeby. Here is Alfred the Great's account of what Ottar told him of the passage south from Oslo fiord:

And from Skiringsal he said that he sailed for five days to 'Ved Hederne' [Hedeby] which lies between the Vender and Saxer and Angel and belongs to the Danes. As he sailed from Skiringsal Denmark lay to port, while to starboard for three days was the open sea; and after that there was a further two days' sail to Hedeby during which Gotland [Jutland,] Sillende [south Jutland], and many islands lay to starboard; here the Angles had lived before they came to this country [England]. During those two days the islands belonging to Denmark lay to port.

The Anglo-Saxon trader, Wulfstan, described to King Alfred his route from the land of Slesvig to the Baltic:

Wulfstan said that he left Hedeby and came to Truso after seven days and nights and that the ship was under sail all the time. Vendland lay to starboard, while to port were Langeland, Lolland, Falster, and Skaane, all of which belonged to Denmark. After that Burgundaland [Bornholm], which has its own king, was seen to port, and, after that, first the land called Blekinge, then Møre, Øland, and Gotland, all belonging to the Swedes. Right up to the mouth of the river Vistula. Vendland lay to starboard all the way.

Such accurate accounts of mariners' routes as these, embodied in King Alfred's history, make up our first real knowledge of the north in those times.

Another and somewhat older source of information (from

c. 880) is Rimbert's biography of Ansgar, whom he succeeded as Archbishop of Hamburg and Bishop of Bremen. Although the work follows the usual pattern of hagiology it provides some eye-witness evidence about the Swedes and the Danes.

But of special interest is the narrative of the Arab merchant Ibrahim Al-Tartûshî, from the Caliphate of Cordova, who made a visit to Hedeby about 950. This Oriental could not have felt at home under northern skies, yet he was an observant traveller, as the following description reveals. He is talking about Hedeby-Slesvig at the end of the Slie Fiord:

> Slesvig is a very large town at the far end of the world-ocean. It has fresh-water wells within the city. Its people worship Sirius, except for a few who are Christians and have a church there. They hold a feast where all meet to honour their deity and to eat and drink. Each man who slaughters a sacrificial animal – an ox, ram, goat, or pig – fastens it up on poles outside the door of his house to show that he has made his sacrifice in honour of the god. The town is poorly provided with property or treasure. The inhabitants' principal food is fish, which is very plentiful. The people often throw a new-born child into the sea rather than maintain it. Furthermore women have the right to claim a divorce; they do this themselves whenever they wish. There is also an artificial make-up for the eyes; when they use it the beauty never fades, on the contrary it increases in men and women as well.

Later he says: 'I have never heard such horrible singing as that of the Slesvigers – it is a growl coming out of their throats, like the barking of dogs, only still more brutish.' This sketch of a Nordic town is far from flattering, but for that very reason, as well as for its selection of detail, it has a distinct credibility.

About 1075 Adam of Bremen wrote a history of the archbishops of that city. His impressions of the Nordic countries are possibly drawn in part from his own direct knowledge and observation; but much of his information, especially about Denmark, is no doubt derived from his superior, Archbishop Adalbert of Bremen, and from King Sven Estridson, whom he knew personally. Adam of Bremen's writings are far from dependable, yet some of his observations about Nordic geography and ethnography – collected in his fourth chapter – are worth attention. Of Denmark he says that it consists almost entirely of islands. The main part of the country, Jutland, stretches north from the river Eider, and from there it takes five or seven days to reach Aalborg. The shortest crossing to Norway begins from the tip of Vendsyssel. The soil of Jutland is thin and sparsely cultivated, and large towns exist only where fiords penetrate the terrain. Jutland is separated from the island of Fyn by a narrow belt which stretches from the Baltic to the town of Aarhus, from where one can sail to Fyn, to Zeeland, or right up to Norway. Adam also mentions fifteen other Danish islands. 'When one sails past the Danish islands,' he continues, 'a new world opens up in Sweden and Norway, two vast northern countries still very little known to our world. The well-informed king of Denmark has told me that it takes a month or more to travel through Norway, and that one can hardly journey through Sweden in two.' He comments upon the fertility of Sweden where the soil produces good crops, abundant honey, and superlative pasture, and notes, too, that the Swedes import a good deal and are short of nothing. Adam subsequently enthuses about the virtues of the Swedes, in a fashion which brings to mind Tacitus's description of the Germans. But he adds that the Swedes are very intemperate about women; every Swede has two or three or more women, according to his means, and the wealthy ones and the princes have many more. They are excellent fighters on land and sea, and although they have rulers of ancient lineage the monarchy rests upon the will of the people. Among Swedish towns which Adam mentions are Birka, Skara, Sigtuna, and Gamla Uppsala. Of the last-named he describes the famous sanctuary, which will be referred to again in a later chapter on the religion of the Vikings.

Norway, says Adam, is the remotest land in the world, and reaches north to an extreme latitude. It is also the least fertile and is suitable only for rough grazing; the herds go far into the waste. The Norwegians are brave warriors not softened by luxurious living. 'Forced by the poverty of their homeland, they venture far into the world and bring back from their pirate raids the goods which other countries so plentifully produce.' They are frugal in their eating as they are simple in their life and habits. Adam mentions the forest and the arctic fauna of Norway; the urus, elk, blue fox, hare, and polar bear. Of the towns he picks out Trondheim. Finally he points out that the northernmost Nordic countries are Helgeland, Iceland, Greenland, and Vinland (in North America).

CHAPTER 3

THE NINTH CENTURY

THE DANES

WE shall first consider the Danish raids. King Godfred, the impetuous and reckless ruler of Denmark, was murdered in 810 while daring, under the very eyes of Charlemagne, to fall upon the coast of Friesland. As we have seen, this threat had taught Charlemagne a lesson, for he now instituted an extensive system of coast defences to guard his northern frontiers. His son and successor, Louis the Pious, continued these precautions. Frankish battle-fleets were stationed in river mouths, not only in Friesland, but also in the north-east of France, including the Seine estuary; and at Boulogne a veritable lighthouse was built on the site of the emperor Caligula's ancient watch-tower. For the first twenty years of his reign, Louis the Pious managed to safeguard the country from northern attacks, except for two minor Viking raids in the year 820, one in Flanders, the other at the mouth of the Seine. What weakened France was not invasions but internecine wars between the emperor and his sons, and in due course the Vikings exploited this situation. In 834 when Louis, by strenuous exertions, had managed once more to stabilize his position, the first big Danish attack to occur since the death of Godfred was delivered upon the coasts of Friesland. The coastal defences were overrun and the Danes pushed on to capture the capital of Friesland, the important mercantile town of Dorestad.

The wealth and prosperity of Dorestad had long been a temptation to the Danish Vikings. The town stood in the middle of Holland, south-east of Utrecht, near the point where a tributary, the Lek, joined one of the arms of the river Rhine, 'the crooked Rhine'. The rivers run in different courses nowadays, but the small town where the junction used to be is still called 'Wijk bij Duurstede' (the 'little place near Dorestad'). Dutch archaeologists have excavated a Carolingian fort built before Viking times, probably by Charlemagne himself; and between this fort and the fork of the Rhine lay Dorestad, a place stretching over half a mile along the river, protected by palisades and gates. It was an important market town ('emporium') and, together with Quentovic (now Calais) farther west, it was during the early Viking period one of France's chief trading ports. Quentovic was the centre of trade with England, equipped with a Customs House and a Mint. But Dorestad was no less important. There, too, coins were minted – Charlemagne's famous 'Dorestad' money, eagerly sought and, indeed, copied by the northerners. From Dorestad, too, sailed the stout big-bellied Frisian vessels carrying the wares of France to Norway and the Baltic countries. During the half-century between 780 and 834 Dorestad was the biggest merchant town in northern Europe.

The Danish plundering of the place in 834 was followed by similar assaults. Despite the strenuous efforts of the Franks to restore the coastal defences the Danes struck several times more at Dorestad. But towns in those days were not easily daunted, and managed to survive both fire and plunder. Wooden houses could be rebuilt, earthworks reinstalled, if the place was a natural centre for trading. Dorestad survived for another generation until, in 864, its great catastrophe occurred. This was not an act of Danish aggression but an infliction of nature: a series of tidal waves which covered the greater part of Friesland and Holland and swept away the vast sand-dunes which had protected the country from the sea. The calamity was described in the chronicles in this fashion:

Strange portents were observed in the sky, and were followed by plagues, gales, and tidal waves. The waters of the Rhine were forced back by the inrush of the sea and drowned masses of people and animals in Utrecht and other places. In later years the river Lek was dammed in with dykes and the Rhine was diverted towards Utrecht, but at Katwijk the Rhine was completely silted up.

The river which was the artery of Dorestad's trade disappeared in another direction, and with that blow of fate Dorestad disappeared, to be supplemented by such river-towns as Utrecht and Deventer.

It was not only the strength of France which had until 834 kept the Danes in check, but also trouble at home. There was strife between King Godfred's sons and a pretender called Harald, who had ingratiated himself with the emperor Louis the Pious by becoming a Christian. In 827 Harald was finally chased out of Denmark by Godfred's son, Horik, who remained king until his death in 854. Before his banishment, however, Harald had managed to secure a foothold in Denmark for that great Nordic missionary Ansgar, who soon set out from Denmark upon his first evangelizing mission to Sweden.

Horik did not favour pirate ventures; if there were to be Viking raids from Denmark he was going to command them. So, in 845, he dispatched several hundred vessels up the Elbe to ravage Hamburg and at the same time sent Ragnar Lodbrog with a smaller fleet up the Seine to capture Paris. A few years before these events, the emperor Lothar had been forced to cede the islands of Walcheren, in the Scheldt, to two Viking brothers called Rorik and Harald – the latter being in all likelihood the Pretender banished from Denmark in 827.

In 840 Louis the Pious died and a period of decline and division in the Frankish Empire began. By the treaty of Verdun in 843, it was shared out between the emperor's three sons – the east being allocated to Ludwig the German, the west to Charles the Bald, and the centre to Lothar. They were not on good terms with each other and, on top of that, had difficulty in controlling their feudal subordinates. Here was the perfect opportunity for the Vikings; and they promptly took it. The great invasions of France by Danes and Norwegians began. From 840 onwards their armies swept across France; Rouen, Paris, Chartres, and Tours were the principal objectives, and the occupying forces were so strong as to be able to winter in France. Charles the Bald was forced to come to terms by buying off the invaders with 'danegeld'.

Back in south Denmark Horik still reigned, a shrewd, far-sighted ruler. Although he himself was not a Christian he saw that diplomatic use might be made of Christian missions and evangelists. It was through Horik, for example, that Ansgar was able twice to visit the Swedes in Birka. But finally his enemies proved too strong for him, and in 854 he fell, with almost the whole of his family except for a young son, also called Horik. Some few years later the Viking Rorik mentioned above, with the help of the Franks, gained a foothold in Denmark again and became the overlord of that portion of southern Denmark 'which lies between the river Eider and the sea' – the region at the base of the Jutland peninsula dominating the trade route to the fiord Slien. How long he exercised this sway is not known. He is said to have been sympathetic to Christianity and to have banished from Slesvig the anti-clerical Earl Hori. After him, and indeed throughout the second half of the ninth century, history does not record any Danish rulers of importance. It was as if Denmark, during this period, was applying all its energies abroad. Its leading figures were independent princes rather than monarchs, chieftains who made convenient and profitable alliances with each other in order to fulfil their aspirations to foreign conquest and pillage. During this period the invasions of northern France and eastern England were primarily carried out by these Danish Vikings, although even then there was some participation by Norwegians and Swedes.

A summary of developments in France arou[nd]
useful at this point. From about 860 a seven-
was waged between the Danish–Norwegian V
Franks in the region of Jeufosse, the island in th
west of Paris. Charles the Bald decided to disl
therners entrenched there, and was joined in this effort by
his brother Lothar. Larger Frankish forces assaulted the island,
but with no success, and this failure was exacerbated by the
action of Charles's hostile third brother, Ludwig the German,
who seized the opportunity to mount an invasion of France.
Subsequently, however, another Viking marauder, Weland,
commanding 200 vessels, offered to clear out the Vikings on
Jeufosse for Charles for a fee of 5,000 pounds of silver plus
sufficient rations for the operation. This kind of offer was by
no means rare among the Vikings, who were frequently
willing to fight as mercenaries against their own countrymen.
In the ninth century there were many Viking chiefs who cultivated the habit of wintering abroad and selling their martial
services, like the Italian *condottieri*, to any good bidder.

Charles the Bald sought other methods than the payment of
danegeld to keep the Vikings out. Fortifications provided
one such method, especially when they included stone or
wooden barriers across the rivers which were the Vikings'
favourite approach. The Vikings did not relish attacking
fortified positions and much preferred to carry them by ruses
and stratagems. Charles the Bald set about constructing a
bridge across the Seine at Pitres, south of Rouen, which would
block the Viking ships from penetrating the Seine valley,
but this barrier does not appear ever to have been completed.
Meanwhile, the Vikings were busy elsewhere in France – in
the west, south of Brittany, for example, where Norwegian
raiders forced their way up the estuary of the Loire. Worse
was in store for France; there lay ahead the great thirteen-
year devastation which was to afflict France, Flanders, Belgium, and Germany. This invasion was, in fact, touched off

ngland, where Alfred the Great's resolute defence cul-
minated in his victory at Edington in Wiltshire in 878. When
the news of this Viking defeat reached a new Danish fleet
which had just arrived in the Thames, a majority of its leaders
decided to turn towards the Continent instead. Reinforced by
other hordes in the neighbourhood, this 'Great Army' sailed
for Belgium and in April 878 penetrated the Scheldt towards
Ghent. For thirteen years western Europe endured a bitter
ordeal. 'There did not exist a road', says a chronicler, 'which
was not littered with dead, including priests, women, and
children. Despair spread through the land, and it seemed that
all Christian people would perish.' The Vikings did, indeed,
meet resistance, the Franks defending themselves bravely.
Eastern and Western Franconia (roughly equivalent to the
Germany and the France of today) were each ruled by a king
called Ludwig. The eastern Ludwig died soon after the invasion began, and his territories were pitilessly overrun. The
western Ludwig, grandson of Charles the Bald, was luckier.
In 881 he defeated the Great Army at Saucourt, near the
Somme, but shortly afterwards this brave soldier, not yet
twenty, was killed – and not in battle. He caught sight of an
attractive girl and spurred towards her. She fled through a
low gateway and he in pursuit ran into it and killed himself.
When his young brother Carloman died in an accident in
884, the responsibility of defending Western Franconia fell
upon the inadequate shoulders of Charles the Fat. He had
already shown his incapacity when, in 882, he faced the enemy,
with a huge army behind him, at Elsloo, near Maastricht –
and bought them off instead of giving battle. Three years
later, when the Vikings were making no headway against
Paris, stoutly defended by Count Odo, Charles the Fat again
arrived on the scene with strong forces, and again played the
poltroon. To begin with, he bought off the enemy, and later
nevertheless allowed them to pass through the protecting
bridges to ravish the country, which they proceeded to do

for several years. Not until 892 was the Great Army checked and dispersed – not by resistance, but by famine and pestilence. The Vikings collected what was left of their men and ships, and returned to their bases in Kent, where their army was disbanded a few years later. But France's respite from the invader was brief, and very soon Viking vessels were again sailing up the Seine. About the year 900, however, the character of the Viking invasions changed. Instead of being merely marauding raids they began to assume a more settled and pacific purpose, and in fact became a deliberate effort at colonization.

In England the penetration began in 835 with a Danish raid on the mouth of the Thames; and during the next thirty years these assaults continued, with varying results. The islands of Thanet and Sheppey were maintained as bases for these attacks. Thus from his camp on Thanet the Danish chieftain Rorik (who had settled in Friesland) plundered both Canterbury and London around 850. The next year, however, he was defeated by King Ethelwulf of Wessex, who ruled most of southern England and who for some years was able to instil into the Vikings a healthy respect for the Wessex fighting man.

In 865, therefore, when the Viking attacks were intensified, they were launched on a more northerly route, from bases in East Anglia. This was the direction taken by a large army led by Ivar the Boneless, a most clever strategist, and Ubbe and Halvdan, the sons of Lodbrog. This army, pressing towards Northumbria, captured York on 1 November 866. The next year it invaded Mercia and captured Nottingham, after which the Mercians paid danegeld and the Vikings retired to comfortable quarters behind the Roman walls of York. When they moved next they went south-east towards Peterborough and Ely, and captured and killed King Edmund of East Anglia. In 870 they fell upon Wessex, which was defended by King Ethelred and his brother Alfred, the latter being the famous leader who was to prove in the long run the only man able to keep the Vikings at bay.

On 8 January 871, the English came off best at the battle of Ashdown. Three months later Ethelred died and was succeeded by Alfred, who, to gain time, was at first content to buy the Vikings off. During 871-2 they wintered in London where Halvdan, who by now seems to have been their supreme commander, struck some new coins. A couple of years later they marched north and split their forces. One part, under Halvdan, moved into Northumbria and, with York as a base, began a definite system of colonization, the first Danish effort of the kind to occur in England. Halvdan distributed tracts of land among his men, fought several battles against the Picts in southern Scotland, and then vanishes from history. One surmise is that he crossed to northern Ireland and died there.

The other part of the Viking army, under three chiefs, made its headquarters at Cambridge, and from there, in 876, resumed violent attacks on Alfred's kingdom of Wessex. Their assault by land from the north was reinforced by naval attacks on the Channel coast, and their pressure on Alfred was so intense that, according to legend, he became an outcast driven into the forests and swamps. But he persevered, and finally, having with the utmost difficulty raised fresh forces, he fell upon the Danes at Edington (Wiltshire) in the spring of 878 and decisively defeated them. The Vikings fell back into East Anglia, where their king Gudrum (who had, incidentally, been christened by Alfred) followed Halvdan's example of distributing land among his men in an effort at colonization. London remained in Danish hands until Alfred liberated it in 886. From now on Alfred was the acknowledged leader of free England. He still had battles to fight, for in 892 the Great Army returned to England and for the next four years there were many clashes between the Anglo-Saxons and the Danes. In 899 Alfred, one of England's great rulers, died.

The position in England at his death was this: the whole of

southern England, under the leadership of Wessex, including London, was free. North of the Thames, to the east of a line roughly corresponding to the Roman Watling Street as far as Chester, was the region conquered and colonized by the Danes – the Danelaw or territories where Danish law ran – covering parts of Mercia and Deira as well as East Anglia. In this area the Vikings became peasants, a society of freemen with their own laws, customs, and language, the last still evidenced in English place-names in this region. The centre of the Danelaw was the area round 'the five Boroughs': Lincoln, Stamford, Leicester, Nottingham, and Derby; and the settled area stretched from the Humber and the Wash in the east to Wales and western Mercia in the west. Farther north Yorkshire had also passed into Viking occupation, sometimes under Danish, sometimes under Norwegian domination. To judge by the traces which survive in its dialect and place-names Lincolnshire was the centre of Danish colonization. More than half of its old place-names are Danish. Many of them end on the old Danish words for a village – *by* and *torp* ('by' and 'thorpe' in English). Country people in Lincolnshire today use 'toft' for a homestead, 'eng' for a meadow, 'wang' for a piece of arable land – all Danish words, and in the dialect such words as lathe, bigg, and bairn (instead of barn, barley, and child) are Danish. Even if other historical evidence were lacking this prevalence of Danish in the local language would be a proof of the Danish occupation of northern England.

The northerners introduced into Anglo-Saxon England their own territorial divisions, and these, too, survive in places. For instance, hundreds are still sometimes called 'Wapentakes' – from *vapnatak,* a word which originated from what used to happen at sessions of the ancient *Thing*. To signify assent to a proposal made at the *Thing* the warriors would bang their shields or rattle their spears. The name given to that noise, '*vapnatak*', became substituted for the *Thing* itself, and subsequently for the region from which the *Thing* was gathered together. The people used to sit on the 'Thing-wall', the judges on the 'Thing-hill', and both Thingoe and Thing-wall are to be found among place-names in the north and east of England. Yorkshire to this day is divided into three Ridings, East, West, and North: a survival of the Danish word *thrithing* meaning a third.

There is little reason to believe that the Anglo-Saxons were pushed out or enslaved by the Viking colonists, although the invaders doubtless helped themselves to substantial properties. The native inhabitants probably suffered a reduction in status within the existent community – but there is little evidence on the subject.

THE NORWEGIANS

Norway, in the ninth century, was not unified by powerful monarchs as was Denmark. Danish kings apparently exercised considerable power in the first half of that century – King Godfred's sway, indeed, extended over territories in southern Norway – but Norway at that period was split into numerous earldoms. In the second half of the century, however, while Danish kings are little heard of, the monarchy in Norway begins to assert itself, through the personality of Harald Fairhair, after his great victory, in 872 or thereabouts, at Hafrsfjord. It was his supremacy, indeed, which largely led to the Norwegian colonizing raids to the Faroe Islands and Iceland, for the men who went on those raids were the malcontents and refugees of his dominion. The earlier Norwegian raids, on the other hand, to the Scottish islands, and to Scotland and Ireland, had been, at first, pirate excursions, and thereafter annexations of new territory.

The treeless islands of Shetland, Orkney, and the Hebrides had long been inhabited when the Norwegians, from the end of the eighth century, began settling there. This is proved by surviving buildings, such as round and cone-shaped towers, as well as by archaeological excavations. This native Pictish population, however, had not been able to put up any effective resistance, and many of the islands became Norwegian bases for southerly attacks upon Scotland and, particularly, Ireland. In the last quarter of the ninth century the situation was changed by the unification of Norway under King Harald Fairhair who, pursuing his enemies across the North Sea, seized the Orkneys and established a strong earldom there under his sovereignty.

Long before that, Norwegian Vikings had begun to settle in Ireland, the green island with the mild climate. This indeed was loot worth fighting for. Soon after the year 800 the Viking raids on Ireland were intensified; the earliest record in the Irish annals dates from 807. The country was divided into numerous chieftainships which were roughly consolidated into two groups, the south-west and the north-east, and the Norwegian advance made rapid headway against these little principalities. Within twenty years the Norwegians were masters of many parts of the country both in the east and west; and they came to stay. Ireland had already been Christian for 400 years, a centre of classical education during the migrations in Europe, and the base for extensive and fanatical missionary activity on the Continent. Its innumerable monasteries were rich in art treasures, many of which now fell into the hands of the Vikings. In 839 the Norwegian chieftain Turgeis arrived with a large fleet in the north of Ireland and declared himself, as the annals relate, 'King of all foreigners in Erin'. He was an energetic soldier and a confirmed heathen. He founded Dublin and tried to replace Christianity by the worship of Thor. In Armagh, the holy of holies of Christian Ireland, he officiated as pagan high priest. But the Irish in due course managed to organize their resistance to this invader and in 844 captured him and drowned him in Loch Nair.

A few years later Danish Vikings made their appearance in

Ireland; and the Irish, wisely taking advantage of the enmity between the Danes and the Norwegians, allied themselves to the newcomers and inflicted a heavy defeat upon the Norwegians in 851. But later in the same year their luck changed. There arrived on the scene another chieftain from Norway, Olav the White, who reconquered Dublin, restored the supremacy of the Norwegians, and finally chased the Danes out of Ireland. For the next twenty years Olav ruled in Dublin, and his brother Ivar in Limerick.

These were hard times for the Irish. One may trace to their experiences at this period their hatred of foreigners expressed sometimes in flowery and colourful language. This passage from a contemporary chronicle is characteristic:

If a hundred heads of hardened iron could grow on one neck, and if each head possessed a hundred sharp indestructible tongues of tempered metal, and if each tongue cried out incessantly with a hundred ineradicable loud voices, they would never be able to enumerate the griefs which the people of Ireland – men and women, laymen and priests, young and old – have suffered at the hands of these warlike ruthless barbarians.

That the Vikings in Ireland were mainly Norwegians is proved beyond question by the chronicles; but even if these were lacking, the evidence of place-names and archaeology would equally establish that conclusion. Ancient ninth- and tenth-century graves in Norway have been found to contain many objects and jewels of Irish origin: scarcely any similar finds have been made in Denmark and Sweden.

About the year 870 Olav the White was recalled to Norway, and the government of Dublin was taken over by his brother Ivar. The rest of the century saw many battles, some between the Norwegians themselves, some against the Danes under King Halvdan in northern England. From these wars the Norwegians came out so badly that in 901 the Irish were able to capture Dublin from them. So much for Ireland herself. But the Norwegians were also active in other areas adjacent to the Irish Sea. Large tracts of south-west Scotland and north-west England were in their power, and their prolonged occupation during this and the next century is shown by the abundance of Norwegian place-names in Cumberland, Westmorland, Lancashire, and even farther east in Northumberland and Yorkshire. The Isle of Man did not escape them either; and here, too, especially in the north of the island, there are many place names which testify to Norwegian settlement.

The Norwegian raiders went south as well. They participated with the Danes in the great battles in northern France, but their favourite hunting grounds in France were on the Atlantic shores where the estuary of the Loire, especially, tempted them to raids into the French interior. One famous raid was that on Nantes in 843, when that flourishing town was sacked and burned by the Vestfalding, i.e. the Norwegians from Vestfold on the Oslo Fiord. After this they settled on the island north of the Loire – Noirmoutier (which means New Covenant) – where they organized themselves for a protracted stay and whence they controlled the extensive water-borne traffic in such commodities as salt and wine. From this convenient base, too, the Norwegians penetrated the lower reaches of the Loire and were able to meddle in the affairs of the more northerly regions of France. Even these areas of expansion did not satisfy the Norwegian Vikings on the seaboard of western Europe. Like the Danes they pushed on to Spain and the Mediterranean. In actions there, two leaders at one time seem to have been Danes – Bjørn Jernside (Ironside) and Hastings.

There are Arab records of two Viking penetrations in these parts, one in 844 into the Iberian peninsula, and one from 859 to 862, again to the Spanish coasts and on into the western Mediterranean. In the Arab narrative the northerners are called *madjus* – 'heathen wizards'. In the expedition of 844 they followed the coast of Galicia to the Christian town of La Coruña; but here they were out of luck and were repulsed by the inhabitants. They went on, under their red sails (as the chronicles relate) along the Portuguese coast to Lisbon, and captured not only this stronghold but, subsequently, Cadiz and Seville as well. It is remarkable that they should accomplish such a feat when the Caliphate of Cordova was at the height of its power. This was the limit of their expedition that year. One interesting fact is disclosed in the Arab narratives: after a battle the Vikings were in the habit of trading back their captured prisoners in return for food and clothing!

The venture of 859–62 was more ambitious and extensive. Led by Bjørn Jernside and Hastings (the presumed Danes) the fleet of sixty-two vessels set out from Brittany. This time they found the coasts of Spain guarded and were only able to sack Algeciras inside the Straits of Gibraltar. From there they crossed to Nekor in Morocco, and eight days later sailed past the Balearic Islands to the southern shores of France, where they encamped on the island of La Camargue in the Rhône delta, and remained for some time, to the annoyance and detriment of the inhabitants of the coastal and delta areas. In 860 the Vikings turned east into northern Italy, where they pillaged Pisa. To this campaign belongs the story, related by Frankish historians, of how Hastings arrived at an Italian town, now vanished, called Luna, which he mistook for Rome itself and which he captured by the famous ruse of the mock funeral. In 862 the expedition sailed back to Brittany, through the Straits of Gibraltar and along the Spanish coast. An Irish source recounts that the Vikings brought back with them to Ireland a number of black prisoners, which seems quite possible.

Other activities of the Norwegian Vikings during the ninth century, notably their excursions into the North Atlantic, still remain to be considered. These voyages, it is true, began before the reign of Harald Fairhair, but were increased and enlarged because of the conditions created by his rise to power in the homeland. Their main destinations were the Faroe Islands and Iceland. According to such medieval sources as the *Faroe Saga* (from the *Flatø Book*) and Snorre's *Harald's Saga*, the first settlement in the Faroes occurred in the time of Harald Fairhair, that is to say, during the latter third of the ninth century. Contemporary foreign sources do not mention the Faroe Islands, although it has been pointed out that the Irish geographer, Dicuil, who lived in France, was probably referring to the Faroes when he mentions, in a document dated about 825, 'the many islands in the northerly area of the British sea which can be reached from the north British islands in two days when the wind is favourable'. And he continues, 'These islands, unnamed and uninhabited from the beginning of time, are now abandoned by the hermits who had sought seclusion there, because the northern pirates have arrived. The islands are full of wild sheep and many varieties of sea-bird.' These references fit the Faroes admirably. The thought that Celtic hermits, in those pious wanderings through the northern seas which history so often records, should have reached this isolated group of islands and settled with their Christian religion and their sheep, is not at all unlikely. When the Norwegian land-starved emigrants arrived in these distant islands about 800, they evidently found them not wholly waste, and the ejection of the Celtic hermits who had sought sanctuary there would be an easy matter. This early colonization of the Faroes by the Norwegians took the form of casual and intermittent arrivals of emigrant groups or families, and was therefore not important enough to be mentioned in the later Icelandic sagas of the Middle Ages. These relate only to the settlements which occurred after Harald Fairhair had driven large numbers of dissidents out of his consolidated kingdom. Thus the *Flatø Book* says: 'The first man to settle in the Faroe Islands in King Harald Fairhair's time was Grim Kamban. In those days many people left the country

(Norway) because of the king's lust for power. Many of these settled in the Faroe Islands and made homesteads there: others went to more remote lands.' There is a story, too, of an outlaw called Nadd-Odd, who settled on a piece of land in the Faroes in the middle of the ninth century.

In Iceland, too, there is reason to suppose some sparse Celtic habitation before the arrival of the Norwegians – despite Snorre's assertion that the colonization of Iceland was due entirely to pressure by Harald Fairhair. Here, too, we have the reference by the Irishman, Dicuil, that Irish monks had found their way to Iceland. And finally, it is related in Are Frode's *Islendingabok* (*c.* 1130) that the Norwegians in Iceland encountered Irish Christians, called *papar,* who soon went home 'because they would not live alongside heathens'.

The Norse records mention three different persons as being the first to reach Iceland. There was the Nadd-Odd mentioned above, who, on a voyage from Norway to his home in Faroe Islands, was cast ashore in a gale on an unknown shore which, on his return, he called 'Snowland'. The second was a Swede, Gardar, who was driven off his course north of Scotland and so found Iceland. He wintered there and, on his return to Sweden, named the island he had found 'Gardarsholm' after himself. The third was a Norwegian, Floke, from Rogaland who had heard of Nadd-Odd's discovery of Snowland and started off in three ships to find it, via Shetland and the Faroes. He reached his destination and wintered there, but found the place little to his liking and named it 'Iceland'. These three journeys in all probability occurred a little before Harald Fairhair's rise to power in Norway.

The most important and authentic source of information about Iceland in the latter ninth and early tenth centuries is the famous Icelandic *Landnámabók* (the book of land-taking) which dates from shortly after 1200. In this are mentioned the names of 400 settlers and, in some cases, the places they came from. They were mostly from western Norway, but some were from the Norwegian colonies on the northern Scottish islands and in Ireland. Few came from eastern Norway or Sweden, and none is mentioned as coming from Denmark. It is important to notice the influx from Ireland, for it supports the opinion expressed by the Norwegian archaeologist, Shetelig, that the Celtic elements may have left on the Icelanders a different mark from that left by the Norwegians, and contributed also a characteristic influence upon Icelandic literature.

The formal and traditional manner in which a settler chose his holding in the new country was to throw overboard, when near the land, his 'throne-poles', the beams of wood which framed the seat of the master of a house. Wherever they landed was the will of the gods, and on that spot the wanderer would build his house and a shrine for his gods. By the end of the century several thousand settlers had thus made their homes in Iceland. One of the earliest of them, the Norwegian Ingold Arnason, found that his throne-poles had been driven ashore on the south-west coast of Iceland, at a spot where there were warm steaming springs. So he named the place 'Røgvigen' which means the 'creek of smoke', and Røgvigen or Reykjavik is today the capital of Iceland. These Icelandic communities evidently retained the Norwegian laws and language, but it was not long after – as the next century revealed – that they began to consider themselves a separate and independent Nordic people.

THE SWEDES

We pass next to Sweden. In an earlier chapter reference was made to Volga Russia during the eighth century with its two Khaganates (or empires) – the Khazar in the south and the Bulgar in the north – and the incentives for trading, by way of the Volga, which these Khaganates offered to an enterprising and expanding northern country. Sweden was in fact just such a country. Its colonizing and mercantile ventures began in the Baltic region, and later developed in an easterly direction towards Ladoga and Onega. This mingling of northerly and southerly currents occurred indeed, not only by way of the Volga, but also by the nearer (though more dangerous and precarious) route of the Dnieper to the Black Sea and Byzantium, and was in active use during the first part of the ninth century. Two convincing proofs, one archaeological and one literary, can be adduced to confirm this. To the north of the little town of Staraya Ladoga (Old Ladoga) which is near the southern end of Lake Ladoga, Russian archaeologists have excavated a large settlement. The deepest and oldest layers of the site prove to be Finnish. On top of them were found the remains of square houses with stone fireplaces, quadrangular wells, stables, and similar relics of an unmistakably Swedish origin which establish the certainty that, from the early ninth century to the middle of the eleventh, there was a large Swedish settlement on this site. When the Swedish colonists or 'Rus folk' arrived on the land which now bears their name it was here that they first settled.

The old Nordic name of this place was Aldeigjuborg. Let us consider for a moment the situation of this ancient town as a junction of communications south and east. Between Lake Ilmen and Lake Ladoga runs the river Volkhov, and Aldeigjuborg stood about six miles south of the river's entry into Lake Ladoga.

In the time of the Vikings anyone seeking to travel south would find a convenient route from Aldeigjuborg along the banks of the river Volkhov to the town of Novgorod (or Holmegaard in Nordic). From there the way continued across Lake Ilmen and along the length of the river Lovat. By this route one would reach the area east of Polotsk, near which three great rivers have their source: the Dyna (which runs into the Bay of Riga), the Volga (which flows to the east), and the Dnieper (which runs south to Kiev and the Black

Sea). If the traveller from Aldeigjuborg wished to journey to the easterly lands he could go either by the rivers Syas and Mologa to the Volga bend, north of Rostov; or he could sail up the river Svir (which joins lakes Ladoga and Onega) and from Onega follow the river to the circular White Sea, where he would reach the trading centre of Byelosersk, and go farther south along the Syeksna towards the Volga. From Aldeigjuborg, therefore, both these ways provided openings for bold, adventurous men who sought trading opportunities. The furs, the honey, and the slaves went by routes which reached from Finland through Permishareds down to the Khaganate of the Bulgars and, by way of the Volga, to the Khazar empire, and across the Caspian Sea to link up with the caravan routes to the Caliphate of Baghdad.

The other proof, the literary proof, of the contact between Sweden and the distant south comes, oddly enough, from a west European source, a Frankish one. It exists by virtue of the coincidence that messengers from the Rus folk to the Byzantine emperor, Theophilus, in the spring of 839, were hindered on their return journey by fighting among tribes on the Dneiper. A Byzantine mission was about to set out, sent by Theophilus to the Frankish emperor Louis the Pious; and this mission took the messengers under its protection as far as the town of Ingelheim, on the Rhine. We know this from a chronicle written some twenty years later by the Frankish bishop Prudentius, who was possibly present on the occasion. He writes that Louis, who had suffered from Viking attacks on his empire, insisted on investigating the Rus messengers who thus arrived at Ingelheim in order to satisfy himself that they were not Norman spies. Whether they did in fact clear themselves, Prudentius does not tell us; but he does disclose two items of great interest to historians. The first is that the emperor Theophilus, in his letter to Louis, said that the messengers declared they had been sent from the Khaganate of Rus; the second is that the messengers themselves told the

Emperor Louis that they were not Swedish but, rather, of Swedish origin. It was the Danish scholar, Stender-Petersen, who first recognized the significance of this evidence. Prudentius tells us nothing more about the messengers; but it is clear that they were men from a Khaganate of Rus, in the north, wherever that may have been situated. Before the middle of the ninth century, therefore, the colonizing Swedes had created in northern Russia an independent settlement, so independent that they could send their own ambassadors to the distant Byzantine emperor.

Stender-Petersen suggests that these emigrant Swedes, the Rus folk, were cultivators who, recognizing the important possibilities of trading in the east, decided to seek them first by way of the Volga, and later the Dnieper. This interpretation is open to doubt, but the fundamental conclusion is sound: that the Swedish expansion was of a mercantile character. Between the Viking activities in western Europe and those of the Swedes in the east there is this basic difference: that the Swedish journeys were not undertaken in search of plunder but in quest of trade. How independent of its original homeland in the kingdom ruled from Uppsala this Rus Khaganate in northern Russia may have been is difficult to determine, but that the Swedish kingdom was connected with its affairs, especially in the tenth century, is proved by the many oriental and foreign coins, as well as other objects, found in Gotland and in the Uppland market town of Birka. Nordic archaeologists and historians in general hold the well-founded opinion that from the ninth century Sweden was politically active in developing trade between eastern and western Europe and securing for itself a strong position not only on the long route to Russia, but also on the North Sea, where in about 900 it came into possession of the harbour of Hedeby.

To call this complex activity 'the foundation of the Russian empire' is to provoke violent disagreement among eastern and western European historians and can, in any case, be misleading. There were independent Khaganates in eastern Russia along the Volga which owed nothing to Swedish colonization, and many independent states, too, in southern Russia side by side with Byzantine territories. Yet the traditions concerning the origins of the Rus people, as related in literature, go back to these Swedish influences, and the birth-myth of the nation has a significant historical essence. The so-called *Old Russian Chronicle,* or *Nestor Chronicle,* dating from shortly after 1100 and said to have been compiled by the monk Nestor in a cave-monastery at Kiev, gives the following account of the origin of the Rus people:

The Varaegars came from beyond the sea and demanded tribute from the Finnish and Slav peoples. They were repulsed, but in due course dissension broke out among the peoples and became so acute that they finally said 'Let us find a prince who will rule fairly and justly over us all'. So they went across the sea to the Varaegers, to the Rus folk (who were called Rus as others were called Svees, Normans, Anglians, Goths) and they said to the Rus: 'Our land is wide and wealthy but it lacks order: come over and rule us.' Three brothers were chosen as rulers, and these agreed to go over, taking all the Rus folk with them. It is further related that the eldest brother, Rurik, came to Ladoga and built there the town of Aldeigjuborg (Old Ladoga); the second, Sineus, settled near the White Sea (at Byelosersk); and the third, Truvor, at Isborsk in southern Estonia. After two years the younger brothers died, and Rurik assumed full power; after which he went south and built on the shore of Lake Volkhov the town of Novgorod (or Holmegaard). From here the Rus folk spread south, to Smolensk among other places.

From this account given in the *Nestor Chronicle* it is fair to assume that when the Khaganate of Rus, in 839, sent ambassadors to the Byzantine emperor, its capital was Novgorod, although Stender-Petersen is of the opinion that the Khaganate came into existence, at an earlier date, in the Upper Volga region. There is so far no conclusive evidence for either contention. It is certain, however, that the Rus folk penetrated rapidly south along the Dnieper as far as Kiev, for we know the names of two rulers: Haskuld and Dyri. In 860 this advance had already progressed so far that the Rus were making attacks on Byzantium itself which, however, was well capable of defending itself. Soon after this we hear of friendly contacts being developed between the Greeks and the Rus. The Rus prince Haskuld, who captured Kiev, became a Christian, although his example does not seem to have been followed extensively by the Rus people, his successors in Kiev maintaining paganism for a long time.

Apart from this Khaganate of Novgorod, which originated as we see from Aldeigjuborg, there are records of another Nordic line of expansion, from Polotsk, on the Dyna. Led by a man called Ragnvald, it pushed south along the Dneiper, and in so doing came into conflict with the Novgorod Rus.

Summing up this Nordic advance into Russia during the ninth century, both in the east and the west, we may describe it as predominantly a widespread development of mercantile activity originated by the 'Vræger' from Sweden. One sign of the extent of this penetration, incidentally, is the prevalence of names in Russia which spring from Nordic origins – Oleg from Helge; Igor from Ingvar; Vladimir from Valdemar. It must, in conclusion, be emphasized that the motive of the far-ranging Swedes was not to conquer or colonize the country with a view to settling in it permanently, but to open up routes and to establish trading centres (which in due course became towns). This trading motive of the Rus was noted by the Arabic writer, Ibn Rustah, in the mid tenth century, who says of the Rus, 'They have no fields but live entirely on what they import from the land of the Slavs'.

By the year 900 Swedish influence had become an important factor in those easterly regions where it had spread; an extensive network of trade-routes had been developed and at least two permanent Khaganates established, one based on Novgorod and the other on Kiev.

CHAPTER 4

THE TENTH CENTURY

THE DANES

THE early part of the tenth century was a thin time for the Danes. Their protracted conflicts in France and England, and especially such defeats as they incurred in Brittany in 890 and at Louvain in 891, had sapped their strength, so that when the Swedes attacked southern Denmark around 900 the Danes were unable to resist them effectively. The king of Denmark, Helge (if he be not a mythical figure), was defeated 'by Olaf who came from Sweden and occupied the Danish kingdom by force'. Our authority for this is Adam of Bremen, who records the event in 1075, quoting as his source his contemporary, the Danish king Sven Estridson. The Swedish Olaf ruled over southern Denmark for some time with his sons Gnupa and Gurd. They were followed by Gnupa's son Sigtryg. Gnupa's wife, Astrid, set up two Runic stones in Slesvig in Sigtryg's memory, both of which were found near Hedeby and which afford ample proof (along with the testimony of Adam of Bremen) that a Swedish royal house reigned in southern Denmark for a generation. We shall hear more of Gnupa when, in 934, he came into conflict with the Germans. In the light of what has been said in the last chapter about the Swedish preoccupation with trade-development, it is not difficult to see why they were so anxious to occupy Hedeby. It provided a base for linking the traffic between the North Sea and the Baltic as far as the Swedish capital, Birka, on the Mälar.

How were the Danish Vikings in northern France faring in the years just before and just after 900? Historical sources are very scanty indeed in this matter. The Saint Vaast annals cease around 900; and the monk of Rheims, Flodoard, does not begin his narrative until twenty years later. Dudo, the monk from Saint Quentin who, a hundred years later, wrote his fulsome panegyric on the dukes of Normandy, is not always reliable. What is certain, however, is that Rollo, later to become the first duke of Normandy, spent the first ten years of the century with his Vikings in the Seine valley, fighting battles, with varying turns of fortune. Dudo declares he was a Dane; Norse sources call him a Norwegian. His army seems to have been predominantly Danish. Rollo established himself pretty firmly in northern France, and in spite of occasional setbacks and defeats, was not easy to dislodge. It is highly likely that he was the virtual ruler of Normandy for some time before the Frankish king Charles the Simple gave him the Norman province on condition that Rollo swore allegiance to him and held Normandy as a buffer state against other Viking attacks. Rollo's formal elevation to the dukedom which took place in 911 at Saint-Clair-sur-Epte, marks an important event in the history of France. For Rollo kept his faith with Charles: he defended the country against other Viking invaders, settled his men to cultivate the land, and stood by Charles in subsequent troubles. When turbulence wracked the king's territories Rollo, in alliance with his Norwegian friends, the Vikings of the Loire, kept order in Normandy until Charles could re-establish his authority. Thus did the province of Normandy develop as a Nordic colony on the banks of the lower Seine, extending in the north-east to Picardy (at the river Bresle), and in the south-west to Brittany (at Saint-Malo), while just across the Channel lay the tempting and prosperous south of England. Rollo's dukedom comprised approximately the modern Departments of Seine Inférieure, Eure, Calvados, Manche, and most of the Orne. The place names of the province bear ample testimony to its Nordic origin, especially round the Seine, the waterway along which the Vikings arrived. There are numerous names of villages with the Nordic suffixes *-tofte, -gard, -lond, -torp*; and others combined with names of Nordic men such as Torbjørn, Asmund, Ulv, and Ragnar. In 912 Rollo was christened. By that time the big Viking invasions of France were over. One or two lesser raids occurred, but in general Rollo and his successors made themselves widely respected.

In England, during the first decade of the tenth century, the Danish Vikings fared far from well. The son of Alfred the Great, Edward, was a bold and skilful soldier who, in alliance with his sister, Ethelfled, 'the Lady of the Mercians', now made war on the Danelaw. The strategy was to set up and garrison many forts which served as strong points for his attacks on the enemy. The Danes were driven back in successive defeats; no reinforcements from their homeland were forthcoming; while in the north of England the Danes were being hard-pressed, sometimes by the Anglo-Saxons, sometimes by Norwegians and Scots penetrating from north-west England and Scotland. By 918 the losses and withdrawals of the Danes had become so considerable that the Anglo-Saxons were masters right up to the Humber. In the north the Norwegian Ragnvald, who had come from Ireland in 920, and had captured York, was forced a year later to make peace with the invincible Edward who, after his sister's death in 918, had added the whole of Mercia to his kingdom.

In 924 Edward died. His son and successor was Athelstan, a brave warrior who in 927 conquered the whole of Northumbria, and York as well. Ten years later he met the combined forces of his enemies in the north and north-west, led by Olaf from Dublin, and defeated them at a place called Brunanburh, which has never been identified. He was one of the great kings of Wessex and England, whose reputation was recognized, for example, when King Harald Fairhair sent him a splendid ship as a present. When he died in 939 he had become the ruler of Wessex, Mercia, Northumbria, York, the Danelaw, and parts of Cornwall. About 940 his brother and successor Edmund ran into trouble and was involved in battles with Norwegian invaders from Dublin. By this time the Danes appear to have become bitter enemies of the Norwegians, for they fought side by side with the Anglo-Saxons. In 945 Edmund was murdered by a returned outlaw, and his brother Eadred assumed his throne. A few years later the Norwegian Eric Bloody-Axe appears on the scene as king of Northumbria and, later, of York, embroiled, among others, with one of the Dublin kings. He was ousted, however, in 954, and his conquests recovered by Eadred, who died childless the following year. For some years to come England was untroubled by Vikings; and at this point we may turn to consider what was happening in Denmark itself.

In the thirties of the tenth century Swedish rule in southern Denmark was drawing to an end. It was not the Danes, however, who were mastering the Swedes, but the Germans. In 934 the Swedish king at Hedeby, Gnupa, attacked the coasts of Friesland, an unwise venture which evoked immediate retaliation by the German king Henry the Birdcatcher, who raided Hedeby, defeated Gnupa, and forced him to be baptized as a Christian. Two years later, King Henry died, and what then led to the termination of Swedish rule in Denmark is told by Adam of Bremen (again quoting Sven Estridson as his authority): 'When he (i.e. Sigtryg, son of Gnupa) had reigned a short while, Hardegon, son of Svend, who came from Nortmannia, took his royal powers from him.' Now 'Nortmannia' can mean either Normandy or Norway; so that it is impossible to say where this Hardegon came from, or who he was. But Swedish rule came to an end soon after 936, and the next dynasty of kings in Denmark derived not from Hedeby but from Jelling in south Jutland.

At Jelling in the years around 940 lived the first king of this Danish dynasty, Gorm the Old, and his queen, Tyre, who is honoured on her runic stone as *Danmarks Bod,* which means

Denmark's ornament, a distinction which tradition attributes to her assiduous improvement of the great defence-dyke, the Danevirke, along the southern frontier. The inscription on the runic stone reads: 'Gorm the king set up this memorial to his wife, Tyre, Denmark's ornament.' Hans Brix has suggested that the inscription can be so read that the phrase 'Denmark's ornament' could refer to Gorm himself, but philologists do not accept this. Gorm was a heathen, and a burial chamber was built in a large mound as a double grave doubtless for him and his wife. Connected to this mound the Danish archaeologist Dyggve traced a large triangular plot of ground framed by upright stones marking a consecrated place, a *vi*. It can be presumed that Gorm died some time in the nine-forties, and no more is known of him. Of his famous son Harald Bluetooth we know much more, for under him Denmark recovered its former strength. This recovery did not, however, begin immediately. To start with there was evidently a strong German influence in the Danish kingdom which revealed itself in the creation of Denmark's first three bishoprics. Adaldag, the German Archbishop of Hamburg became Primate of these bishops. Thus Christianity was introduced to Denmark about the middle of the tenth century when Harald himself was still a heathen. In due course, however, Harald, presumably under German pressure by Otto I, was christened by the priest Poppo, who in the presence of Harald endured ordeal by fire, an event which occurred about 960. Shortly before, Harald had gone to war against Norway, incited by his sister Gunhild, the widow of that Norwegian king Eric Bloody-Axe who had been driven out of England some years earlier. Gunhild wanted to drive her late husband's younger brother, Haakon, from the throne of Norway. Her brother Harald agreed to her project, but at first had no success. Haakon not only drove him back, but took the offensive in 957, raided Jutland and Skaane, and even took possession of the whole of Zeeland. After this episode the tide turned again in Harald's favour; he drove the Norwegians out of Denmark, invaded Norway, in a decisive battle in Hordaland defeated and killed Haakon, and by about 960 made himself sole monarch of both countries.

It is this achievement which King Harald Bluetooth, with justifiable pride, commemorates on the stone he set up at Jelling to his parents, King Gorm and Queen Tyre. This famous 'Great Jelling Stone' is a remarkable work of art, decorated with carvings of Christ and a great beribboned lion; its runic description runs: 'Harald the king caused this memorial to be made to his father Gorm and his mother Tyre: Harald who won all Denmark and Norway and made the Danes Christians.' This memorial has been called 'the Danes' certificate of baptism', and certainly the consolidation of Christianity in Denmark was the most lasting of King Harald's three great achievements.

Unrest soon began to develop in Norway. Harald Graafeld, a son of Eric Bloody-Axe, usurped the power there, but was, in turn, attacked by a prince he had banished and whose father, Sigurd, he had burnt alive. This prince, Earl Haakon, supported by Harald Bluetooth, killed Graafeld in battle in the Limfjord in north Jutland. Norway was now divided. In the north Earl Haakon settled as an independent ruler; in the west he governed an earldom owing allegiance to Harald Bluetooth; in the south Harald himself was king. Such was the situation immediately after 970. But then a serious danger confronted Harald Bluetooth, coming this time from the south. In revenge for Danish attacks on Holstein the German Emperor Otto II in 974 assaulted the Danevirke and Hedeby. King Harald summoned assistance from Earl Haakon, but, even then, could not hold back Otto, who proceeded to penetrate the Danevirke and master a whole district where he set up a strongly garrisoned fortification. This defeat produced quarrels between Harald and Earl Haakon, disputes deepened by the fact that Harald had insisted on the latter's being baptized. The result was that Haakon assumed independence in his part of Norway, while Harald's efforts, from southern Norway, to subjugate him proved fruitless.

To add to his troubles Harald Bluetooth's son, a violent and virtually heathen character called Sven Forkbeard, now began to assert himself, although Harald was still the nominal ruler of Denmark. The Danes turned on the Germans in the south and broke their power. In 983 the castle which the emperor Otto II had built near the Danevirke was carried by a ruse and burned down, and after that Hedeby was besieged. Two runic stones near Hedeby commemorate warriors killed on that occasion; as one inscription says: 'When men sat round Hedeby'. The other stone, also naming the Hedeby fight, proclaims itself erected by Sven the King – which must refer to Sven Forkbeard who presumably (as his father's deputy) commanded the Danish forces in this battle. Soon afterwards an open breach occurred between Sven and Harald. The latter, wounded, escaped to a stronghold – possibly built by himself – on the east coast of Germany – Jumne or Jomsberg, where Wollin now stands. And here the great Harald Bluetooth died, about 986, 'wrongfully wounded and banished for the sake of Christ', as the pious Adam of Bremen writes. He was buried not in Jelling, but in the church of the Holy Trinity in Roskilde. In Jelling Harald had previously erased his father Gorm's heathen *vi* by erecting over its southern end a big memorial mound, and had as it seems prepared a transfer (*translatio*) of his parents' remains from the wooden chamber of the northern mound to a Christian burial-place.

Sven Forkbeard was an assertive, ambitious ruler. Without being a Christian himself he accepted Christianity and, for political reasons, tolerated the Church and supported the Jutland bishop, Odinkar. His first action, after securing the southern border of Denmark, was to attack Norway, an effort in which he was assisted by the Joms-Vikings from Wollin, led by Earl Sigvald. But the attempt failed. Earl

Haakon won a decisive sea battle at Hjørungavaag in west Norway, which must have taken place around 990. There is, too, an unauthenticated story to the effect that Forkbeard waged unsuccessful war against the Swedish king Erik Sejrsæl, who had conquered parts of Denmark, and that Sven was captured by Slavs and, finally, ransomed at great cost. In the final decade of the tenth century Forkbeard's eyes turned towards England.

After Eadred's death in 955 there was a prolonged period of peace in England, lasting a quarter of a century. Eadred's handsome successor, Eadwig 'the All-fair', died young, and his brother Edgar became king. His coronation was delayed, but when it did take place, at Bath in 973, the holy anointing was combined with an occasion of much splendour. Acting as oarsman in the king's boat were Nordic and Celtic princes, and Edgar adopted the proud title of 'King of England, and ruler of the Islands and the Sea Kings'. He is known to have allowed the Danelaw some degree of autonomy. With his death in 975 the peace was broken and bad times returned again. His eldest son, Edward, a violent and turbulent prince (who nevertheless was later recognized as a saint) was murdered after four years by henchmen of his half-brother, Ethelred, an unstable youth, who thereupon became king: Ethelred the Redeless, Ethelred the Unready. His accession was untimely, for it was now that the Viking raids were resumed. Between 980 and 982 there were minor descents on the coasts; but from 988 onwards the attacks were heavier and were made not only by the Danes but, particularly in the west, by the Norwegians as well.

The year 991 was a bad one for England, for then began the fatal method of buying off the Vikings by payments of danegeld – thousands of pounds of silver, year by year, which brought no more than a temporary respite. The Vikings sailed from place to place and sold local peace for cash payments. In the south the Normans observed with sympathy and interest this successful policy of their relatives and, indeed, made their harbours available to them. This form of support, however, was checked by a Papal negotiator who arranged a treaty between the English and the French which was confirmed at Rouen in March 991, but proved, in fact, short-lived. In the same year the Viking raiders on English shores included the famous Norwegian Olav Tryggvason, by then already christened; and when in 994 he arrived in the Thames he was accompanied by the Danish king Sven Forkbeard. With a joint fleet of about 100 longships and presumably at least 2,000 men they attacked London; but the city beat off the assault and the Danes had to be content with plundering south-east England and, finally, accepting 16,000 pounds of silver to go away. Olav Tryggvason definitely departed, to resume the task of conquering Norway; but Sven Forkbeard, on the other hand, came back to England – though not for about nine years. The occasion of his return will be discussed again later. Meanwhile, the Viking raids continued intermittently, throughout the 990s, along the coasts of England.

THE NORWEGIANS

In Norway, too, the tenth century brought troubled times, and varying fortunes for different rulers, interspersed occasionally with periods of peace and progress. Three years before his death, Harald Fairhair resigned his throne to his son, Eric Bloody-Axe, who was evidently more of a Viking than a king, for he retained the throne for only a few years and preferred, when his younger brother Haakon Adelstensfostre (later called the Good) was recalled to Norway, to quit the country without challenging him. He went to England, where he twice acquired a throne, but soon afterwards died. His widow, the Danish Gunhild, Harald Bluetooth's sister, returned to Denmark and, as previously described in this chapter, incited the Danes to attack the

Norwegian king her brother-in-law, Haakon Adelstensfostre. In the second of these attacks, in 960, Haakon was killed. He had proved a good monarch: drew up legal codes – the Gula Thing- and the Frosta Thing-laws – organized a land-militia which enabled him to retain personally only a small body of house-earls, and yet be ready for sudden attack. In addition he refrained from enforcing Christianity upon completely heathen peasants. He seems to have deserved the title Haakon the Good.

The sons of Eric Bloody-Axe now returned home from England, among them Harald Graafeld, who became King of Norway and proved a sharp contrast to Haakon the Good both in himself and in his actions. He was harsh to great and small alike, and was so hostile to heathen religious practices that he sought to suppress them by force. His reign was accompanied, too, by failure of crops and famine. But he did not rule for long, and as noted earlier in this chapter was slain in battle on the shores of the Limfjord in Denmark by Earl Haakon, who thus (with Harald Bluetooth's aid) avenged the murder of his father, Sigurd, by Harald Graafeld. After this event, which occurred around 970, Norway, as we previously noted, was divided into three dominions. We noted, also, the sequel to this division: how Harald Bluetooth, assisted by Earl Haakon, was defeated by the Germans at the Dane-virke, and how enmity subsequently developed between Bluetooth and Haakon. Earl Haakon returned to his own territory and, some years later, successfully beat off at Hjørungavaag an attack on western Norway by the Joms-Vikings. He met his end, finally, when Olav Tryggvason, the most picturesque figure of all the Norwegian Vikings, returned from England in 995, newly confirmed in the Christian faith by the English king at Andover, and determined to conquer and christianize Norway. Earl Haakon was now murdered by his own men, and Olav proclaimed king by the Trøndelag people. His problem was now to weld together the long straggling territories of Norway. What happened up at Trøndelagen in the north was very different from what might be done or said in the south and south-west, especially in Olav's own homeland, which was the province of Viken. But in his endeavours to unify and consolidate, Olav came up against the demands and pretensions of the Danish king, Sven Forkbeard, who asserted a traditional Danish supremacy over southern Norway. It was inevitable, too, that Earl Haakon's two sons, Erik and Sven, should manifest hostility to the Olav who had taken their father's throne.

Olav Tryggvason seems to have been more warrior than diplomat. In any event he failed to prevent Sven Forkbeard, by a series of skilful marriage alliances, from getting on his side the Swedish king Olav Skotking, son of Erik Sejrsæl. He married one of Earl Haakon's sons, Sven, to Skotking's sister, and the other, Erik, to his own daughter, and to round off the relationship Sven Forkbeard himself married Skotking's mother, the widow of his one-time enemy Eric Sejrsæl, thus creating a cleverly spun web of alliances.

His quarrel with Olav Tryggvason came to a head at the naval battle of Svolder in the year 1000. It is disputed whether the location of the battle was in Øresund or off the German Baltic coast. To Olav Tryggvason the situation was characterized by dissensions and defections among his own forces (especially the Joms-Vikings under Earl Sigvald). In spite of Olav's own personal bravery, and in spite of heroic efforts in his famous vessel, the *Long Dragon* – the biggest warship ever seen in the north – Olav's fleet proved too weak for a superior force; he was defeated and fell. Sven Forkbeard's rewards were considerable. He now became overlord of the whole of Norway, although the two Earls, Erik and Sven, who had allied themselves to him, exercised authority under him in the north of the country.

Such was the situation, then, about the year 1000, in Norway and Denmark. Let us look at what happened in the tenth century in the Norwegian sphere of influence in the west, in the old Viking hunting-grounds of the Atlantic coasts and islands; to begin with, at what developed in Ireland and in the Irish-Scottish-English areas. We completed our last survey of these regions with the Irish reconquest of Dublin in 901. This was a hard blow for the Norwegians who, however, from their bases in the north-west and north of England, and especially in Northumbria, set about preparing for their revenge. They struck back twice, in fact, in battles at Confey in 916, and Climashogue in 919, where the Irish were defeated in a gruesome massacre; and by these victories secured the mastery of great parts of Ireland for over half a century. This was the period when the Ivar dynasty flourished in Ireland, a dynasty which included such famous names as Sigtrygg, Gudrød, and Sigtrygg's son, Olav Kvaran. It was during the latter's time, says an Irish Chronicler, that Ireland was really penetrated by Norwegian influences: 'There was a Norwegian king in every province, a chief in every clan, an abbot in every church, a sheriff in every village, a warrior in every house' – a very effective scale of billeting! In addition to his hold over Ireland, Olav Kvaran, like Sigtrygg, held extensive sway in north and north-west England. Christianity now spread among the Norwegians in Ireland: Olav Kvaran himself died as a monk, in 981, in Iona monastery. The year before this the Norwegians suffered a heavy defeat at Tara – the first Irish victory of any substance for many years. With this the Irishmen's fortunes improved: and in Brian Boroimhe they obtained a king of remarkable political, as well as military, prowess who by 1000 managed to secure the sovereignty of all Ireland, including Dublin.

In northern England, and particularly in Northumbria, the Norwegians had greatly strengthened their positions during the tenth century, against both the English and the Danes, largely by virtue of the leadership of such warriors as Ragnvald and Sigtrygg (who died a Christian). After 926 Northumbria was incorporated with England, and Olav Kvaran later pushed into north-west England, to be beaten finally, as already related, at the battle of Brunanburh in 937. About 940 he and Eric Bloody-Axe were alternately kings in York; then came a long period of peace in England under King Edgar. Before we leave this résumé of Norwegian influence in English, Irish, and Scottish regions mention must be made of the celebrated figure of Sigurd Digre, mightiest of the Orkney earls, who became the sovereign of all the Scottish and Irish islands, including the Isle of Man. The Manx tenth-century stone crosses display a significant mixture of influences and traditions – Norwegian and Celtic, heathen and Christian.

South towards France, from Ireland and the Irish Sea, the Norwegian raids continued in the tenth century as they had done before. Reference has already been made to the part the Norwegians played in colonizing Normandy: Rollo may have been a Norwegian. On the Île de Croix, off the coast of Brittany, one memorial of Norwegian activity has been found, in the shape of a burial-mound erected over a Norwegian Viking, about 900. The mound was found to contain relics from a funeral by fire: a ship, shields, weapons, household articles, and fragments of clothes ornamented with gold. On this spot some far-voyaging Viking, perhaps from northern Ireland, had died and been buried with heathen rites. During an Irish raid on a Norwegian settlement at Limerick in 968 there were captured (according to a chronicler): 'Treasures of Viking property; their beautiful foreign saddles; gold and silver, exquisite woven cloth of all colours and kinds; satins and silks in scarlet and green; all kinds of cloth.' It sounds like one of the treasure-dumps where the Vikings stored the spoils captured in raids upon the Mediterranean and Spain. The Norwegians were also active in the Loire region during the tenth century, as we know from their alliances with Rollo's Vikings from the Seine. And we have knowledge, too, of raids still farther south, in the nine-sixties, on Lisbon and on

Asturias, where the pilgrim shrine of Santiago de Compostela was attacked. Clues to Arab contacts in the western Mediterranean have been provided by finds in western Norway of Arab silver coins minted in southern Spain and Africa. There is no doubt that the Norwegians' penetration was very extensive.

What of their voyages in the north Atlantic; first of all, to Iceland? On the evidence of the *Landnámabók* the emigration to Iceland was coming to an end about 930. Each family arriving on the island needed to claim and settle a substantial piece of land. It was varied land, some good, some bad. It was treeless and difficult to cultivate. Nevertheless, it had tracts of good grassland, birds and eggs were plentiful on the rocks, there was an abundance of fish in the rivers, no lack of seals and whales upon the coasts, and driftwood on the beaches. Large flocks of sheep were gradually spreading in the interior. One man, it is said in the *Landnámabók*, began counting his sheep but had not the patience to continue when he got as far as 2,400. Horses, too, were numerous as time went on.

Some of the early settlers improvised a court of law, but it soon became necessary to organize justice on a wider scale. It is said that a man called Ulfljot was sent home to western Norway to study methods of law and justice. Three years later he returned to Iceland and then, in 930, the Alting was set up and Ulfljot became Iceland's first *lovsigemand* (lawspeaker). The annual summer session of the Alting was held in a place called Thingvellir in the south-western part of the island. Here the people gathered to hear the laws proclaimed, to lodge their suits, to worship their gods, to display their sporting skill, and to buy and sell. Several local Things were held elsewhere in the island.

The story of how Iceland became christianized is as dramatic as everything else in the history of the Saga Island. It began with several unsuccessful endeavours at the end of the tenth century. First, in 981, the Icelander Torvald came home to the island accompanied by a Saxon priest called Fredrik; their ardent missionary efforts, however, ended in murder, outlawry, and their banishment from Iceland. Next the zealous, fanatical, Olav Tryggvason sent missionaries to Iceland on two occasions. First he dispatched Stefne, in 987, but Stefne seems to have been a man of Olav's vehement temper, for he too was chased off the island. Olav's second proselytizers, in 997, were an Icelander and a German (Tangbrand) who, after some initial progress, found themselves involved in murder and banishment. At last came success. Two Icelanders, Hjalte Skaggeson and Gissur the White, arrived from Norway. They began boldly by pulling down a shrine (hov) to the gods and then, with a crowd of followers, went to the Thing and proclaimed Olav Tryggvason's message invoking the islanders to accept Christianity. At that moment a volcanic eruption occurred and was promptly interpreted as a sign of the wrath of the ancient gods. The restless crowd was now taken over by a judge called Torgeir, who proved himself master of a difficult situation. On the third day of the Thing he delivered his judgement on the matter, and warned the people that division would destroy them and that they must reach agreement on this solemn issue. His exhortation succeeded and, says the Icelandic source, 'It was then agreed by law that all should become Christians and that all who were not christened must become so. But certain ancient laws were retained – such as the practice of exposing children and the eating of horse meat. Blood sacrifice in secret was also permitted, but if witnessed by others involved the participants in banishment for three years. A few years later this relic of heathen practice was abolished.'

The decision to retain secret sacrifices for a time may seem naïve, but it was doubtless a safety valve. Torgeir, himself a heathen, knew very well what he was doing, and his qualification of the main resolution was a wise act. This remarkable occasion, probably unique, on which an entire people, although a small one, decided to change its religion, suggests that the situation was ripe for such a radical transfer of faith and that the traditional religion had lost its power. In this simple and dramatic manner did Iceland adopt Christianity in the year 1000.

About a hundred years before this occurrence Greenland was visited by a Norwegian called Gunbjørn. His visit was involuntary, for on a voyage from Norway to Iceland he was blown off his course, and made a landfall off the east of Greenland, but felt no temptation to get to know it better. On his return to Iceland the land he had sighted was called Gunbjørnskær. It was almost a hundred years before that land was seen again. In 982 a man called Erik the Red, originating from Jären in Norway, was outlawed from Iceland for three years for committing a murder. He decided to employ his period of banishment on a westerly journey to look at this Gunbjørnskær which people still talked about. So he found Greenland. It must be presumed that with his companions he worked his way down the icebound and impenetrable eastern coast of the great island in a southerly direction, rounding Cape Farewell and eventually reaching the more accessible and agreeable south-westerly part of the country. Somewhere here the daring band of men wintered, and in the following summer made a camp in a fiord which Erik the Red named after himself. He then went on along the west coast (towards Godthaab) and, say the records, 'gave his name to many places'. He stayed in the country two more winters, and then, his banishment over, returned to Iceland from his resourceful journey. Wishing to return to the discovered country, accompanied by as many people as possible, Erik called the country Greenland, hoping that this attractive name would persuade people to go with him. He succeeded in this, for there were many in Iceland anxious to travel farther, possibly because there was already a dearth of land there. So in the following summer, with a fleet of twenty-five vessels containing emi-grants, their women and domestic animals, he set out – and a small majority of the voyagers reached their destination, after a hazardous journey, in 985 or 986. We may assume that further colonization occurred rapidly in the succeeding years. Greenland and Iceland were rather similar in conditions for living, and the climate there was approximately the same as it is today (i.e. milder than in the Middle Ages). Erik the Red chose to settle up Ericsfjord, where he built a farm (Brattahlid) which has been excavated by the Danish archae-ologist, Poul Nørlund.

The colonization of Greenland proceeded in two extensive and separate districts: 'the Østerbygd' (east settlement) in the south, where Brattahlid was located and where a Thing-site was chosen at Gardar, near the present-day Julianehaab; and 'the Vesterbygd' (west settlement) in the north, south of the present-day Godthaab. Danish investigations have found the remains of 200 farms or holdings in the Østerbygd and about 100 in the Vesterbygd, a quite substantial total, although not all these places were established in Erik's time. Agriculture was never widely practised in Greenland, and the people lived off their domestic animals (cows, horses, sheep, pigs, and goats) and off the products of those animals (meat, butter, milk, and cheese) as well as from hunting and fishing. Erik the Red's farm in Brattahlid, where he lived the rest of his life, consisted of a house with several rooms, built of stone and turf, in addition to a great hall (with a well in the middle) round which were the stables and stores. Thick walls of turf sheltered the habitation from wind and cold, and a little farther up the hill were the barns and sheepfolds.

The introduction of Christianity to Greenland and the Norse discovery of America were both effected in the year 1000 by the same man, the son of Erik the Red, called Leif Ericson. We shall return to this achievement later.

THE SWEDES

Sweden at the beginning of the tenth century was as strong as Denmark was weak: hence the Swedish occupation of parts of southern Denmark at that time. We know from Wulfstan's Travels that not only Gotland but also Øland and Blekinge were under Swedish rule. This sphere of Swedish domination was now extended down to South Slesvig, where a Swedish prince settled at Hedeby and controlled its foreign trade. Between Wulfstan's Travels, which make no mention, in the 890s, of Swedish rule in southern Denmark, and Hardegon's eviction of the Swedish king Sigtryg from Hedeby shortly after 936, there is a period of about forty years, representing the span of Swedish domination of southern Denmark. How much of Denmark was under Swedish occupation is not known.

On political conditions and events in Sweden itself in the early tenth century the sources are scanty. Two runic stones from Skaane describe in similar terms a battle at Uppsala which ended in a defeat for the Danes. One of them says of Toke 'He did not flee at Uppsala'; the other says of Asbjørn, 'He did not flee at Uppsala but fought as long as he had weapons.' This information, combined with what is revealed by later Icelandic sources, suggests that the kingdom of Sweden at Uppsala under Erik Sejrsæl had been attacked by the Danes, and by Erik's nephew, the famous Viking Styrbjørn, who sought the Swedish throne, but that Erik had won a decisive victory in the battle fought on the plain of Fyris near Old Uppsala. (Adam of Bremen's further information – that Erik also took Denmark from Sven Forkbeard – is not considered trustworthy.) Sweden fought another famous battle soon afterwards, the battle of Svolder, where, as related earlier in this chapter, Erik's son King Olav Skotking and his allies defeated Olav Tryggvason.

When we come to consider Sweden's efforts abroad to wage war or develop colonies and commerce in the tenth century we find, as we did of a previous period, that its expansion lay primarily in the east, although it undoubtedly took an active part in several developments in western Europe. There were, for example, Swedes with Rollo in Normandy. But Russia was the principal theatre of Swedish foreign activity in the tenth century. The great Volga route through the Khaganate of the Bulgars and the Khazars was still travelled over by Swedish merchants; and by a lucky chance an Arab eye-witness wrote down what he saw of the activities of the Rus people in the Volga regions. This was Ibn Fadlan who, shortly after 920, was an ambassador from Baghdad to the Khaganate of the Bulgars and stayed for some time in the capital, Bulgar. His spirited narrative describes his strenuous journey via Samarkand and Bokhara, and recounts how, on the Volga, he meets the Swedish traders and their women, whom he discusses in a lively and vivid manner. His comments are quoted later, in another context.

To judge by the quantity of Arab coins found in Swedish soil, the silver stream from Arab sources in the southern parts of central Asia diminished during the tenth century and dried up altogether in the eleventh. The silver mines were worked out and commerce found other routes. For the Rus folk, or Swedes in Russia, this compelled a fuller use of western trade routes, especially the one which followed the Dnieper to the Black Sea and Byzantium. In two treaties in 911 and 944 between the Rus people and the Byzantines there appear several Nordic names – more in 911, though, than in 944. The impression emerges that Swedish influence as such was declining, and that the Rus folk were becoming assimilated with the Slavs.

In 965 the Prince of Novgorod, Svyjatoslav (or Sveinald), conquered the Khazar stronghold of Sarkel. Of his two sons the first, Vladimir (or Valdemar) was given Novgorod, while the other, Jaropolk, was given Kiev. Assisted by reinforcements from his Swedish homeland Vladimir advanced on Kiev in 980 and killed his brother. The two Khaganates of Novgorod and Kiev were now combined, and Kiev became the capital of a Rus kingdom which extended over the whole of western Russia from the Dnieper to Ladoga. Vladimir was baptized in 987, became an ardent Christian, and after his death, in 1015, was proclaimed a saint. He maintained the friendship with the Byzantines.

CHAPTER 5

THE ELEVENTH CENTURY

THE DANES AND THE NORWEGIANS

In Denmark at the beginning of the eleventh century, Sven Forkbeard stood out as a strong invincible monarch. Since the assault on London in 994, and the ensuing raids on southern England, he must have had England frequently in his thoughts. Conditions were not unfavourable for realizing these ambitions of conquest. Ethelred the Redeless had committed a blunder which has been described as a political crime, and which was certainly a political *bêtise,* by ordering the mass assassination of all Danes in his country, an event which occurred on 13 November 1002, St Brice's Day. This massacre, in which Sven Forkbeard's sister, Gunhill, was murdered, aroused violent anger, and Sven launched two vengeance raids in 1003 and 1004 upon Wessex and East Anglia. Other raids followed in the ensuing years, although not under Sven's leadership. From 1009 the Danish raiders in England were commanded by Torkil the Tall (perhaps a brother of Sigvald the Earl of Jomsborg) who in due course, however, switched his services to Ethelred. Then, in 1013, Sven Forkbeard took over again, and with a well-found fleet and army launched a rapid and skilful campaign against England. In a short time he overran Ethelred's kingdom and then advanced on London, now defended by Torkil the Tall. The city held out, and Sven decided to waste no time besieging it, but seized Wallingford in order to secure his hold on Wessex, and from there went on to Bath. Then London surrendered and Ethelred fled to his brother-in-law, Duke Richard II of Normandy, with whom his wife, Emma, had already taken refuge. Torkil the Tall remained in England, but with a strength so inferior to Sven's as to cause the latter no anxiety. Sven's task was accomplished and he was generally accepted as the sovereign of England. But, on 3 February 1014, he died suddenly at Gainsborough.

The immediate consequence of his death was that the Anglo-Saxon nobles in England turned again to Ethelred, in Normandy, and made a pact that, under certain conditions, Ethelred should return home and resume the battle against the Danes. The Danish leader in southern England was now Knud, Sven's son, who had already campaigned with his father in England while his older brother, Harald, stayed in Denmark. He was undertaking a big task for a young man, a task made the more arduous by the fact that Ethelred's bellicose son, Edmund Ironside, was one of the English commanders. Knud was so daunted by the harsh prospect that he went to Denmark in order to raise, with his brother Harald's aid, fresh forces for a final attack on the English. His luck was in. For one thing, Torkil the Tall, who had so long been in Ethelred's service, joined him: a valuable ally well supplied with ships if not with judgement. His second piece of fortune was to win the active support of his brother-in-law, Earl Eric of Norway.

In England, meantime, Edmund Ironside, against his father's wishes, had taken over, about 1015, the government of the 'Five Boroughs', the Danelaw. Shortly after, in the same summer, Knud and his brother Harald arrived with a large fleet off the south coast. Here Knud was faced by Edmund Ironside and Eadric of Mercia – the latter an unreliable character who, during subsequent developments, changed sides more than once. Engagements between the rival forces occurred with varying results. Knud made headway in Wessex and (via Mercia) in Northumbria as well, where the Anglo-Saxon earl was deposed in favour of the Norwegian earl Eric. Then Knud, avoiding the Danelaw where Edmund was too strong, went back through Mercia to Wessex and, with the following summer in mind, prepared for an attack on London where Ethelred and Edmund were both camped with their armies. Ethelred died there in April 1016, and Edmund was acclaimed by the Londoners as his successor. Before Knud had time to seal off the city, Edmund broke out and reconquered Wessex; upon which Knud, leaving a force to besiege the capital, went after Edmund. Edmund proved to be as good a warrior and strategist as his opponent and, after Knud's failure to capture London, Edmund beat him in a battle at Otford, and so far gained the upper hand that the opportunist, Eadric of Mercia, changed sides from Knud to Edmund. But this proved a dubious advantage when the rival forces faced each other again in a big battle at Ashingdon in Essex; for here, at a critical moment, Eadric and his army fled, transforming what had seemed to be an impending victory for Edmund into a heavy defeat.

Both sides were now exhausted and ready for a settlement. They met on an island in the river Severn, and made a treaty under which Edmund was to have Wessex, and Knud the rest of England, including unconquered London. Hardly was this peace concluded when the brave Edmund, who had been worthy of the nickname Ironside, died suddenly in November 1016. The consequence was that Wessex now acknowledged Knud, who thus became king of the whole of England. Under him Earl Eric ruled in Northumbria, Torkil the Tall in East Anglia, and the untrustworthy Eadric in Mercia. Knud connived at Eadric's assassination soon afterwards. He assumed the direct rule of Wessex himself to begin with, but soon after split this province (and Mercia as well) into smaller earldoms.

In 1018 Knud declared that he did not want England to be regarded or treated as a colony, but as an independent kingdom with himself as its chosen ruler. To demonstrate this he sent the big fleet back to Denmark and paid off its men with the biggest danegeld ever levied: 10,500 pounds of silver from London and 72,000 from the rest of the country. He retained for himself a personal fleet of forty ships, later reduced to sixteen. His second act calculated to illustrate England's independence was to summon a national assembly at Oxford, where it was agreed that the new constitution should be adopted as a continuation of that which had been law in King Edgar's time. Soon after these events, Knud's brother, King Harald, who was childless, died in Denmark, and in 1019 Knud returned to his homeland, partly to assume the throne there, partly to ensure that no Viking raids against England should be mounted. Having achieved both objects he returned to England, where, for reasons we do not know, he outlawed Torkil the Tall, who thereupon went to Denmark. But it soon became apparent to Knud that it was imprudent to have as an enemy a man with such powerful connexions as Torkil had in Denmark, and so, in 1023, Knud went to Denmark and was reconciled with Torkil on terms which reveal the strength of the latter's hand: namely, that in Knud's absence Torkil should govern Denmark, and that each of them should adopt the other's son as a foster-child – i.e. as a hostage. Later on, after Torkil's death (probably in 1024) his place in this curious pact was taken by Earl Ulf, who was married to Knud's sister Estrid. The son of Knud and Emma, Hardeknud, thus became Ulf's foster-child.

About this time a new danger began to threaten Knud, this time from Norway. Here one of Harald Fairhair's descendants, Olav the son of the Norwegian noble, Harald Grenske, was making trouble. In his youth he doubtless had experience of Viking raids on England, under Torkil, as well as service with Duke Richard of Normandy. He saw his chance, while the Earl Eric was in England, to usurp power in Norway and, by 1016, had defeated Eric's brother, Earl Sven, in the northernmost regions of Norway (Trøndelagen). Olav Haraldson, later Saint Olav, was master in Norway, although he had many enemies who not infrequently asked assistance from Knud in England. But Knud had his hands full and decided to postpone his settlement with Norway. Olav thus gained time to plan his tactics, and used it to some purpose. His natural ally was Sweden, whose ruler, King Anund Jacob, a son of Olav Skotking, was concerned about the disturbance of the Scandinavian balance of power which would result from Denmark, England, and Norway all being under one king; and Anund's interest in the situation was further emphasized by the fact that his sister was married to Olav. The year 1026 was chosen for their joint attack on Knud, and Olav and Anund were counting a good deal on the strained relations which had developed between Knud and his brother-in-law Earl Ulf to make the latter their potential ally. As the place of battle the Swedes and the Norwegians chose the mouth of the river Helge, in eastern Skaane, and to this rendezvous came Anund's ships from the north-east and Olav's from the west, followed by Knud's fleet which came from the Limfjord through the Kattegat. Seldom has such an important battle been reported in such contradictory accounts. The Swedes are said to have held their own, but all the military and political consequences of the battle point emphatically to Knud as the victor: the Swedes were checked, Olav went back to Norway, and Denmark was no longer threatened by him. A Jutish runic stone of the period, set up over a man called Full, perhaps refers to this battle in the words 'who found his death in the east, in the sea when kings fought'.

Shortly after this battle, the tension between Knud and Earl Ulf was resolved by Ulf being killed at Roskilde, on the initiative of Knud, who proceeded to atone for the deed by bestowing large estates on Ulf's widow, who was his own sister Estrid. At Easter in 1027 Knud was in Rome for the coronation of Conrad II as emperor of the Holy Roman Empire, and was accorded the highest honours as one of the world's leading monarchs. He made friends with Conrad, and came to an agreement with him to safeguard the southern borders of Denmark. All that remained for him to do now was to secure his North Sea empire, where the only remaining problem was Norway.

There was still Olav Haraldson to be reckoned with. He was now in armed conflict with several of the earls of Norway, and the situation was so ripe for intervention that in 1028 Knud led a combined Danish and English fleet into action and, landing at a number of places along the Norwegian coast, soon occupied the country. Olav retired to Oslofjord, and from thence fled east to 'Gardarige' (Russia). Knud now summoned a parliament at Trondheim (Nidaros) and there proclaimed his son Hardeknud as king of Denmark and Earl Eric's son Haakon as king of Norway; and in the winter of 1029 he left Norway, taking with him a number of hostages to ensure that the peace was not disturbed. Yet disturbances there were nevertheless. During the same year Haakon was drowned while on a visit to England, and in his place Knud installed his young illegitimate son, Sven, as the ruler of Norway under the regency of the boy's mother Elfgivu. She failed in her attempts to introduce the Danish systems of taxation and justice into Norway, and almost before she began her unsuccessful government of the country a sensation occurred: Olav Haraldson returned, via Sweden, at the head of an army, to regain Norway. He was beaten by the peasants of Trøndelag in the famous battle of Stiklestad in 1030 (of which more later). But soon after this the Norwegians seemed to repent of their hostility to Olav, the devoted and gallant fighter for Christianity; such an intense current of feeling developed against Elfgivu and her son that they were compelled to retire, first to southern Norway in 1033, and later, in 1035, to Denmark. The successor to the Norwegian throne was now Magnus the son of St Olav, who was brought home from Russia by Norwegian nobles.

There is no doubt that Knud the Great was a powerful personality. Not for nothing was he his father's son. There was a strain of violence in him which not infrequently asserted itself; but first and foremost he was a statesman of profound acumen. So far as his principal kingdom, England, was concerned, he concentrated on two ends: first, to consolidate good relations with the Church; and secondly, to cultivate the principle that his government should be a continuation of the national Anglo-Saxon government of King Edgar's time. He was internationally-minded also: he prudently secured Denmark's southern frontiers, and towards the end of his life arranged a diplomatic marriage between the emperor Conrad's son and his own daughter Gunhild. He safeguarded the pilgrim routes from England and the north to Rome, and developed amicable relations with the ruler of Aquitaine. The only foreign power with which he failed to get on to good terms was Normandy, where Richard II, who died in 1026, was succeeded a year later by the ambitious Robert, who was not well disposed to Knud.

Whether Knud really expected that his North Sea empire comprising three widely separated countries could survive him it is not possible to say. But even a man of such determination as he was could not be unaware of the difficulties of such a union. It was difficult, for example, to eradicate from the Anglo-Saxon mind the feeling that he was a foreign conqueror, for he had perforce to surround himself with his 'house-carles', his Nordic bodyguard of highly disciplined warriors. The process of assimilation might have proceeded more rapidly if Knud, who carried out his code of administration and justice, had lived longer – but he died in 1035, and almost at once the process of disintegration began.

Two sons were now candidates for the English throne. One was the Danish king Hardeknud; the other was Harald Harefoot, one of Knud's sons by Elfgivu. In 1035 Hardeknud was in Denmark, Harald in England. Both the mothers,

Emma and Elfgivu, pressed their respective sons' claims in England; and after some confusion Harald was made King of England in 1037 (though without coronation or anointing) and Queen Emma, Hardeknud's mother, was exiled to Flanders. Knud's North Sea empire was thus split again, although Hardeknud in Denmark still nursed his ambitions for the English throne. This he showed, in 1040, by sailing to his mother in Flanders, with a strong fleet, on his way to attack Harald Harefoot. But Harald died suddenly, and Hardeknud now succeeded without difficulty in assuming the throne of England. At the same time, however, he lost his Danish throne, which was taken from him by King Magnus of Norway. An attempt by the Danes soon afterwards to recover it, led by Sven the son of Earl Ulf, and Knud the Great's sister, Estrid, was a complete failure. Moreover, Hardeknud was not fated to enjoy the English throne for long: he died in 1042 and was succeeded by his half-brother, whom he had presumably nominated, Edward the Confessor, son of Ethelred II; and with Hardeknud's death the period of Danish kings on the throne of England came to an end. But it was not the end of Danish Viking raids on England; as we shall see, not even the Norman conquest of 1066 put an end to them.

In Denmark the Norwegian Magnus occupied the throne. Under him Sven Estridson ruled as the Earl of Jutland, and he was with Magnus when he met and defeated a powerful Wendish army in south Slesvig. In the middle of the 1040s, however, St Olav's half-brother, Harald Hardrade, came back home from Byzantium and claimed the right to be co-ruler with Magnus. At the same time he formed an alliance with Sven Estridson, who had now broken with Magnus and was living in exile in Sweden, where he had been brought up in the royal house, and from which he received support. Next, however, Magnus and Olav came to terms, and agreed to share royal power in Norway. Just as things began to look really black for Sven Estridson, Magnus died in 1047 by

falling off his horse. Sven Estridson was immediately proclaimed king of Denmark in Jutland, and there followed a
strenuous period of seventeen years (with a gap in the 1050s)
during which Harald Hardrade attacked Denmark in a series
of incursions which Sven was unable to ward off. Yet although
so frequently defeated he managed by toughness and per-
sistence to survive, and at last, in 1064, to compose a peace of
sorts with Harald, who went to England, where he died two
years later.

Sven Estridson, eagerly though he wished to renew Forkbeard's and Knud the Great's conquests of England, was not
now disposed to commit all his forces on such a venture. He
compromised by dispatching, in 1069, a fleet of 250 vessels
against England, commanded by his brother Asbjørn – an
expedition in which three of his sons sailed, and in which there
were many Norwegians as well as Danes. Arriving off Kent,
this fleet sailed north along the coast to the mouth of the
Humber. Here the army went ashore and was joined by substantial Anglo-Saxon forces who had mustered to resist Duke
William the Conqueror. The combined armies marched upon
York, which the small Norman garrison promptly set on fire,
and there they won a battle. If the two armies had been better
led they might have altered the course of history; but they
began plundering in and around York, and when a rumour
arrived that Duke William was approaching, the Danes went
back to their fleet and entrenched themselves on Axholme
Island. Duke William therefore turned upon the Anglo-
Saxon army, and while he was so engaged the Danes advanced on York again and captured it. William then decided
to leave York alone for the time being, but set about method-
ically laying waste by fire and destruction large areas of
Yorkshire so as to drive away the inhabitants and prevent
future risings against him in those parts. He applied this ruthless 'scorched earth' policy also against Mercia and Northumbria, again to ensure that future foreign invasions should

attract no local support. Meanwhile, the Danish fleet lay in the mouth of the Humber, and here King Sven himself arrived from Denmark in 1070. In the spring, Danish and Anglo-Saxon forces captured Ely and Peterborough, but during the summer Sven and William the Conqueror came to a settlement, for which William probably paid a consideration. Ely was given up by the Danes, and Sven went home with the fleet the same year.

In Denmark Sven Estridson now pushed on with various reconstruction schemes and with plans of church politics, in which his aim was to ensure a development on different lines from England and from Germany as well. He ruled Denmark wisely and ably until his death in 1076.

He was succeeded by his five sons, one after the other. The second of these, Knud (later called Saint), laid plans, in conjunction with his father-in-law, Count Robert of Flanders, to conquer England. A large fleet was assembled, in 1085, in the Limfjord in Jutland, but before it could sail a rebellion broke out in Denmark, in the course of which Knud was killed, and with him perished the last Nordic threat of invasion against England. The Viking times, as far as Denmark is concerned, had come to an end.

THE NORWEGIANS

In Norway, as we have seen, the result of the crucial battle of Svolder was so to stabilize conditions that Sven Forkbeard gained supreme sovereignty over Norway, and exercised direct rule in the south, while under him Earl Sven governed Westland and Earl Erik Trøndelag. Both earls were the sons of Earl Haakon. This parcelling-out of power displeased, among others, the young and ambitious chieftain, Olav, son of the south Norwegian noble Harald Grenske. After the death of Sven Forkbeard in 1014, and while his son Knud, together with Earl Erik, was fully occupied in England, Olav went home to Norway, advanced rapidly through the south, which was his own homeland, and in 1016 gave battle to Earl Sven in a naval encounter at Nesjar in the mouth of the Sognefjord. For some years after this he was king of Norway, and proved himself an implacable ruler who made many enemies, not least by his Christian zeal for the repression of the traditional forms of religious worship. Olav, expecting an attack from Knud (later the Great) allied himself with the Swedish monarch Anund Jacob, and thus originated the battle, already mentioned, of the three kings at the river Helge, in which Knud triumphed. Olav remained for the time being in Norway, restless and unsettled, and when at last Knud the Great moved against Norway in 1028 with his massive Danish–English fleet, Olav, as we have noted, went to Russia, until, in 1030, he returned home via Sweden where Anund Jacob helped him to raise a new army. Olav, who was presently to become known as St Olav instead of Olav the Stout, then proceeded westwards through Jæmtland, in north Sweden, determined to recover his lost kingdom of Norway. It is because, in centuries to come, Olav was regarded by Norwegians and Norwegian Christianity as their greatest sovereign and saint, that we now consider this crucial campaign of his in some detail.

Anyone travelling today in Jæmtland, westwards along the ancient route from Sweden to Norway, will pass the little island of Frøsøn (the god Frøj's island) which stands in the middle of Storsjøn, the holy lake of the Jæmt people. On it is an open-air amphitheatre, a beautifully sited grass-covered gradient facing to the west; and from above the amphitheatre one looks west across the lake and the low blue hills which fringe it until the eye discerns the distant barren mountain range of Kølen which marks the boundary of Norway. On this open-air stage there is often performed nowadays the modern musical drama *Arnljot*, which takes its theme from St Olav's campaign. Arnljot was a Swedish warrior, mentioned by Snorre, outlawed for committing a murder on Frøsøn. He volunteered to join Olav, became a Christian, and fell fighting under Olav's banner at the great battle of Stiklestad. This open-air pageant affords modern travellers to Sweden an excellent introduction to the saga of Olav.

Trøndelag is accessible by three routes – as it probably was in Olav's time as well – which begin from a bulky mountain, 4500 feet high, called Åreskutan, a mass which overhangs the valleys and which affords, towards the east, a view over half of Jæmtland. From here King Olav set out, with an army probably of 2000 men, for Norway. Snorre asserts that he chose the middle one of the three routes, that which nowadays passes numerous mountain huts and crosses the Kølen range down into the Norwegian Inn Valley south of Stiklestad. On the Norwegian flank of the Kølen they met a peasant who complained to the king that the soldiers were flattening his crops. From now on, the king predicted, the man would have excellent crops – and so it proved! When Olav rode over the Kølen he saw, in a vision, the whole of Norway spread out before him – and then he went to the battlefield which he had chosen – Stiklestad.

He arrived there with his mercenaries a few days ahead of the enemy, determined to defeat the nobles and peasants of the Trøndelag. Their army, led by the great landowners Kalv Arneson and Tore Hund, was much bigger than Olav's; a factor which determined the result of the battle. The battle of Stiklestad, as we noted earlier, was the first land-battle of any size that we know of in Norway's history: all through the ninth and tenth centuries the Norwegians' engagements were always naval. Harald Fairhair, St Olav's great-grand-father, conquered Norway from his ships. The technique of battle in those days went on this pattern: both sides launched a hail of arrows – as many as possible 'so that the sky was darkened'. After this volley (this discharge of artillery, so to speak) came the hurling of spears against each other and, finally, the hand-to-hand mêlée with sword and axe. Snorre relates vividly and precisely the progress of the battle; the narrative contains such graphic items as the death of Tormod, Olav's minstrel, after the battle. As he stood there dying he pulled the arrow out of his breast and said 'Well has the King fed us; I still have fat round the roots of my heart!' (Incidentally Snorre's narrative discloses many interesting sidelights on the medical skill of the Vikings, of their treatment of wounds, etc.) King Olav, Snorre tells us, had carefully selected the field of battle and took up his position on slightly higher ground from which he led such a vehement charge as almost carried him to victory. But numbers began to tell, and before long King Olav was hemmed in and fell under his banner slain by blows from all the Vikings' three main weapons: sword, spear, and axe. His half brother, the fifteen-year-old Harald Hardrade, who was to become the last and perhaps the fiercest of all the Viking kings, was 'blooded' on this bitter occasion and managed to escape after the battle. Stiklestad was fought on 29 July 1030. When Snorre dramatically declares that the sun went out during the battle we must correct him, for the eclipse of the sun took place in the following year.

Norwegian historians have disagreed violently on the nature and significance of this battle. Older scholars asserted that Olav's enemies in Norway were the nobles and landowners, and that his supporters were the peasants and common people, and have gone on to conclude that Olav was ideally motivated by a faith in the future of his country and was willing to give his life for his idealism. Authorities of later generations, however, hold that Olav's cause was adopted by the lesser nobles who were at odds with the more substantial nobility and many of the earls. They find no particularly idealistic motives in Olav, but rather a passion for revenge and a typically Viking love of battle. It is worthy of note that he promised his troops, who were mainly mercenaries, rewards of land in Norway after victory had been achieved. Olav's last battle was certainly not fought in the cause of religion. There were, in fact, many Christians among the Trønder army which beat him at Stiklestad, and a Danish bishop, indeed, harangued them before the fight began. By that time Norway was already christianized; Olav's campaign was not a crusade against a heathen horde. We get nearest the truth, perhaps, by regarding the men of northern Norway as the natural defenders of the Trøndelag – and therefore of the realm of Norway – against a Viking king bent on revenge.

Snorre's saga of Olav does not disclose any saintly qualities in its hero. He seems no more sympathetic a character than most Viking leaders – certainly less so than Olav Tryggvason. And yet after Stiklestad the legend develops which transforms Olav the Stout into St Olav, and we hear stories of miracles and astonishing cures. Evidently the Church was taking a hand in the game. It was on the verge of a notable accession of strength in Norway, and its rising fortunes could be strengthened and stimulated by a Saint, especially by a royal Saint. Such a one the Church certainly contrived to get in Olav, and the results may be calculated by the estimate that, 200 years later, there was a priest in Norway for every 150 inhabitants – 2,000 of them in all. Olav was a powerful factor in the Church's attainment of such strength and power.

Near Stiklestad lies the old royal estate of Haug. Some time after the battle Olav's son, the young King Magnus, was discussing the fight with two chieftains, Ejnar Tambarskælve and Kalv Arneson. Snorre relates what happened: 'Go with me', said Magnus, 'to the battlefield and show me where my father fell.' Ejnar answered, 'You had better ask your foster-father, Kalv, for he fought there that day.' Kalv hung back, but King Magnus insisted. When they came to the place Kalv said, 'Here he fell.' 'But where were you then, Kalv?' 'Here', said Kalv, 'where I now stand.' Magnus's face darkened –

'So your axe could reach him?' 'But it did not reach him,' cried Kalv – and he leapt on his horse and galloped away. The same night he fled the country, as Tore Hund, another of the victors at Stiklestad, had done some time ago. And now King Magnus embarked upon a campaign of extermination against those who had led the Trønder men against his father at Stiklestad, so that discontent grew and multiplied amongst the Trønders. The situation was taken in hand by Sigvat, who had been Olav's favourite minstrel. He now composed a ballad – the equivalent of what would be in our times an Open Letter in the newspapers – in which he warned King Magnus not to make divisions between the throne and the people, as Olav had done. The warning went home and Magnus broke off the persecution of his father's conquerors. He caused a constitution to be drafted, became popular, and earned the sobriquet 'the Good' – which his father had never enjoyed.

Magnus did not become full king until 1035, when Elfgivu, nominated regent for his and her son by Knud the Great, was driven from Norway. Magnus left behind him a good name in his own country as well as in Denmark, which he conquered. About 1045 his father's half-brother Harald Hardrade returned home from Byzantium, famous and rich, and shared the kingdom of Norway with Magnus until the latter's death two years later. Then, for nineteen years, Harald held the supreme power and became the most doughty warrior of his time. He had a passion for fighting and engaged in frequent Viking raids against Sven Estridson in Denmark; he succeeded, indeed, in gutting Hedeby in 1050. Finally he made peace with Sven, an enduring peace, and turned his turbulent thoughts to a descent upon England, this time from the north.

Harald assembled his ships and men on the Orkneys, and from there sailed south in September 1066, aided partly from Scotland and also by the exiled Anglo-Saxon Earl Tostig, brother to the English king Harald Godwinsson who had succeeded Edward the Confessor. Wafted by that same north wind which was holding up William the Conqueror's battle-ready fleet in the estuary of the Somme, Harald Hardrade now sailed south along the Scottish and English coasts with a fleet, it is said, of 300 vessels, entered the Humber, and anchored in the river Ouse. Landing there the Norwegian army marched towards York and on 20 September, at Fulford, south of York, won a battle – assisted, it is said, by some local sympathy for the invaders. Harald now returned to his fleet, after making pacts with the people of York for their assistance in the future in his further attempt to conquer England. He now summoned hostages from several places and received them in his camp at Stamford Bridge, a few miles east of York. Meanwhile, the English king Harald Godwinsson was not idle. By rapid marches he advanced from the south, reached the undefended York on 24 September and the next day took the Norwegians by surprise at Stamford Bridge. This skilful campaign gave the English Harald a complete victory, in which both the Norwegian Harald and Tostig were killed. Harald's son, Olav, was compelled to make peace, and he sailed back home with the remainder of the army, having given his oath that he would never again attack England. The valiant and skilful Harald Godwinsson had brief enjoyment of his brilliant victory. Three days later the Duke of Normandy made his fateful landing in the south of England; Harald made another forced march to meet him, and in the celebrated Battle of Hastings on 14 October 1066, Harald fell. The Conquest had begun.

Harald Hardrade's son and successor in Norway, Olav Kyrre, reigned for over twenty-five years, almost to the turn of the century, and proved himself a man of peace. With him the Viking period, as far as Norway was concerned, came to an end.

We must next take a look at the Nordic spheres of interest in the West, and note the course of Viking activities in that quarter. The Orkneys, about 1000, were ruled by the powerful independent Earl Sigurd Digre (the Stout) married to the daughter of the Scottish king Malcolm. He held sway over not only the Orkneys themselves, but also over Caithness, the Hebrides, and the Isle of Man. In Ireland in 1012 Brian Boroimhe (Irish: tribute), the supreme monarch, fell foul of the King of Leinster, who allied himself to another of Brian's subsidiary princes, Sigtrygg Silkbeard the Norwegian ruler of Dublin. Sigtrygg, fearing that Brian Boroimhe would recapture Dublin, called upon Sigurd Digre for aid. A fierce and bloody battle was fought at Clontarf, on 23 April 1014, in which the Irish prevailed, but both Brian Boroimhe and Sigurd Digre died on the field. Dublin itself was not attacked, and Sigtrygg, who had not taken part in the battle of Clontarf, continued to reign as King of Dublin for many years. He was, incidentally, the first king in Ireland who minted coins. Sigtrygg, like his father, ended his life a penitent monk in the monastery of Iona.

In Ireland during the rest of the century there was a succession of quarrels and affrays between the Norwegians and the Irish in which no outstanding personage figured. But in the Orkneys arose Thorfinn the Mighty. Embroiled, in the 1040s, in a quarrel with a relative, Ragnvald, whom he managed to kill, this Thorfinn was, for the next twenty years, the chief earl in the Orkneys until his death in 1064, by which time he had, indeed, become widely acknowledged as ruler of the whole of north-west Scotland. The Isle of Man, too, acquired a strong man (around 1050–95) in the Icelandic-born Godred Crovan, who succeeded in extending his rule to Dublin and Leinster. At the end of the century the King of Norway visited these old Viking stamping-grounds on three occasions. This was Magnus Barfod, son of Olav Kyrre, who finally brought the Orkneys, the Hebrides, and the Isle of Man under Norway. He fell in 1104 during a campaign in Ulster. This attachment of the Orkneys to Norway persisted,

with little break, until the fifteenth century, when King
Christian I of the Danish-Norwegian union gave the islands
as security for his daughter's dowry to King James III of
Scotland.

ICELAND AND GREENLAND

The story of the independent Icelandic Christian states in the
eleventh century can be briefly told. The adoption of Christianity went smoothly, for the people, as we know, had
chosen of its own free will. It may be presumed that the
heathen sanctuaries soon disappeared and were supplemented
by simple turf-built churches. In the eleventh century Iceland
had three eminent Christian administrators, all called Gissurr,
father, son, and grandson. The first of these was Gissurr the
White, who was present at the decisive meeting of the Alting,
in 1000, when Christianity was accepted. He sent his son,
Isleifr Gissurrsson, to Germany for an ecclesiastical training,
and in 1056 this second Gissurr was ordained by Bishop Adalbert of Bremen as Iceland's first native bishop, with his seat
at Skalholt. He died in 1080, worried (the story goes) over
the manifold difficulties which beset a bishop. His son, Gissurr
Isleifsson, the third Gissurr (1072–1118), followed as bishop,
and proved well endowed with wisdom, persuasiveness, and
authority. He was evidently one of those admirable prelates
in whom physical and spiritual strength and courage are
matched. During his time, it is said, there was peace throughout Iceland; people could go their ways without weapons;
and so great was Gissurr's prestige that 'every one, young and
old, poor and rich, women and men, sat or stood as the
Bishop ordered'. This period of tranquillity, which lasted not
only throughout this third Gissurr's time, but through most
of the eleventh century, cannot be entirely attributed to the
achievement of a few men. But what other factors existed it
is difficult to say. There was no lack of trouble both before

and after the period of the Gissurrs. Iceland's constitution, constructed in 930 on the Norwegian pattern, had an Alting consisting of the legislative assembly presided over by two law-speakers, and a law-court, divided into four, one for each quarter of the island, supplemented after 1000 by an appeal court. But in spite of this the country had not enjoyed peace, and the decisions of its courts often proved to carry insufficient authority. Thus the century or so from 930 had been racked by blood-feuds and strife. Then for another hundred years there came this pacific age of the Gissurrs – to be followed again by turbulence in the twelfth and thirteenth centuries. But it is time to leave Iceland for the northernmost Nordic colony, Greenland.

The sources do not always agree, but it is said that Leif son of Eric the Red visited Olav Tryggvason in Norway in the autumn of 999. There he was baptized, and ordered by the king to return at once to Greenland to preach and proclaim the Christian faith. For this mission he was given two assistants. Leif accepted the task, without much enthusiasm, and soon found that his evangelism displeased his father – who, we may presume, never accepted Christianity. His mother, on the other hand, was allowed to build a small chapel where she and other converts could gather for prayer. To this extent Christianity was introduced to Iceland and Greenland almost at the same time, about the turn of the century. But it was not until the beginning of the twelfth century that Greenland had its own bishop.

THE DISCOVERY OF AMERICA

One final Viking deed must be recorded, which occurred in the farthest confines of the Norwegian sphere of interest: the discovery of America. According to the Sagas Bjarni Herjulfson and his followers sailed from Iceland to Greenland in the year 986. They lost their course on the journey and three times sighted land, but did not go ashore. The first land they saw was well-wooded coast, and so was the second; but their third landfall was a rocky island with glaciers visible upon it.

Some time later Leif Ericson bought Bjarni's ship, and in 992 (probably) left Greenland with thirty-five men to find and explore the land which Bjarni had reported. He found the glacier island. Between the shore and the ice there was nothing but stone, and the island which he named 'Helluland' (Stoneland) seemed to him to be 'without any good things'. But next he reached a flat and forested land which Leif named 'Markland' (wood-land); and two days later they came to an island on which they found abundant grass and sweet dew. Between this island and the mainland they discerned a strait in which their vessel grounded itself on a sandbank at low tide. They got off at high water, and on going ashore by a river decided to winter in this place, where there was good timber to be got, for building their huts, from the adjacen forests of maple. In the rivers and in the sea they found salmon bigger than any they had ever seen before; there were no frosts in the winter and the grass scarcely withered at all. Day and night were of much more equal duration than in Greenland and Iceland. During the short days the sun rose in the east-south-east and set in the west-south-west.

Leif now divided his company so that some stayed by the camp while others went to reconnoitre the district. During these explorations a man called Tyrk, who hailed from Germany, one of Eric the Red's old friends, was reported missing one night. Presently they came across him, and found him in a state of great excitement: babbling in his German mother-tongue, grimacing and rolling his eyes. He had found, so he said, vines and grapes – and he would certainly know, for he was born in a land where vines were familiar. In the time that followed they collected grapes, cut vines, and felled timber, loading all this on to their ship; and in the spring they broke camp and sailed home from the land which they christened 'Wineland'. On their way back they rescued some shipwrecked men from a rock and got safely home to Brattahlid, Erik the Red's house at Ericsfjord in Greenland. Elsewhere it is told that after this voyage Leif was called Leif the Lucky.

The next story to be told in the Sagas is of Leif's brother, Torvald, who, borrowing Leif's vessel, sailed away with thirty men and safely reached Leif's huts in Wineland where they settled down for the winter. In the following summer they explored the westerly coast of the country which they found very beautiful: with forests, white sandy beaches, numerous islands, and shallow waters. On one island they came across a kind of wooden shed, but otherwise found no sign of human habitation or activity. In the autumn they returned to their base at Leif's huts, and employed the next summer in exploring the eastern and northern coasts. They broke off their keel in a storm while rounding a headland (*næs*) and, after fitting a new one, they set up the broken one on the headland which they called 'Kølnæs' (Keelness). Continuing their journey to the east they came upon wooded fiords. They lay to alongside a promontory so beautiful that Torvald exclaimed: 'This is a fair land, here I will build my farm'. But on the beach they came upon three skin boats with nine men; they fought and killed eight of them. Soon afterwards they were attacked by a large number of men in skin boats, and these 'Scrarlings' shot at them, but finally fled. Torvald, however, was pierced by an arrow and died of his wound. They buried him at his desire on the promontory, and put up a cross at his head and another at his feet. They called the place 'Korsnæs' (Crossness) and then returned to Leif's huts for the winter. They collected grapes and timber for cargo and when spring came they sailed for home and came to Ericsfjord 'with great tidings for Leif'.

Another narrative tells how the Icelander Torfin Karlsevni goes to 'Wineland' with three ships and 160 men. They first reach Helluland and after that Markland, and then after sailing along strange, long, sandy beaches, reach the promontory with the ship's keel, 'Keelness'. Near here they turn up a fiord and dispatch two scouts, a Scottish runner and his wife, who return three days later with grapes and self-sown wheat. They go on, into another fiord with an island at its mouth, where there are so many sea-birds that a man can scarcely put a foot between the eggs. A powerful current runs around the island, and so they name the fiord 'Strømfjord' and the island Strømø (strøm – current). They winter here with their cattle. There is plenty of grass, but little food for human beings. In their hunger they pray to God; but Torhal the Hunter, on the other hand, appeals to Thor. A whale drifts in, of a variety unfamiliar even to Torfin Karlsevni, who is knowledgeable about whales. It proves to be uneatable, they become ill and fling the whale meat into the sea. As spring comes they manage on birds' eggs, hunting, and fishing. By this time Torhal the Hunter is discontented and anxious to return to Greenland, and therefore taking one ship and nine of the men he sets off. They are driven by an easterly gale to Ireland, and there Torhal dies. The others sail south for a long way until they reach a river running through a lake into the sea; only at high water can they get into the river. They call the place 'Hóp'. Here on the low ground grows self-sown wheat; on the high ground vines. Every brook teems with fish. Where they find the highest tidewater they dig pits and at ebb tide find halibut in them. The forest abounds with animals of many kinds. Here they spend the winter. No snow falls; the cattle can be kept out of doors. Now they encounter the inhabitants of the country, the 'Scrarlings', and to begin with barter peaceably with them, giving them red cloth and milk (which was unknown to the natives) in return for furs. But a quarrel arises, a roaring ox having stampeded the natives who now come in hordes, in skin boats, terrifying the Norsemen by flinging great stones sewn into painted skins from tall poles. Men fall on both sides, the Scrarlings fight with slings and stone axes; they are astonished at the iron axes of the Norsemen. After this Karlsevni judges it too dangerous to remain in the land of Hóp and, abandoning the idea of settling there, returned to Strømfjord half-way between Hóp and Keelness. Leaving most of his people there he takes one ship to the north to look for Torhal and after a vain search returns to winter at Strømfjord. There a son, Snorri, is born to him. Next spring they all go home via Markland, where they capture and take along with them two Scrarling boys. One of their vessels turning out to be worm-eaten, founders, but Karlsevni's own ship finally gets back to Ericsfjord in Greenland.

The last story in the Sagas about Wineland tells of Freydis, a natural daughter of Erik the Red, a violent Viking woman. She sets out on a voyage to Wineland in two ships, accompanied by her two brothers Helge and Finnbogl. They reach Leif's huts in Wineland, where they winter. Trouble breaks out; Freydis carries out a plan to murder both brothers and, with her own axe, moreover, slaughters all the women. Early next summer she returns to Greenland.

This is the essence of what the Sagas tell us about Wineland and the Norse discovery of America. Some scholars, in former times, were sceptical of this traditional material as historical evidence. That attitude has changed, and in its place there is a recognition of the truth that lives behind these tales, namely, that the Norsemen of Greenland, somewhere around 1000, really did discover and explore an extensive non-Arctic country which can only have been some area of the North-American continent. Where was it? Where did Wineland lie? Many speculations have been made, without reaching any conclusive result; there is not enough evidence, nautical, astronomical, or anthropological, in the Sagas to pin-point the locality of Wineland. Nor has North America provided any archaeological clues of any worth or significance. To my mind there is no reason whatsoever to doubt that the Nordic colonists in Greenland did find America at the close of the Viking period, and did endeavour to establish a permanent foothold there. In the latter effort they evidently did not succeed. America, unlike Greenland and Iceland, was not uninhabited when the Norsemen discovered it, but had a population which was apparently hostile – for which they are certainly not to be blamed, considering the behaviour of the Norsemen! The Sagas seem to confirm that the men from Greenland made serious efforts to colonize in North America, but that the task was too much for them. Their lines of communication with the homeland were too extensive and fragile, their bases on the new continent too weak. But the attempt in itself may fairly be regarded as the final expression of Viking adventurousness and daring. That it fizzled out was due, I repeat, to the fact that the source and mainspring of the effort was too distant from America: otherwise world history might in several ways bear a different aspect today.

It would be a fine thing if we could trace Wineland by finding the sites of Leif's huts; or of any other Norse houses like those which have been excavated in Greenland by the Danish archaeologist Poul Nørlund – such as the ruins of Erik the Red's own house in Brattahlid. Such discoveries would confirm the presence of Norsemen in America, long before the days of Columbus. It would be worth while making a systematic search along the treeless Atlantic coast for such evidence by aerial survey from low-flying and slow-moving planes. Danish archaeologists have carried out such an investigation in Greenland.

THE SWEDES

Of Sweden's political history in the eleventh century little is known, for sources are scarce. In earlier pages something was said of Olav Skotking who, with Danish and Norwegian aid, fought Olav Tryggvason at Svolder) in 1000; and of the son Anund Jacob who, in 1026, suffered defeat at the Helge, in company with Olav Haraldson, by Knud the Great. Both these Swedish kings were Christians, and so, too, forty years later, was King Stenkil. But it must not be assumed that Sweden became christianized in the early part of the eleventh century; on the contrary, the religious battles appear to have continued until after 1100. Of the three Scandinavian countries, then, Sweden was the last to abandon the traditional heathen faith. As we shall see later, the heathen temple at Uppsala was flourishing when Adam of Bremen wrote in the 1070s.

In Sweden's Russian sphere of interest ('The Great Svitjod') much had changed during the eleventh century. The two Rus Khaganates of Novgorod and Kiev had combined into a single Christian West Russian Empire, in which the Swedish element gradually gave way to Slav predominance and where Byzantine influences slowly penetrated. The eastern trade route along the Volga had lost its importance, since the production of silver by the Caliphate of Baghdad had fallen off; from the Swedish point of view the major trade route was the Dneiper, leading to the Black Sea and Byzantium. The Greek Emperor in Constantinople had recruited a Nordic bodyguard – the Værings – of which Harald Hardrade had been a member; and the word 'Væring', which had formerly signified a merchant, now stood for a Viking warrior. The Swedes got as far as Athens. The big marble lion found in the harbour of Piraeus, and now set up in Venice, has a Swedish runic ribbon round its shoulders, but the inscription on it has unfortunately weathered away.

In late Icelandic literature we are told of an outstanding Nordic feat – an expedition launched from Sweden, around 1040, against far-eastern Mohammedan countries ('Särkland') led by Ingvar Vidfarne, Emund's son. His campaign is commemorated on many Upp-Swedish runic stones, the so-called 'Ingvar stones', but there are no reliable records of it. During the reign of St Vladimir and his son Yaroslav (who was married to Ingegerd the daughter of Olav Skotking) in the first part of the eleventh century the Kiev empire was powerful enough to make the Dneiper route safe against attacks by eastern nomads.

Two factors later combined to undermine the West Russian Empire based on Kiev: the Crusades encouraged Oriental trade to come in directly across Europe, instead of by the more devious route of the Russian waterways; and the Asiatic nomads, the Kumans, multiplied their raids upon the west so that the Dneiper route became increasingly dangerous. But when we look back on the record and achievement of the Rus folk we can truly say that it was Swedish activity that created the following Russian towns: Novgorod, Izborsk, Polotsk, Byelosersk, Rostov, Murom, Smolensk, Chernigov, and Kiev.

This extensive development of the eastern routes by Swedish merchants and warriors in the eleventh century had profound reactions upon Sweden itself. There is evidence of this in archaeological finds. The many thousands of Arabic coins picked up on Swedish soil – the Kufic dirhems – which must all have been brought by the Volga route, belong to the ninth and tenth centuries. There are scarcely any from the eleventh. By that time the Volga route had become insecure, and the Baghdad Caliphate had lost its silver mines to eastern invaders. But to compensate for this Sweden got a substantial share of danegeld from England from the end of the tenth century and through the first half of the eleventh: as witness the thousands of Anglo-Saxon coins of this period which have been found in Sweden, especially in Gotland.

The last of the great Swedish Viking expeditions, almost lost in legend yet authenticated by runic stones, is the one mentioned above – Ingvar Vidfarne's campaign to Särkland. And then, during the last half of the eleventh century, the Swedish Viking period comes to an end.

CHAPTER 6

WEAPONS AND TOOLS

WEAPONS

THE offensive weapons of the Vikings consisted of sword, axe, spear, and bow and arrow. The most favoured of these were the sword and the axe, which every Viking of any quality always carried about with him.

The Viking sword is familiar from numerous finds in Scandinavia: over 2,000 in Norway, many in Sweden, but comparatively few in Denmark. This uneven distribution is accounted for to some extent by the fact that these ancient swords are usually found in graves, and Christianity, which forbade the burial of weapons with the dead, came earlier to Denmark than to Norway and Sweden. The sword was undoubtedly the Vikings' principal weapon, with the axe as a close runner-up. During the epoch immediately preceding the Viking period the most popular kind of sword, especially in Norway, had been the one-edged sword; but the Vikings preferred the long, usually broad, two-edged iron sword with a hilt in the shape of two cross-bars and a triangular or semi-circular pommel. The blade was frequently worked in dama-scene, and the hilt inlaid with gold, copper, silver, or *niello*, so that the Viking sword was often a weapon of great splendour. The Vikings, indeed, loved grandeur and colour in their weapons and their clothes. Few scabbards have been found, but many bronze ferrules of scabbards have been discovered: triangular in shape and frequently decorated with animal ornament. The oldest Viking swords are rather simple, the later ones more elaborate. Archaeologists have carried out much research on Viking swords, and have classified them into more than a score of categories – Norwegian, Danish, Swedish, primitive, late, etc. Many specimens have been un-earthed also in the various Viking spheres of interest – in England, Ireland, France, and Russia.

Where would these Viking swords have been manufac-tured: in the Nordic countries, abroad, or both? The probable answer is that some were home-produced and some imported. A sword is a complicated product, and its various parts were doubtless not all made by the same craftsman. There may well have been different specialists for blades, hilts, mountings, and so on. For example, a hilt decorated with Nordic orna-ments, such as the 'gripping beast' design or the Jelling pat-tern, must have been made in Scandinavia itself. On the other hand, a blade bearing the 'factory' trademark of *Ulfberth* or *Ingelri* was certainly forged abroad, probably in France. Nordic smiths were unquestionably able to manufacture swords; the quantities of iron and native iron tools found among Viking remains, notably Norwegian, witness to the high standard of the Scandinavian smith. Yet there is some-thing to show that the best sword-makers were the Franks. One source of this evidence is the embargo on the export of swords and other weapons which Charlemagne and Charles the Bald imposed, even to the extent of a death penalty for infringement. Charlemagne's ban included the east and the north as well, both the Avars and the Vikings; and clerics were enjoined to obey it, which suggests that weapons were often forged in the smithies of monasteries. Charles the Bald's prohibition was expressly directed against the Viking market: why should his craftsmen supply these bloodthirsty robbers with the choicest weapons in the world? The region of the Rhine and Cologne in particular was an important centre of manufacture. England is said to have imported 'good Cologne swords'.

An illustration of the superiority of Frankish over Nordic swords is to be found in the anecdote told in *Gesta Caroli*

Magni (The History of Charlemagne) of the emperor Ludwig
the German sitting on his throne to receive gifts of homage
from 'the kings of the Normans'. Among these gifts were
Nordic weapons, which Ludwig tests with his experienced
hands: and only one sword satisfies him! The anecdote may
well be an invention but even so its tendency is clear enough:
to point out the inferiority of Nordic swords. Another
pointer of the same kind occurs in the remarks of the Arab
Ibn Fadlan, who specially noticed the swords which he saw
the Rus merchants carrying among the Bulgars: broad, flat,
with grooved blades 'after the Frankish pattern'. And other
Arab writers testify to the importation of swords to the
Orient, partly from France (through Jewish middlemen) and
partly by the Rus folk. They record, moreover, that the Arabs
sometimes robbed the graves of Rus warriors to filch the
splendid swords buried with the dead; and these Rus swords
were most likely weapons bought originally from the Franks.
The Arabs, who were themselves no mean swordsmiths,
would scarcely have given such praise to Nordic weapons.
These surmises have archaeological support, too. A Swedish
authority has noted a discovery from the Viking period, at
Øland in the Baltic, consisting of five damascened sword-
blades bearing the signature of the manufacturer (Ulfberth):
apparently these blades were imported from the Franks to
get their hilts made in Sweden, for the Nordic craftsmen were
famous for their production of hafts and hilts in bronze with
various inlays.

Whereas the sword was common to all countries, the axe
was a characteristically Nordic weapon, and one, moreover,
far older than the sword. It is not difficult to see why this
should be so. The sword is really an elongated dagger, and
it was not developed until man, in the long course of his
development, found a material which could produce such
an artificial product as a sword – first bronze and subsequently,
iron. The axe, on the other hand, existed already in the Stone

Age, long before the sword appeared. During the Viking period the battle-axe was, in Europe generally, outmoded, and had little more than a ceremonial or heraldic significance. In the Nordic countries, however, the battle-axe remained a favourite weapon, and to the much afflicted peoples of western Europe the long-handled broad-edged battle-axe was a sinister symbol of the bloodthirsty Viking. The Lindisfarne Stone bears a typical picture of Vikings carrying their two principal weapons, axe and sword, raised high above their heads. The Viking battle-axe had many varieties of design, but there were two main types: the older one, called the *Skægøxe* or beard-axe, was an inheritance from the eighth century, while the broad-axe with its powerful concave edge was in vogue about 1000. The cutting-edge of the broad axe, made of specially hardened iron, was often welded on to the weapon. Both axes had a polygonal neck and were sometimes decorated with exquisite silver inlay on blade and neck. One exceptionally beautiful silver-inlaid broad-axe was found during the excavations of the Danish Viking camp at Trelleborg.

The spear, too, was familiar to the Vikings; in fact it was their third main weapon. No shafts have survived, only the spear-heads, which are blades of an elegant shape with a sharp mid-rib and a hollow conical base, fitted on to the end of the shaft. Sometimes this base has a pair of short side-wings, no doubt of Frankish origin. Some late specimens of the spears are richly inlaid with geometric silver patterns across the base of the blade; presumably such beautiful specimens were brought back to the owner after a battle, if he were victorious.

Finally there is the bow and arrow, an ancient weapon which, as the Sagas confirm, played an important part in Viking battles. None of the actual bows have survived, but they were probably long-bows; nor have any arrow-shafts been saved. What have been found in abundance in graves (including women's graves) are arrow-heads having a considerable penetrative power when shot from a long-bow. Sometimes they lie alongside the dead in bundles of anything up to forty, some of them in cylindrical quivers.

Another Viking weapon – which was also a tool – was the knife. The simple single-edged knife, with a handle of wood or bone, was carried by men at their belts, by the women (as Ibn Fadlan relates in his Volga narrative) on a chain worn on the breast. In graves of the Viking age it is common to find the dead woman lying with her knife on her chest or by her side.

The most important defensive equipment of the Vikings was the wooden shield, the iron coat of mail, and the leather or iron helmet. Few specimens have been found, but they are familiar from pictorial records and from descriptions in the old literature. The shield was round, flat, and not very thick, often painted and fortified by a broad disc or boss in the middle. Shields of this kind hang in rows along the gunwales of the famous Norwegian Viking ship at Gokstad. Chain armour and helmet were worn by the nobles alone, and fragments only have survived. But pictorial records show (leather) helmets of a conical shape (rather like a storm hat), presumably of oriental origin. Woven tapestries from the Norwegian Oseberg ship depict white-painted armour covering the whole body and ending in a hood on the head.

An analysis made some years ago of the weapons recovered from Danish graves revealed the fact that the four staple weapons – sword, axe, spear, bow and arrow – were never found together; and only in one were sword, axe, spear, and shield found with the warrior. As a rule only two weapons were found with the body, and of these the most frequent were first the axe, second the sword, and third the spear. This investigation however only covered Danish material, of which much less is available than of Norwegian and Swedish.

While on this subject of Viking weapons it is perhaps appropriate to make some reference to that strange species of Viking warrior known as *berserk*: half-crazed fighters who revealed incredible strength while possessed of battle intoxication and who relapsed into a stupor when their unnatural exertions were over. Snorre, in *Ynglinga Saga,* speaks of this kind of warrior as being inspired by Odin's rage. He writes: 'Odin could so devise it that his enemies in battle were struck with blindness, deafness, or terror, so that their weapons were no better than sticks; whereas his favoured men, scorning armour, fought with the madness of dogs or wolves, biting the shield-edge; they had the strength of bears or bulls. They beat down all opposition, and were themselves touched by neither fire nor iron.' The word *berserk* has been derived from *bare serk,* meaning 'only a shirt' – that is to say, without armour. Another suggested meaning is *bjørne serk* or 'bear shirt', a reference presumably to the animal skin in which this kind of warrior habitually fought being then, as was believed, transformed into the animal concerned. (There were other fanatical fighters called *ulfhednar,* which means 'wolf skins'.) These berserks frequently turn up in Nordic literature. Nils Lid thinks they are to be regarded as psychopaths selected for their exceptional strength and ferocity and organized into special corps in the service of the king or chieftain. During battle they were supposed to be able to incite each other to a frenzy.

The favourite animal of the Vikings was the horse, and a warrior's charger (and his dog) were often buried with him. The rider's outfit – spurs, stirrups, bridle, reins, saddle, collar-harness, etc. – afforded ample opportunity for fine decoration. In a grave at Birka in central Sweden there was found a bridle made of leather decorated with silvered studs, and on the south Danish island of Langeland there was found a chieftain's grave containing spurs and stirrups adorned with silver inlay in elaborate patterns. A Viking horseman in his splendour must have been a noble sight. Across the horse's mane lay the carved 'chair', a bronze-mounted piece of wood (collar-harness) with a hole through which the reins were passed (Pl. 3c). Saddles, as found in Norway, were made of wood, and seem to have been placed well forward on the horse. Stirrups – originally invented (in leather and wood) on the steppes of Eurasia and from there penetrating west to Europe – were in Viking times made of iron. One of the two Viking variations is more or less a strap made of iron, while the other has a rectangular foot-rest of wood inside the iron step, imitating the original one of wood. The vertical bars of the stirrups were frequently decorated with silver or copper inlay (Pls. 3A and B). Another item in the riding outfit, on Norwegian evidence, is the so-called 'rangel', a rattle probably intended to keep evil spirits at bay.

TOOLS

There is no lack of archaeological evidence to show that the Vikings were skilled craftsmen, quite apart from the products they imported from abroad. Their home manufactures included ships, carts, sledges, textiles, jewellery, as well as the numerous tools for artisan use. The basic worker in iron age communities is evidently the blacksmith: without the tools of iron he fashioned there would be poorer ploughs, houses, and weapons – in short, a lower standard of life. The three Nordic countries had long learned to extract iron from the ores they found in swamp-land. The fact that they had home-produced iron is confirmed in many ways, such as finds of concealed 'depots' of raw material (hundreds of home-made iron bars). The Nordic blacksmith was a highly-regarded member of the community; and on his death his smith's tools were buried with him for further use in the beyond. Egil's Saga tells how Egil, on the death of his father Skallagrim, built a mound for him at the far end of a promontory and laid him inside it, with his horse, his weapons, and his black-smith's tools. Even the chieftain mastered smithing! It seems likely, however, as Sigurd Grieg has suggested, that each village had its special community blacksmith to perform the jobs which were too difficult for the layman. Grave-dis-coveries have established the nature of the blacksmith's kit in Viking times – light and heavy hammers, tongs with bent or with straight beaks, files, chisels, scissors, and anvil.

The equipment of many other kinds of artisan has also come to light in Swedish and Norwegian graves – such as the car-penter's knives, chisels, drills, axes, plane-irons, awls, and saw-blades. Of agricultural implements there have been found plough-irons, scythes, and sickles for cutting grass and corn, and knives for cutting branches and leaves from trees; of fishing-gear, hooks, spears, and stones for sinking the nets. Of women's household equipment there have been found most of the things necessary for spinning and weaving – needles, spinning wheels, weights, flax rakes, scissors, smooth-ing irons – and the full battery of kitchen utensils, such as kettles of bronze or iron, racks and chains, frying pans, spits, grills, hooks, and wooden bowls, as well as pots made of soap-stone. Swedish and Norwegian discoveries have been especially fruitful. In Norway soap-stone quarries have been excavated from which it is possible to trace the procedures in this ancient industry, from the ring-shaped cuts in the rock wall where the soap-stone was quarried through the make-ready processes right down to the finishing-off of the smooth bowls and pots. Only one traditional craft, which had for-merly been skilfully practised in the North, seems to have been neglected in Viking times – ceramics. In Norway it seems as if pottery disappeared, to be replaced by wooden vessels, soap-stone pots, and iron kettles. Some Danish ceramics of the period exist, mostly spherical bowls, in black or brown, without handles or legs. Only in Sweden have ceramics of quality been encountered – well burnt and decorated. Some of these come from Birka, perhaps imported from Finland. The fact that, both in Birka and Hedeby, which were trading centres, there have been found excellent ceramics, often painted and decorated, which were imported from Friesland or the Rhine region, cannot conceal the truth that the potter's art was neglected in the Viking homelands, although less in Sweden than in the other two Nordic countries.

Two final kinds of Viking handiwork must be mentioned: glassware and coins. In Hedeby crucibles and other witnesses to glass-production have been found; although this does not invalidate the view that the fine glasses found in the graves of the mighty were imported products. As for coins, it has been established that the Nordic countries were minting them as far back as the ninth century. But more of that later.

CHAPTER 7

DRESS AND ORNAMENT

How did the Vikings – and their women – dress? Imagination plays upon what they must have looked like, what total impression their costume would make upon us. Three sources will help us. First, archaeological discoveries: fragments of Viking dress which afford some clues to technique and details, and also Viking pictures of themselves, which give a general impression. The second source is provided by pictures in Europe *outside* the Viking countries, and the third comprises descriptions of Viking dress in literature.

The archaeological find in the north which affords the best impression of Viking costume in the ninth century is the Oseberg ship in south Norway, that inexhaustible treasure of knowledge, discovered about fifty years ago. From this ship there came a tightly-packed bundle of textiles from which, after patient treatment of its damage, some remarkable things were salvaged: pieces of a woven tapestry showing pictures designed to hang in the hall, a parallel to the famous Norman Bayeux tapestry, more than two centuries younger, showing William conquering England in 1066. In the old Norwegian language such a narrow woven tapestry was called *refil* or *tiald*. The Oseberg specimen is only twenty centimetres high, a fact which Robert Kloster has explained by saying that it had to be placed in the hall so that people sitting around could see and study it. If it were hung high in the dark and smoky hall it would not be seen at all; if it were hung too low it would be obscured by the heads of the people at table. So it had to be a rather narrow piece of cloth. The original colours of this Oseberg tapestry were mainly red and yellowy brown. It had numerous figures on it, and an ornamented edging serving as a frame. The themes of the tapestry apparently were myths, tales, and heroic poems. We see warriors in plenty, berserks in armour, armed women, horsemen; there are carts and covered wagons, the latter looking like prairie wagons. Between these pictures, to fill in empty spaces, we find birds, zigzag lines, swastikas, plaited patterns, and so on. The weapons depicted are mainly spears and bows and arrows, but there are also swords and axes. The predominance of the spear is emphatic – not only in the warriors' hands but stuck into the ground as well. At first glance the warriors seem to be standing in clumps of tall flowers, but what seem to be giant flower-stalks are really man-killing battle-spears. The scenes on the Oseberg tapestry are taken from a land-battle: no ships are in sight. They are difficult to interpret; but one of them, a particularly vivid battle-scene, with spears, shields, berserks and a single chariot warrior has been explained by Bjørn Hougen as illustrating the battle of Braavalla, with King Harald Hildetand in the chariot.

The costumes on the Oseberg tapestry are very interesting. The warrior wears a helmet and a coat of mail, and has a white oval shield and spear. But some of the men apparently are in 'civilian' clothes – yet they too carry the ubiquitous spear. These clothes appear to consist of a thick woollen coat, reaching to mid-thigh or a little above it. The sleeves are long, and the coat, though occasionally belted, usually hangs loose. This coat, strangely enough, is 'tailor-made': it fits snugly into the waist. The coat or jacket is familiar from other Viking discoveries in the north – for instance, from the Gotland carved stones, a Norwegian runic stone, and a bronze statuette discovered at Skaane. It is also the same kind of coat as is shown on the Lindisfarne relief mentioned earlier in this book.

Two kinds of trousers are depicted in the Oseberg tapestry. They are either long and tight (again the Gotland and Lindisfarne stones) or else wide and baggy, rather like plus-fours.

This type of trousers, too, with a rather different cut, appears on some of the men shown on the Gotland stones. The Arab Ibn Rustah, in the tenth century, said of the Rus traders that they used exaggeratedly full trousers gathered at the knees. The two Vikings shown on the Smiss-i-När stone from Gotland are depicted in a duel and their wide trousers stick out horizontally below the knee to such an extent that one is inclined to believe they are supported on some sort of inner framework like a crinoline. Trousers of this abundant, baggy kind, which used so much material, would of course be appropriate to rich and noble persons who liked to display their wealth; and it is a commonplace that, always and everywhere, fashions are dictated not least by vanity and the desire to flaunt the wearer's riches.

There is yet a third male garment shown on the Oseberg tapestry. This is a long cape or cloak ending in two points reaching almost to the ground and worn in either of two ways – with the points at each side or else at back and front. This cloak again, is well represented on the Gotland stones. One is reminded that Ibn Fadlan wrote that the Rus traders wore their cloaks thrown over on one side so as to keep one arm free; and this the Gotland pictures confirm. This long cloak, hanging freely from the shoulders, is a stately garment. Its appearance is not in the least military, but it has a dignity which consorts well with the other 'civilian' clothing of the Vikings. Where Nordic nobles of Viking times are shown (rarely) in pictures from other lands, they are wearing this impressive cloak over the long-sleeved knee-long jacket. Thus is Knud the Great shown in an illuminated English manuscript, which displays the king and his queen, beneath flying angels, placing a large cross of gold upon the altar in the new minster at Winchester.

In the Oseberg tapestry are several women dressed alike in long costumes which are also to be seen in different Swedish sources: the Gotland carved stones (Tjängride for instance), and four small middle-Swedish silver figures. The textile authority, Agnes Geijer, in her painstaking analysis of the bits of cloth from the graves at Birka, has thrown much light on our knowledge of the clothes worn by well-to-do women in Viking times. From this evidence it is established that next to her skin the Viking woman of standing wore a fine chemise, sometimes pleated; and over this a sleeveless dress, in two parts, which hung from bronze oval buckles worn on the breast. The dress reached to the ground and even had a train. Over the dress was worn a sleeveless cape which when thrown back exposed the celebrated white arms of the Nordic woman. She must have been an impressive figure striding along in her flowing dress, adorned with pearl necklaces and oval breast buckles from which hung, in fine chains, her scissors, a container for needles, knife, and keys. We shall be reminded of her appearance when we refer later to Ibn Fadlan's remarks about the women of the Rus folk. The hair was worn gathered in a thick knot at the back of the neck, gathered into a hair net or under a cap. That young girls were evidently permitted a less solemn appearance is shown by the gay young girl on the Oseberg wagon wearing a short skirt and long boots.

It is not unusual to see the men depicted as wearing a pointed or round-topped hat, made of leather or cloth, with a round aperture over the temples. The women are sometimes shown with caps or cap-like headdresses. Finally, we learn from the Oseberg find that the women wore sewn shoes of tanned leather.

The Vikings loved luxury and splendour; and in their graves remnants of the most exquisite and decorative clothes have been found, especially in the Birka graves. These finds have included precious materials, such as Chinese silks, elaborate gold-thread embroidery from Byzantium and the Orient, *passementerie,* heavy gold brocades, and braided cords of the finest design and quality. The silks, and many of the other materials, are of course imports from foreign lands, but sometimes the brocade shows an unmistakable Nordic style. One example of Nordic splendour, not from Birka but from Mammen in Jutland, was found in a grave there. With the dead warrior lay his silver inlaid battle-axe; under his head was a pillow of down; only fragments of his cloak remained, but it was beautifully embroidered. His two bracelets or cuffs of wool covered with silk and threaded with gold were well preserved, and so, too, were a couple of long silk ribbons, like pennants, the broad parts of which showed delicate gold embroidery in an elaborate tendril pattern. These ribbons were probably the ornament the Viking wore on his forehead, called *hlad* in the sagas. Even the toughest warriors enjoyed dressing in such finery; according to the saga the most ruthless of all the sons of Njal, Skarphedin, wore his elegant silk *hlad* when he went to the Thing.

In this Jutland grave, as in about sixty of the Birka graves – and in Gotland finds too – there appeared wool and silk ribbons made by the technique called 'tablet-weaving', an old method of manufacture in Nordic countries. In the grave of the Oseberg queen was found a ribbon loom set up as though ready to function, and containing no fewer than fifty-two tablets. Another ancient weaving technique, the *sprang,* is illustrated by finds in graves at Birka.

It is not easy to determine whether the finer textiles found in these graves were imported or home-made. The silk itself, of course, came from abroad, but it is very probable that a great quantity of the beautiful textiles mentioned were of Nordic manufacture. An example of what was doubtless an import is the material, found both at Oseberg and Birka, which resembles a worsted fabric, so precisely woven as to be evidently a standardized product manufactured with a skill and on a scale that could not have been achieved within the Nordic countries. Agnes Geijer is inclined to think that these fine quality cloths are of Frankish origin, and she identifies them with the famous Friesian cloth, called in Frankish literature *pallia fresonica,* which Charlemagne considered worthy enough to present to the Caliph Haroun al Raschid in exchange for a white elephant.

In concluding these comments upon the costume and cloths of the Vikings it is appropriate to mention a *revle,* or picture-tapestry from the village of Skog in north Sweden, now preserved in the museum at Stockholm. It belongs to the last years of the Viking period, and shows a collection of figures, human beings and gods, dressed in clothes which include wide baggy trousers of much the same kind as those in the Oseberg tapestry. The fashion, it seems, lasted right through the time of the Vikings, from the ninth century to the eleventh.

ORNAMENT

How did the Vikings adorn themselves and their womenfolk? The men's only ornament, apart from the *hlad,* mentioned above, was the armlet, the braided or twisted ring made of gold or silver so often named in the sagas as the gift which a king or earl gave to his house-carles or his minstrels. The women had more decorations – gold and silver rings for the neck or the hair as well as sets of buckles worn on the breast. This breast-set was a standard affair of two oval buckles of bronze and between them a three-lobed one of bronze or silver. Close examination reveals that this breast-set is partly of Nordic, partly of foreign origin. The oval buckles are native, of a well-known Scandinavian prototype. In earlier Viking times they were of a simple shape, decorated with clearly recognizable animal designs. But later on they assumed a more elaborate form; over a smooth gilt bowl there now appeared a second plate of openwork pattern, like a net, and the simple animal designs gave way to superimposed figures and heavy ornamentation. These younger oval buckles give a strong almost severe baroque impression. The three-lobed buckle was not Nordic but Frankish in origin, and began as an ornament for men. Frankish male dress included many straps – shoulder-straps, belt, sword-straps – with oblong bronze tags at their ends, decorated with leaf designs, especially of acanthus foliage. Where three of these strap tags met it was natural to combine them – hence the three-lobed ornament on the shoulder which one sees in Frankish miniatures. These were no doubt among the loot which the Vikings brought home from their raids. One such three-lobed gold buckle, splendidly decorated, was found in a Norwegian hoard dating from the ninth century. This three-lobed type of buckle, then, embellished with Charlemagne's characteristic leaf-ornamentation, found its way to the North: but as the Viking warrior's costume did not particularly require it he gave the buckle to his wife. Thus did it come to adorn the Nordic bosom, and before long its foliage decoration, so foreign to the Nordic eye, was supplanted by homely designs of animals. Ornaments, too, can have a history of their own.

There were other varieties such as the long bronze buckle which originated as a means of joining the metalled ends of two straps; or such as the round silver filigree buckle, divided into four quarters and adorned with animal designs. It is the type of ornamentation, of course, which determines the age as well as the origin of these objects. Those bearing the Charlemagne plant designs or the Irish animal ornaments are clearly imported; but the Viking goldsmith was a skilled craftsman who copied according to his own taste, though it must be admitted that, for all his ingenuity, he did not achieve the finish and elegance of the foreign products.

From about the year 900, however, less than half-way through the Viking period, the Nordic workers in gold and silver came into their own. Their apprenticeship to foreign example was over, and from that time they revealed an independent skill in making ornaments. One of the favourite types, especially in eastern Scandinavia, was the penannular brooch or buckle; another was the thick silver armlet pitted with knobs or studs; a third was the spiral bracelet, indented with ornamentation and knobbed at the ends. All these are probably of Baltic origin.

Some types of silver ornaments have rarely been found in Viking graves, but rather in those depots which are called, by archaeologists, 'silver hoards' or 'treasure finds' and which are abundant particularly on Gotland. These treasures are not thought to have been votive offerings to the gods, but are explained by two other suppositions. The first of these is that the objects were buried because they would be useful in the Beyond. (Snorre's *Ynglinga Saga* of the thirteenth century observes that what a man buried in the ground he would enjoy in Valhalla.) The second theory is that in time of war or other misfortune people concealed their valuables in the earth and did not live to reclaim them. Both explanations are plausible, though some scholars seem to use the second one in a somewhat exaggerated way.

Silver hoards from the ninth century are not so numerous, but many have been found belonging to the later Viking period. They consist of three different ingredients: trinkets, 'broken silver', and coins. Gold objects are very scarce, for during the entire Viking period silver had replaced gold as the primary metal of value. Silver production, especially from the Arabic mines, had ousted the late-Roman gold.

A principal type of ornament found in the older silver hoards is the spiral bracelet, already mentioned, with its characteristic end-knobs or bosses. In the later hoards have been found twisted and braided armlets and necklaces; round filigree brooches ornamented with spiral and vine ornaments (originally Frankish patterns); and long finely-made chains (which follow textile design) ending in animal heads and, sometimes, bearing amulets shaped like the hammer of Thor. It must be emphasized again that these objects are rarely found in graves, a factor which suggests that definite laws or, at least, traditions must have governed the choice of objects fit and proper for burying with the dead.

The 'broken silver', the second component in the hoards, especially the later ones, was used for making payment by weight for goods purchased in trade. Sometimes the balances themselves are found as well (and, indeed, in this case, in graves too). They are small collapsible scales, equipped with weighing bowls, and the weights themselves are contained in round bronze boxes. The broken silver itself consists of bits of rings and other ornaments, little bars and splinters of silver, and coins which evidently were used not as currency but as weights. The presence of the broken-up trinkets suggests that, when business required it, the Vikings did not hesitate to mutilate and fracture pleasing works of art.

The third element in the hoards consists of coins, mostly complete and undamaged, and these help considerably in dating the treasure-finds. The coins which predominate are those of the east. Not only in the ninth century but through most of the tenth as well the hoards contain masses of Arabic coins – dirhems (with so-called 'Kufic' inscriptions, named after the town Kufa, south-west of Baghdad) coming in the main from the Samanide chieftains in Samarkand – but rather few Carolingian or Anglo-Saxon coins. Not until the payment of danegeld by England at the end of the tenth century and during the first half of the eleventh did Anglo-Saxon coins become plentiful. At the same period, German coins appear, from Saxony and the Rhineland, which agrees with our knowledge that silver-mining began in the Harz round the middle of the tenth century. Byzantine coins are rare throughout the entire Viking period. The region in which most of these foreign coins are found is Gotland, which shows that this large island was the main trading area of the Baltic and the whole of Southern Scandinavia. A count made some years ago of the coins found on Gotland resulted in the following: Arabic, 25,000; Anglo-Saxon, 18,000; German,

30,000. For the whole of Denmark the corresponding figures were: 3,800, 4,000, 8,900; and for Norway they were smaller than for Denmark.

All this, of course, concerns foreign coins. But the Vikings also minted their own coins, both at home and abroad, and to this matter we shall return.

CHAPTER 8

TRANSPORT

SHIPS

THE ships of the Vikings were the supreme achievement of their technical skill, the pinnacle of their material culture; they were the instrument of their power, the pride of their existence. What the temple was to the Greeks the ship was to the Vikings, the expression of their natures in a harmonious pattern. Whether it was the black ship on its 'cool keel' gliding away from the land, or, 'like the goat of the sea', gaily butting the waves with its bows, it was always the Vikings' favourite object of contemplation, created by his skilful hand and affectionately commemorated in his poetry. It is appropriate that Norway in particular should have yielded up specimens of its vessels of the Viking age, for because of their lengthy coast the Norwegians know the sea as do few other nations. An Icelandic poet of the Viking period, Egil Skallagrimson, called the breakers that smash against the rugged rocky Norwegian coast 'the island-studded belt round Norway'. Here in Viking times were built three great mounds, by the sea's edge, each of which bequeathed a ship to posterity. The three ships were found at Tune, Gokstad, and Oseberg, and they can be seen today in the 'Hall of the Viking Ships' outside Oslo. The three sites where the ships were discovered lie on the Oslo Fiord: Tune on the east of it, Gokstad and Oseberg on the west.

The Tune ship was excavated in 1867, in a huge grave mound about 250 ft in diameter. The ship was lying north-south, and was embedded in blue clay which had preserved its timbers for so many centuries. Athwart the stern was a platform of poles, their ends penetrating the clay beyond the ship's bulwarks, and on this platform had been built a burial-chamber of oak with a flat roof above it. The chamber had been penetrated and ransacked in ancient times, but within it the excavators found the incinerated remains of a human male skeleton and a horse, the latter apparently buried in a standing position. Little else had survived: a wooden spade, some carved bits of wood, fragments of clothing and weapons, and a few beads. The ship itself, now somewhat defective, was about 60 ft long, $13\frac{1}{2}$ ft in the beam, and rather less than 4 ft deep from its rail to the bottom of the keel. It was made of oak, with a rudder of pine. It had been placed in the mound with its mast standing, but its eleven pairs of oars had been removed before the burial. Shetelig describes this Tune ship as a good solid workmanlike vessel, devoid of decoration, sitting low in the water, and very suitable for sailing in shallow waters, such as estuaries. Its date is approximately the end of the ninth century.

The Gokstad ship (Pl. 8) was dug out in 1880 from a mound 150 ft wide and 15 ft high on a subsoil of blue clay. It was deeply buried in the clay and was well preserved, with its stern pointing to the sea. The mast had been cut off at the height of the roof of the timbered burial-chamber which was again built athwart the stern of the vessel. This chamber, too, had been pillaged long ago, as was proved by a large hole in the ship's side and in the wall of the chamber. Within it there had been buried a chieftain, lying finely dressed and armed in his bed. An examination of the skeleton showed a powerfully-built man of middle age, about $5\frac{1}{2}$ ft tall. He was well provided with gear: three rowing boats and five beds in the prow of the ship; an abundance of kitchen utensils amidships, such as bronze and iron kettles, plates, cups, candlesticks, barrels, and wooden spades; and a game board and a decorated sledge. In the chamber there were scraps of wool and gold-embroidered silk, the remains of a leather purse, an axe, an iron belt-buckle, and strap mountings of lead and gilded bronze. Outside the chamber were found the bones of a peacock, and near the ship the remains of eighteen slaughtered animals – twelve horses and six dogs. The grave is dated around the year 900.

The ship, built of oak, is well preserved; it is about 70 ft long, 16 ft in the beam, nearly 6 ft deep from the rail to the bottom of the keel, and weighs a little over 20 tons. A facsimile of the ship, made in 1893, with a tonnage of nearly 32 tons, successfully sailed across the Atlantic. The main components of the Gokstad ship are keel, bows, ribs, and planking. Compared with older vessels, dating from the Iron Age in the north, the Viking ships show several advances in construction: the flat bottom plank is replaced by a real keel which serves as a backbone and is strong enough to resist the pressure of the water outside. The keel, bows, and stern are each made of one solid piece of timber; of the sixteen rows of planking nine are below the water line, and the planks are riveted together, caulked with tarred rope, and by means of thick perforated cleats lashed to the ribs. This construction gave the vessel considerable elasticity in rough seas. Amidships was a heavy block of oak in which the mast was set, and on top of this block was another one, shaped like a fish (the mastfish) with a hole in its middle, to support the standing mast.

Apart from mast and sail the ship was equipped with sixteen pairs of oars. As it stood in the mound where it was discovered it bore along each rail thirty-three shields, two for each oar-hole, hung in such a way that each shield half covered its neighbour. The shields were painted alternately black and yellow and formed a continuous line from the prow to the stern of the ship. This 'ornamental' display was only for a Viking vessel in harbour, not when under way, and we shall return to this point when we come to consider the original significance of the ship-burial. The rudder was a single piece of oak, shaped like the blade of a huge oar, about 10 ft long, made fast to the starboard side of the ship by a stout riveted cleat; through this cleat, through the rudder, and finally through the ship's side and the rib ran a hole for a thick rope of osiers. In the rudder-neck the tiller was put in at a height fit for the steersman on the rising poop. When the Norwegian Captain Magnus Andersen sailed the facsimile of the Gokstad ship to America in 1893 he reported: 'This rudder must be regarded as one of the conclusive proofs of our forefathers' acumen and skill in shipbuilding and seamanship. The rudder is a work of genius . . . a man could steer with this tiller in all kinds of weather.'

The ship's mast, considered to be about 40 ft high, was made of pine. The sail was probably square, but further details of its shape and colour have not been verified. The sagas, however, tell of blue and red striped sails, or of entirely red ones. The Gotland Stones usually depict chequered ones. In the bows of the Gokstad ship was found its iron anchor completely rusted; and here, too, were the oars, some 16 ft long and some a little longer (up to 17½ ft), their blades small and lancet-shaped. The oar-holes were a little higher towards the prow and stern than they were amidships. Neither in the Gokstad nor the Oseberg ship were any thwarts for the oarsmen found, and there was no chance, says Shetelig, to test the ship's qualities under oars during the voyage of the facsimile simply because no trained rowers were available. It is possible that the rowers used their sea-chests, fastened in some way, as seats.

The gangway of the Gokstad ship also came to light: a narrow plank of pine, some 22 ft long, with a pole at one end for securing it, and cut-out steps in its top side. There were also found in the ship four strong planks, ending in carved animals' heads; these are thought to be the gables of a tent which was put up alongside the ship when it was moored to the land. The animals' heads were not intended merely for decoration but to scare away evil spirits from those who slept under the tent. No fewer than eight beds, or fragments of them, were found with the Viking buried in the Gokstad ship, two of them with beautifully carved animals' heads to guard the sleeper. Scraps of blankets and eiderdowns came to light, too, of which the surviving colours were mainly black and yellow and, in a few cases, red. Both Shetelig and Captain Magnus Andersen testify to the remarkable attention to detail which distinguishes the Gokstad ship.

Finally we come to the Oseberg ship (Pl. 10), that celebrated revelation of the Viking art and spirit. It was found in 1903, and excavated in the following year from a mound originally nearly 20 ft high and over 120 ft in diameter, made of peat which – with the subsoil of thick blue clay – acted as the preservative which safeguarded the wonderful wood carvings of the ship. This vessel, like the other two, faced north and south, but with the bows towards the sea. Subsidence and pressure in the mound had damaged the ship a good deal, and grave robbers had been busy in olden times. The ship was moored to a large stone inside the mound, and the timbered grave-chamber in the stern contained the remains of two women. The skeleton of one of them, a young woman, was broken up: only a little of it was inside the chamber, some more of it outside. The grave-robbers had evidently been particularly concerned with removing her body. The other woman was older, 60 to 70, and her skeleton bore signs of a bone disease such as arthritis. It is reasonable to conclude that the younger woman was the mistress, the noble lady (since it was her body the robbers had tried to remove), and the older one her servant. The Norwegian archaeologist, A. W. Brøgger, has advanced the attractive theory that the lady in the grave was Queen Åsa, mother of King Halvdan Svart and grandmother on the father's side of King Harald Fairhair. This supposition accords with the dating of the Oseberg find, for the time of the burial (fixed by plant-deposits to August-

September) must have been some time in the second half of the ninth century. The ship, however, was an old one at that time, for its decoration, on stylistic grounds, belongs to round about the year 800, to the beginning of the Viking period. On this basis the Oseberg ship is a hundred years older than those from Tune and Gokstad.

The two women had been given a generous burial: beds, pillows, blankets, eiderdowns, several chests and barrels (one of which contained wild apples), four magnificent carved head-posts adorned with animal heads, the tapestry already mentioned, a couple of looms, and some iron rattles probably intended, like the animal-headed poles, to frighten off evil spirits. The grave-robbers had broken in from the south, had excavated a tunnel 9 ft wide to the prow of the ship, cut away its great spiral, and finally reached the burial chamber which they entered by making a hole in the roof. In the front part of the ship lay many things of the greatest historical and cultural value: first of all a four-wheeled wooden carriage with carved pictures, and four sledges, three of them ornamented with magnificent carvings. Then there were two tents, three beds, a chair, a handloom, a round pole inscribed with runes, two wooden barrels, a number of battens and oars, a large baler, an anchor stock, wooden tubs, landing planks, and much else. Aft was found kitchen equipment: an iron knife and axes with handles, wooden plates and jugs, two iron kettles and a kettle-stand, a grinding mill, and on a couple of oak planks was laid out an ox. Here and there in the ship were found fruits, grain, and seed: two kinds of apple, walnuts, hazelnuts, wheat, cress, and the blue dye-plant called woad.

The Oseberg ship is well preserved. It is built throughout of oak, except for parts of the rails, which are made of beech. The dimensions are about 65 ft long, $15\frac{1}{2}$ ft in the beam, and nearly 5 ft deep from rail to keel. Although its design and construction are of the same pattern as the other two ships',

the Oseberg vessel is evidently less strongly built than they.
It contains fewer store chambers for supplies, the oar-holes
cannot be closed from outside, as was essential in heavy seas,
and the oars (fifteen pairs) were shorter (11 to 12 ft) and were
clearly newly made and decorated for the funeral. The mast
and the rudder were new and not designed for practical use.
For these reasons Shetelig is inclined to believe that the ship
used for the Oseberg burial was an old vessel which had been
laid up, and was refurbished for its last journey. But even
when this ship was new it could not have been intended for
hard use or long journeys; it was a luxury ship, and its elegant
lines and superb decoration still bewitch the eye of anyone
who looks at this ancient relic, standing in its wing in the
Ship Museum near Oslo. No one has better described it than
Haakon Shetelig, the affectionate interpreter of the Oseberg
discoveries. He writes: 'The rails run low above the water in
a long straight line, to accommodate the oars at an even
height, and then rise at each end of the ship in a steep curve to
more than 15 ft above the waterline, finishing in a slender free
spiral.' The lines of the Oseberg ship are inexpressibly fine
and pure.

The prow is decorated on each side with elegant friezes
which look like vegetable scrolls but are not. They are in
fact authentic ancient Nordic animal designs of the kind
produced around 800 by men who were masters of decorative
art. The examples on the Oseberg prow convey a vivid
impression of a traditional native art which was already nearly
300 years old at the beginning of the Viking period and had
not yet begun to degenerate in careless or indifferent hands.
Elsewhere on the Oseberg ship is quite another style of
decoration, again based, it is true, on animal ornaments but
executed in a baroque manner with no concern for delicacy
of line. This style is devoid of all elegance and relies for its
effect upon bizarre presentation and robust humour. It is a
new style of the young Viking period inspired, surely, by the

Vikings' apprehension of Frankish lion-pictures of Charlemagne's time. These half-naturalistic creatures seem to have attracted and amused the Vikings, who proceeded to make variations on the theme – and thus produced such novelties as posturing comic beasts with broad faces and strong paws, the so-called 'gripping beasts'.

The bows of the Oseberg ship rise, as we said, to a high spiral ending in a snake's head. The top of the stern of the ship is missing, but presumably it showed the snake's tail. The whole ship, then, looked like a fabled monster as it breasted the waves, its head and tail glistening, and its thick body filled with men.

Viewed in a nautical European perspective, the Viking ship represents the completion rather than the beginning of an evolutionary process. It marks the end after several centuries of the development of the rowing-boat which appears, finally, as a craft equipped with keel, mast, and sail. And through the Viking period this 'long ship' became steadily larger. The biggest vessels of Knud the Great were probably twice as big as the Gokstad ship, but they remained the same in principle – vessels designed for battle as well as for commerce. The Bayeux Tapestry, whose date matches the late Viking period, depicts the same type of ship for all purposes. With the end of the Viking period this unity of function ceases and two separate types of ship are evolved – one built for speed and mobility in battle, the other for its carrying capacity as a trader: one for war and one for peace.

CARTS AND SLEDGES

If the long ships ruled the waves how did the Viking get about on land? His best individual method of transport was – and had been for 2000 years – the horse, and we have already noted the Viking's high regard and affection for his mount. But apart from that the Vikings had two old kinds of transport – the cart and the sledge. In the Oseberg ship was found the famous four-wheeled cart (Pl. 9), equipped with heavy wheels and a central rib. The curved body of the vehicle is covered completely with decorative carvings illustrating, no doubt, some myths and legends. It may be said that this is evidently a sacred, ceremonial carriage of some kind and, therefore, no proof that four-wheeled carts were in general use as a means of transport in Viking times, especially as their roads cannot have been very advanced or practicable. One answer to this argument is that, in fact, good cobbled roads already existed in Denmark in Roman times; and we must not be tempted to assume from Adam of Bremen's grim descriptions of Jutland and other Northern territories that the north lacked roads. Other evidence to this effect is found in the Oseberg tapestry which depicts at least two varieties of four-wheeled transport – one open and the other covered. Across wide stretches of the Scandinavian lowlands four-wheeled carts and coaches, protected by horsemen, were doubtless able to drive. Yet another confirmation of the existence of passable roads in the later Viking period is found in the many Swedish runic stones which, in paying tribute to the man over whom they are raised, often mention that among his good deeds was the making of a bridge, and this phrase 'to make a bridge' usually meant to lay a firm surface across swampy ground. There is good reason for agreeing with Sune Lindqvist that this frequently implies the improvement or renewal of existing routes used by horsemen and carriages. There is every reason to believe that carts and carriages were extensively used in the north during the summer, and in southern Scandinavia in spring and autumn, too, when the snow was absent But what about the winter? The answer is that in winter transport was easier still, for the Vikings had the sledge.

We find in the Oseberg relics three well-preserved, fine carved wooden sledges, toboggan shaped, richly decorated on the sides (Pl. 12). There is also a fourth, less ornate, a simple working-sledge. And in the Gokstad ship, too, there were remains of a sledge. It is evident that the extensive tracts of snow and the ice-covered lakes and rivers in the northern winter encouraged long journeys on sledges and skis – for the Vikings also used skis. The fact that, in winter, the Vikings preferred to travel by land rather than by sea is revealed in the sagas. St Olav, for example, made his long winter journey to Russia and back by land. It must have been much easier.

CHAPTER 9

TOWNS, EARTHWORKS, AND CAMPS

TOWNS

NORDIC communities had developed so much in Viking times that towns grew up rapidly, and these towns were sited with two considerations in mind – to develop trade and to protect that trade from the consequent risk of piracy. For these reasons towns were built well up narrow but navigable fiords and fortified with earthworks. There was always the danger that raiding enemies would suddenly attack, but the sea-going traders were armed and knew how to use their weapons. Yet things often went wrong: ships were plundered and towns burned down. The fear of such misfortunes could not, however, deter the townsmen and the merchants from seeking to develop their trade.

Along the North Sea and the Baltic, like blind eyes, lie the vanished towns of the Vikings, the sites of northern Europe's oldest trading centres – the Friesian Dorestad, the Danish Hedeby, the Nordic-Slav Wollin, the Estonian Truso, and the Swedish Birka. What do we know of these deserted cities? Where were they and what traces remain?

We have noted earlier something of Dorestad and its final destruction by natural forces. Let us now look at Hedeby.

Hedeby

It lay at the end of the narrow but navigable fiord, the Slie, which cuts deep into south Slesvig from the Baltic. 'Hedeby' means 'the town at the heaths'. On three sides, north, west, and south, it is protected by a semicircular defensive wall; on the east it is open to the water. The protective earthwork, now grass-grown, has sunk upon its long-rotted, vertical wooden frame. Within these perished defences the town, now fertile fields, covered some 70 acres, and in circumference was the largest town in the North during the Viking period. There were two gates in the wall, south and north, and probably a third in the south-west. From the year 1900 until the outbreak of the Second World War German archaeologists, with some interruptions, were digging in and around old Hedeby. The result of their excavations showed that the semicircular wall was originally not as high and as broad as it subsequently became. It began as a simple low earthwork with a defensive stockade and a moat, but was built up in several stages to a large and complex rampart; its circumference, however, remained unchanged. Either the wall was originally built round an area greater than the actual size of the town, with an eye to the town's expansion, or else it was not built until the town had already grown to its final proportions.

In Viking times a rivulet ran through the place, entering through the wall in the west and flowing into the cove 'Haddeby Nor'; here was the oldest part of the town. This modest stream was important because it supplied Hedeby with drinking-water. It has proved valuable, too, to the archaeologists, for it has enabled them to date various objects found in its bed; the deposits in the lower levels are, as a rule, older than those in the upper layers of the river bed. The excavators were also able to observe the changing relation between buildings in the town and the river. Sometimes the houses, whose sites were clearly observed, were built close to the stream which was then fenced in by a wooden palisade; at others the houses were built well back from the river, separated from it by an open space. In this low-lying part of Hedeby the inhabitants of nearly every house had dug a well and installed a wooden pipe in it, a discovery which agrees with the fact that the Arab merchant during his visit to the town in the tenth century (p. 144) specially noticed its fresh-water wells. The damp ground near the water has preserved the nether-most parts of the houses admirably, and anyone who visited the site, where whole fields at a time were uncovered, got the fanciful impression of a vast stubble-field over which the angel of death had passed his scythe, slicing away the upper nine-tenth of these perishable huts of mortals (Pl. 13). From the remains of these habitations it was found that some of them had been stave-built (close vertical planking), others half-timbered (wattle-and-daub), others, again, constructed like log huts. The houses had their gable ends to the street, with barns and stables behind. The hearths were in the middle of the floor. In the later, higher, western end of the town some small half-buried houses were found built of wattle-and-daub with the fireplace in a corner.

Various crafts flourished in Hedeby. There are traces of iron-smelting, weaving, boneware and antler manufacture, bronze casting, glass making, and minting of coins. A sub-stantial quantity of pottery was discovered, mostly of Rhine-land origin, but very few farming implements. Inside the semicircular wall, both in the western part of the town, were two burial places, one containing coffins (lying east-west) but very few funeral objects, and the other containing wooden chambers and many burial gifts such as weapons and orna-ments. The animal bones found in many parts of the town were for the most part the remains of meals, and they show that pigs and cows were the most plentiful or popular meat; after them sheep and goats, very little horse and chicken – and no game-birds. Dogs and cats had evidently lived in the houses. Many varieties of plants and fruit were found: barley, wheat, hazel-nuts, walnuts, apples, cherries, plums, sloes, elderberries, blackberries, raspberries, wild strawberries, and hops.

The cove Haddeby Nor provided a natural harbour for Hedeby. Many poles were found there, which had served as moorings or were, perhaps, the remains of piers and jetties. At a depth of about 9 feet the excavators came across the wreckage of a burnt ship, made of ash, about 48 ft long and 9 ft wide, a rather flat-bottomed vessel, presumably of some kind of local construction. And there are said to be traces of another ancient wreck in the harbour.

Evidence about the origin and age of Hedeby will be considered when we come to discuss its relationship with the adjacent earthwork, the famous Danevirke. But the town clearly owed its existence to the trading-route between the North Sea and the Baltic. It was a mercantile centre, sometimes in Danish, sometimes in German or Swedish possession. (There is, indeed, reason to believe that it was the Swedes who constructed the semicircular wall when they captured the town around 900. But more of that later.) The evidence about the final fate of Hedeby is clearly presented not only in literature but also by archaeological confirmation. History testifies very plainly to the situation which arose in the middle of the eleventh century, when King Sven Estridson of Denmark and King Harald Hardrade of Norway came to grips with each other. Around 1050, while Sven was engaged in the south with the German emperor, Harald seized the opportunity to fall upon Hedeby, and plundered and burned it completely. As Sven, returning from the south, approached the place, Harald's ships, loaded with loot, made off. Sven pursued him and caught up with him at Læsø in the Kattegat where Harald, to lighten his vessels and escape, was forced to throw his plunder overboard – so that it flowed on the windswept Tutish sea as the minstrel Torleik Fagre says in his song. Another minstrel, a Norwegian who was with King Harald (according to Snorre), celebrated the fate of Hedeby in jubilant song – 'Burnt in anger was Hedeby, from end to end. It was a valorous deed and one which will injure Sven. High rose the flames from the houses when, last night, I stood on the stronghold's arm'. This 'arm' is probably the northern extremity of the great semicircular wall, where it runs into Haddeby Nor and from where, even today, one can command a view of the whole site.

During the excavations in the areas of Hedeby near the harbour the top layer in many places proved to consist of the debris of fire – charcoal and sooty earth – evidence of the catastrophe by burning which brought the town's existence to an end. On top of this layer there was no trace of refuse, and no other indication of human activity or survival. In the uppermost deposits in the river-bed were discovered the burnt remains of two men and a horse: these, like the ship in the harbour, seem to be relics of the great fire which destroyed Hedeby for ever.

In Nordic ecclesiastical history Hedeby is famous as the scene of the first Christian mission to Denmark, where the monk Ansgar was active between 826 and 829 as the forerunner of the full introduction of Christianity to Denmark which was to occur 150 years later. According to the Arab trader who visited Hedeby in the mid tenth century, the place was not without Christians, but the religion did not really take root until Harald Bluetooth was converted. However the oldest Christian church in Denmark was undoubtedly Ansgar's, in or near Hedeby. But all efforts to locate it have failed. It was doubtless built of wood and, as we have seen, much of the lower parts of timber buildings were preserved in the swampy soil near the harbour. But nothing has been found there which might have been Ansgar's church.

Slesvig

Near Hedeby, north of the Slie fiord, lies the town of Slesvig which, by archaeological evidence, could not have existed before the eleventh century. The suffix 'vig' is from the Latin *vicus* ('town') and was embodied, as Walter Vogel has shown, in the time of the Vikings – and earlier as well – in the names of many important trading centres in north-west Germany, on the Channel coast, and in England: among these are Brunswick, Wijk-bij-Duurstede (Dorestad), Quentovic, Lundenwic (London), Eoferwic (York). Slesvig, then, signifies 'the town at the (fiord) Slie', and Hedeby 'the town at the heaths'; the latter meaning conforms to the designation 'Hæðum' 'at the heaths', given to the place in Alfred the Great's World History (*c.* 900) by both of the two narrators: the Norwegian Ottar and the Anglo-Saxon Wulfstan. Furthermore there is the famous declaration made a hundred years later by another Anglo-Saxon writer, Ethelweard, that the capital of the province of Angel 'is in the Saxon language called Slesvig, but in Danish Hedeby'. Thus there is every reason to believe that the town at the bottom of the fiord Slie in the time of the Vikings was Hedeby and that this town had two names, the Saxon Slesvig and the Danish Hedeby. After the destruction of Hedeby in 1050 the survivors moved to the north of the fiord and founded the present Slesvig, and the former name 'Hedeby' was gradually supplanted by 'Slesvig'. It is necessary to add that these deductions have not been generally accepted by scholars.

Wollin

The next Viking town to be considered lay at the north of the Oder in the Baltic, on the southern fringe of Nordic culture. By Adam of Bremen, in the 1070s, it is described as 'the well-known town of Jumne, which affords to the barbarians and Greeks (i.e. Greek Orthodox merchants) in those parts a much employed anchorage'. He continues:

As so many almost unbelievable tales have been told in praise of this town, I think it is worth mentioning some matters of interest: it is, for example, the largest town in Europe, inhabited by Slavs and such other people as Greeks and Barbarians. Even visiting Saxons are permitted to live there on equal terms so long as they do not disclose they are Christians. But though the inhabitants are still bound by their heathen error, they are nevertheless more honourable and hospitable than any other people. There is an abundance of merchandise from the Nordic countries, and the town is plentifully provided with good and precious things.

Other commentators who mention the town at the mouth of the Oder do not call it Jumne but Jumneta (or distorted: Vineta), Julin, or Wollin. Philologists have concluded that these are two names for the same place, comparable with Hedeby-Slesvig; on this basis Jumne or Jumneta are the Nordic names for it, Julin or Wollin the Slav names, a conclusion all the more acceptable since the town probably had a mixed Slav-Nordic population. Archaeologists, on their side, have tried eagerly to locate the site or sites concerned. The Oder has three outlets: Peene in the west, Swine in the middle, and Dievenow in the east. On which of these three estuaries lay the town which Adam of Bremen so favourably mentioned? Answers to this question differ, but extensive excavations in and around the present little town of Wollin on the Dievenow suggest that it may well have been there. Let us then call the Viking town Wollin.

The most significant finds were located in the very middle of the town square at Wollin: thick layers of debris of which the lower strata date back to later Viking times. The remains of buildings and pottery have been dated with pretty fair accuracy; the various forms of house construction – staves, half-timbers, log huts – represented on the site include Viking as well as post-Viking buildings (the latter from around 1200). There is a similar mixture of styles and manufacture in the pottery, some of it Nordic and some Slav. The conclusion, then, is that here, where the present Wollin stands, on the eastward outlet of the river, the Vikings began to settle about the year 1000 and became assimilated with the existing population. There were doubtless good trading opportunities at such a place, though Adam of Bremen's eulogies were probably pitched too high.

A problem which has long occupied the interest of historians is whether this Wollin or (Nordic) Jumne is identical with the mythical 'Jomsborg' mentioned in Danish writings of the twelfth and in Icelandic sagas of the thirteenth century (Sven Aggesen, Saxo, the *Jomsviking Saga,* and the *Knytlinga Saga*). The Danish tradition is that when Harald Bluetooth was banished from Denmark by his son Sven, he took refuge in the land of the Wends, taught them the practice of piracy, and created a base for piratical operations at Jomsborg. Another version is that while at the height of his power in Denmark he built up a stronghold at Jomsborg, gave it a Wendish garrison, and installed Danish chieftains there as commanders. The Icelandic sagas tell a more romantic story. According to them Jomsborg was a kind of Nordic military 'academy' run on Spartan principles, where no women were permitted, and where great warriors and heroes were developed: figures of fame such as Palnatoke, Sigvald, Bue the Stout, Vagn Aagesen, Styrbjørn. It was the celebrated citadel of the Joms-Vikings, governed with harsh discipline; from its well-designed artificial harbour, capable of accommodating 300 longships, the Joms-Vikings set out on those historic campaigns which included Hjørungavaag in Norway, Svolder in Wendland or in Denmark, Fyrisvold in Sweden. The splendour of their feats resounds through the ages and was not diminished in defeat – for the Joms-Vikings seem to have distinguished themselves in the paradoxical business of suffering brilliant defeats!

Behind the highly-coloured pictures the sagas present there is certainly the historical fact that, throughout the Viking period from the time of King Godfred at the beginning of the ninth century to that of Jomsborg's destroyer Magnus the Good, just before the middle of the eleventh, the Danes had vital interests along Germany's extensive Baltic coasts where the Slavs – Obotrites and Wends – lived. And there is a historical nemesis in the fact that Viking Denmark, when its lust for plundering had abated, itself became the victim of raids by the Wends who, in the twelfth century, showed themselves so adept in the slowly acquired art of piracy that it was not until the 1160s that the Danes and Saxons managed to check them.

The question whether Wollin was in fact Jomsborg is not at present settled. The solution of the problem would be assisted if the town and its neighbourhood could produce archaeological evidence of a Nordic Viking site corresponding in some measure to the narrative of the sagas. No such evidence is forthcoming. If, indeed, the Viking relics discovered in Wollin had come to light *outside* the happy hunting-ground of the Jomsborg theorizers, no one would dream of identifying them with Jomsborg.

Truso

Our next vanished Viking town is Truso. It is first mentioned by the traveller Wulfstan in the foreword to Alfred the Great's edition of Orosius's *World History*. His reference was picked up a long time later – in 1689 – by the English geographer Richard Hakluyt, and since then it has been much studied by scholars. As mentioned earlier (p. 39) Wulfstan describes his journey from Hedeby to Truso; seven days and nights, he says, their vessel was continuously under way; on their right was Wendland, on their left Langeland, Lolland, Falster, and Skaane – all belonging to Denmark – then Bornholm, a sovereign state with its own king, then Bleking, Møre, Øland, and Gotland, all Swedish. Wendland lay continuously to their right the whole way as far as the mouth of the Vistula. Then follows a somewhat complicated account of Truso's position in the Vistula delta. In their endeavours to locate the place scholars have come to realize how little they could depend upon Wulfstan's vague description. Only the discovery of traces of a Viking colony could give them firm ground to build upon, and in this connexion German scholars have advanced the claims of the town of Elbing, at the bottom of the Gulf of Danzig. No actual site has been uncovered there, but scattered deposits of Viking weapons have been found and, more important, a large and partly Viking burial place has come to light near Elbing railway station. Elbing's position fits Wulfstan's remark that the Vistula formed the frontier between Wendland in the west and Esterland (Estonia) in the east; and the name Truso may be connected with the half-dried-out lake near Elbing called Lake Drausen. If Truso were indeed here, it must have had a mixture of populations and excellent trading possibilities. The wide river Vistula led toward the south-east, deep into the continent, and its distant source was not far from the Dniester which flowed into the Black Sea and provided a route to Byzantium.

While we are in the Baltic, incidentally, it is appropriate to mention a commodity of the greatest importance in these regions many centuries before the Vikings. This was amber. In the Bronze Age the main source of amber was the west coast of Jutland. But by the time of the Iron Age this situation was entirely different. It is significant that Pliny, when describing the quest of Roman traders for amber, does not mention Jutland or other North Sea regions, but speaks only of their going to the Baltic for their amber. The supplies of amber in Jutland had become exhausted by the time of the Vikings, but the precious stuff was still plentiful in the Baltic. Truso must have been a very convenient mart for amber trading.

Birka

The last of the vanished Viking towns, and the most famous of them all, is Birka, the Swedish mercantile centre on the little island of Björkö in Lake Mälar in eastern Sweden. The island, like Hedeby, is well hidden from the open sea; to reach it one must penetrate the Swedish archipelago, sail through the narrows, where Stockholm now stands, and out into the wide expanse of Lake Mälar in the east. And here, in the middle of the fairway, where the north-south and east-west sailing routes intersect, lies the island of Björkö, lonely and secluded nowadays, but in Viking times seething with activity and bustling with commerce. Birka lay on the north-western promontory of the island; and its fame as a market for furs and other Nordic wares attracted foreigners from many lands: Frisians, Anglo-Saxons, Germans, Balts, Greeks, and Orientals. That it was indeed such a cosmopolitan centre is evidenced by the discoveries in its many graves, in which have been found Arab silver, Byzantine silks and brocades, Rhineland glass, Frisian cloth, and Frankish weapons. Nordic merchandise, too, has come to light in those ancient graves: furs especially, of bear, fox, marten, otter, and beaver, and also such valuable commodities as reindeer-antlers, walrus teeth, amber, and honey.

The sources of information about Birka are partly literary and partly archaeological. The latter evidence is derived not only from the grave discoveries, but from other remains which stand revealed to the present day. Some description of the scene is appropriate. A visitor approaching the island of Björkö from the south will first catch sight of a bald rock directly south of Birka, surmounted by a modern stone cross (of Irish design, oddly enough) erected in memory of the monk Ansgar's mission to Birka in the ninth century. (Sweden and Denmark share Ansgar, but Denmark has the predominant interest in him, as he lived some years in Hedeby before visiting Birka. On the other hand, he was on two occasions – with an interval of twenty-five years between them – with the Swedes in Birka, first in the reign of Good King Bjørn and later during the reign of the savage King Olav.) This rock must have been the fortress and refuge of the town, for it is surrounded by a wide oval wall, 25 ft by 46 ft, of earth and stones in which there were three gates, one north, one south, and one east, into the town. Outside the northern gate there have been found many relics of the garrison of the fortress. In a north-easterly direction from this gate lies an area called the Black Soil – and this is the actual site of the historic town of Birka. Excavations here have not yielded, as at Hedeby, the lower parts of houses, but only fragments of burnt clay of two different shapes from which it is deduced that there were two kinds of house in Birka, one built of wattle-and-daub, and one of clay and timber. The soil on the site is full of deposits of ashes and organic moulds; in short it is a 'dark culture soil', and this black area covers a space of thirty acres, or less than half the area of Hedeby. The gravel protective wall of Birka, 21–36 ft wide and 6 ft high, is lower and weaker than that of Hedeby. Only the northern part of this defensive wall, stretching from the fortress to the western harbour, survives, to the length of about 1,500 ft; it may have been reinforced by a row of square wooden towers. Birka possessed three harbours: an artificial one to the west, which has completely disappeared, and two natural harbours on the northern coast – Kugghamn in the west (named after the Frisian type of vessel, the Kogg), and Korshamn (= cross-harbour) in the east. Still farther east, where Salvik now stands, there seems to have been a flat-bottomed harbour. 'Salvik' means the centre of commerce, and 'Korshamn' may have been a corruption of an original 'Kornhamn'. One of the experts on Birka, the archaeologist Holger Arbnan, has drawn attention to the latter possibility, and also to the likelihood that the great markets of Birka were probably held in the winter when the finest furs would be available. He cites in support of this the fact that many of those buried in the Birka graves had frost-nails at their feet, and that in the Black Soil there have been found many ice-axes and skates made of animal bones.

Though Birka is smaller than Hedeby it has a far larger and finer collection of graves: thousands of them, indeed, which have provided the famous collection now in the Museum at Stockholm. No other ancient Nordic town has yielded so many and such various objects and relics as this. To the east of the defensive wall, on a somewhat hilly field, there are 1,600 burial mounds, large and small, huddled close together under pine and birch trees. This is Birka's biggest burial-place. There are several others, however; between the Black Soil and the hill-top fort, for instance, there are a number of mounds, and in the area south and south-east of the fort 400 scattered barrows have been located. Farther to the east there are several other groups of graves. Some of the richest burial-remains on Birka have been found not under mounds but in subsidences containing the rotted remains of large wooden chambers. Two such burial-places have been found, one close to the north gate of the fort, the other south of Kugghamn inside the defensive wall of the town.

How long did Birka, the most thriving of all Swedish Viking towns, exist? Not as long as Hedeby, which perished in the catastrophe of 1050 already mentioned. To judge from what has been found there, Birka seems to have been declining before 1000. It is not that Birka, like Hedeby, was destroyed by fire, leaving behind thick layers of ash; it is simply that there are virtually no relics and remains dating after the end of the tenth century. There have not, for example, been found in Birka (as elsewhere in Sweden) those coins of the English king Ethelred II in which the last substantial amounts of danegeld were paid; and indeed no coins later than those of the mid tenth century have been discovered there. The latest dateable find is a hoard of silver unearthed in the Black Soil in which no coin is later than 963 or 967. It may be presumed, though not with certainty, that Birka was destroyed by the Danish Viking forces which set out to conquer Sweden at the end of the tenth century but were defeated by King Erik Sejrsæl at the great battle of Fyrisvold described on the

runic stones. Whether this was so or not, Birka drops out of
history about 975; its function as the centre of the Baltic
trade was taken over by Gotland, and the more local trade of
Lake Mälar was divided among several other places on the
lake, principally Sigtuna, half-way between Birka and
Uppsala.

Sigtuna

Sigtuna was favourably situated, on the south of a peninsula
in the broad part of Lake Mälar. Excavations there have
yielded material in the main later than 1000. It is a 'long
town' stretching about 1800 feet along the border of the lake,
and about 600 ft towards the land. It had been christianized
early, probably from its foundation, and had many churches.
The earliest verified minting of coins in Sweden was at Sigtuna: Olav Skotking's coins, copied from Anglo-Saxon
designs, and most probably made by an Anglo-Saxon mint-
master. They bear the inscription SIDEI, which stands for
SI(TUNE) DEI or 'God's Sigtuna' – a piece of propaganda,
possibly, directed against the neighbouring heathen temple in
Old Uppsala. Olav's son, King Anund Jacob, also had coins
minted at Sigtuna. It is possible that coins were struck at
Birka, too, in its time, but there is no certainty of this. Two
Swedish runic stones of the first part of the eleventh century
tell of a guild of Frisian craftsmen in Sigtuna, and an Icelandic
poem declares that King Magnus the Good and King Harald
Hardrade stopped at Sigtuna on their way home from Russia.
Adam of Bremen describes the place, in 1070 or so, as a large
town (*civitas magna*) and records that it was the episcopal seat
of Sweden's first bishop, Adalvard the younger. It is highly
likely, though not certain, that the ancient Sigtuna lay at
Signhildsberg, about 2½ miles away from the present town,
and that its layout followed an Anglo-Saxon plan. Excavations in Sigtuna have revealed, as at Birka, a thick dark layer
of early culture, a Black Soil in which were found fragments

of primitive houses with clay floors and wattle-and-daub walls, as well as larger log houses.

Other Viking Towns

Apart from Sigtuna there are three other existing Swedish towns which have origins dating back to the later Viking period: these are Skara in Västergötland, Lund in Skaane, and probably Tälje, the modern Södertälje near Stockholm.

Denmark possesses one more lost town of Viking times, an abandoned site with a semicircular defensive wall at Brovold on the isle of Als, where Viking relics establish the age of the place. There are also, however, many modern Danish towns which have their roots in Viking times, some of them reputed also to have been episcopal seats. In Jutland there are Slesvig, Ribe, Aarhus, Viborg, Aalborg; in Fyn there is Odense and, in Zeeland, Roskilde and Ringsted.

In Norway the present towns of Oslo, Bergen, and Trondheim (Nidaros) can trace their origins back to later Viking times. There is also a lost town, mentioned by the merchant Ottar, called Skiringsal, in the south of Norway. Although its site has not been identified it is possible that it may have been somewhere near the so-called Kaupang farms in the south of Vestfold, where many Viking graves have been found (including several boat-graves), containing objects of foreign origin from the ninth century, such as Irish and Anglo-Saxon metalware and bits of finely woven Frisian cloth.

Several reasons together – or possibly one alone, if broad enough – could account for the establishment of a town in Viking times. The commonest, no doubt, is trade, especially maritime trade, which requires harbours and transit points such as were afforded by Birka and Hedeby. Towns came into being in the interior too at points where land-routes intersected and where legal decisions on commercial matters were formulated, such as Viborg and Ringsted. Religious shrines, again, whether heathen or Christian, would have the effect of bringing large numbers of people together as permanent residents; and so would a royal centre. But the most potent factor in the creation of a town was the existence of a market place where merchants could buy and sell and where the craftsmen would find a ready and stable demand for their products.

EARTHWORKS

The Danevirke of South Slesvig

In the Frankish annals – *Annales Regni Francorum* – there is described under the year 808 the historic enterprise initiated by the Danish king Godfred after he had sacked and destroyed the north German Baltic town of Reric. Godfred, says the chronicle, 'carried the merchants off with him and sailed with his whole army to the harbour called Sliesthorp. Here he stayed for some days and demanded that his country's frontiers with the Saxons should be fortified by a wall, so that this earthwork stretching from the eastern bay called Østersalt to the western ocean would protect the entire northern shore of the Eider river and would have but a single gate for carriages and horses to travel to and fro. After he had distributed this task among his chieftains he returned home.' This great earthwork across the base of Jutland, from the bottom of the Slie fiord right across to the west, was subsequently known (and still is) as the 'Danevirke' (the Dane-Work), and a good deal of it is still visible (Pl. 14A).

This protective system of earthworks, securing Denmark in the south, is the most extensive monument of the past to be found in the Nordic countries. As the sketch-map on page 156 shows, the Danevirke is a barrier across the narrowest part of south Slesvig from the bottom of the Slie fiord in the east to the meadows by the Trene and Rheide streams in the west. And on the east, furthermore, the 'Østervold' (the East Wall) ran at the base of the Svansen peninsula.

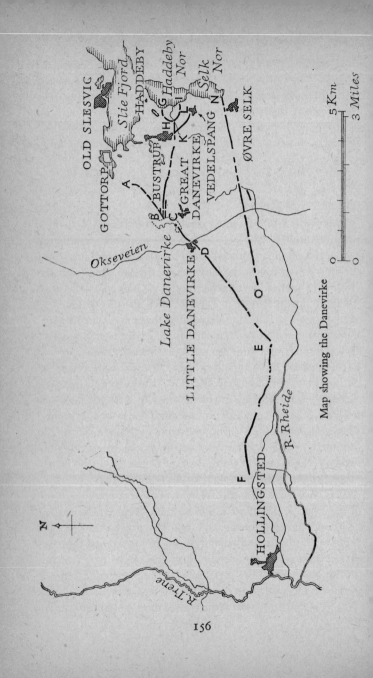

Map showing the Danevirke

The main component of the system is the Main Wall (A–F on the map) which stretches with some interruptions for nearly nine miles from the Gottorp meadows to the Hollingsted meadows. One gets the impression that, apart from the isolated mound called Tyraborg (C), the Main Wall was constructed as a complete unit; and it may well be identified, therefore, with the wall reaching from sea to sea referred to in the Frankish annals. To this conclusion the objections can be made that this Main Wall does not, in fact, stretch from sea to sea, though the force of that objection is somewhat reduced if we combine the Main Wall with the East Wall. But one cannot expect a literary source like the Frankish annals to be wholly in accordance with the object it is endeavouring to describe. There may well be a margin between the Frankish chronicle and the great monument itself. Moreover, in summertime at least, a wall linking meadow to meadow and swamp to swamp would give the impression of a continuous barrier from sea to sea. Another conflict must be noted: the expression in the Annals about the wall protecting 'the entire northern shore of the Eider river' does not strictly fit the Main Wall. On the other hand, however, the gate for traffic is doubtless the so-called 'Kategat' (D) where the ancient route (known as the 'Army Road' or the 'Ox Road') from south to north through Holstein, Slesvig, and Jutland intersects the Main Wall. From C to D the Main Wall covers a length of some 1,850 ft, and is about 18 ft high and 90 ft wide. The middle part of the Main Wall (D to E) carries on for over $2\frac{1}{2}$ miles in a south-westerly direction to 'Kurborg' (E). This part of the wall is of very considerable dimensions and, according to German archaeologists, was built in several different periods. It was strengthened by palisades and a flat-bottomed moat in the south-east, and its rear sloped down to an inner road well protected by the wall along its whole length. At some period this middle section of the Main Wall (D to E) was reinforced by a stone parapet 9 ft broad and 9 ft high: the celebrated 'Granite Boulder Wall' constructed with a facing of stones set in a zig-zag pattern and bound with clay. In front of this parapet there was a round-bottomed moat. A further and final reinforcement of the middle section was supplied by a brick wall 6 ft wide and 18 to 20 ft high which was equipped with buttresses and probably with battlements and gallery as well. This addition, made in the 1160s by King Valdemar the Great, is still preserved in parts, and it is the only part of the Danevirke which can safely be dated from literary sources – i.e. by the writings of Sven Aggesen and Saxo and by the inscription on a leaden tablet in Ringsted Church in Sjælland. In the final 1,100 ft before the bend near Kurborg (E) the middle section again becomes comparatively low – 6 to 9 ft high – and no more than 60 ft wide. The western section of the Main Wall (E–F), which traverses the Hollingsted meadows, has the same dimensions. Sections cut by archaeologists in this part of the Main Wall lead to the conclusion that it was constructed at up to four different periods, and that there was, here too, a road along the inner side of the wall. There was no moat on this front.

Between the Main Wall of the Danevirke and the semi-circular defence wall of Hedeby there runs a connecting earthwork (B–H) getting on for two miles long. It is about 15 ft high for most of the way, and its western end is twofold. It traverses the low ground south of Bustrup and joins the semi-circular wall at the place where the rivulet runs through. German archaeologists are of the opinion that this connecting wall was built during three different periods, and that from the very first it was protected on the south by a moat.

Hedeby's defensive semicircle of earthwork (G–I) is over three-quarters of a mile in length, while its height varies between 12 and 25 ft (Pl. 14B). Near its northern gate, according to German experts, there is evidence of no fewer than nine periods of construction, but this figure is probably an exaggeration. Outside its south-western stretch there has been an advanced earthwork as well, of which only slight traces remain. North of Hedeby lies the 'Højborg', a steep hill with a flat top on which there are a number of shallow burial mounds ringed round by a low wall; this whole system, however, seems to be older than the Vikings. About a mile and a quarter south and south-west of Hedeby there used to run, from the bottom of the Selk cove to the meadows by the river Rheide a dead straight wall (N–O) about 3¾ miles in length and 6 ft high, with a sharp-bottomed moat to the south; it is called the 'Kovirke' and is now partly destroyed. Stretching across the peninsula of Svansen, from the Slie fiord to the Vindeby cove, was the 'Østervold', some two miles long. It has now almost wholly disappeared.

This complex Danevirke is an impressive feat of military engineering, covering 350 years of Danish history from its beginning in Viking times to the addition of King Valdemar's brick wall in the 1160s. Much of these long broad earthworks still remains as a testimony to Denmark's ancient history and activity; but during the Second World War – and especially in the spring of 1945 – several sections of the Danevirke were badly damaged by the deployment of German heavy tanks against an anticipated attack by British forces. These cuts were insignificant and have now been refilled but what cannot be repaired is the demolition by the Germans of large sections of the Kovirke (N–O) in building an airfield.

The investigation and dating of the Danevirke has been going on now for almost a century, and has yielded much difference of specialist opinion which cannot be enlarged on here. One such clash of opinion exists between the conclusions reached by the German Herbert Jankuhn and his colleagues who examined the Danevirke in 1930, and those reached by the Danish scholar Vilhelm la Cour in 1951. 'Even today,' wrote la Cour in 1951, 'the unsolved mysteries of the Danevirke are more numerous than those which have been solved.'

Perhaps I may offer my personal view on the matter, a view which I had reason to qualify after reading la Cour's last book.

King Godfred's wall, mentioned in the Frankish annals of 808, seems to be the one which can be identified with the Main Wall (A–F) of the Danevirke. The location of the harbour of Sliesthorp, which according to the annals, was used by Godfred, is uncertain, but, as it must have been protected by his new wall, it was most likely somewhere on the north side of the Slie, near the present Gottorp or Slesvig. Later in the ninth century there grew up the marketing centre of Hedeby-Slesvig at the cove 'Haddeby Nor'; and around 900 this place was captured by the Swedes and protected by the semicircular earthwork which was then joined up with the Main Wall of the Danevirke. (This assumes, evidently, that the Main Wall was also in the possession of the Swedes at that time.) After the end of the Swedish occupation the Main Wall was reinforced in the tenth century by the 'granite wall'. At the end of the same century the Kovirke was built. In 1050 Hedeby was destroyed, the inhabitants moved to Slesvig on the north bank of the Slie, and soon the name of Hedeby was forgotten. This outline of developments I agree, is not conclusive; I am especially puzzled about the problem of Sliesthorp. I appreciate, too, the fact that the absence in the present town of Slesvig of archaeological finds from earlier than the eleventh century is hardly in itself a substantial enough reason for saying that the town did not exist in Viking times. *Non liquet*. We must wait and see.

Other Earthworks

There are no other massive systems of defence like the Danevirke elsewhere in the lands of the Vikings. One would not expect otherwise, for defences of this elaborate kind of earth, stone, and timber were only necessary at the one place where Viking territory met that of a considerable and hostile

A. Danish sword-hilt

B. Simple iron sword

c. Ornamented Swedish sword-hilts

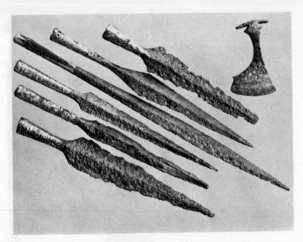

A. Swedish spear-heads and an axe-head

B. Ornamented Danish iron axe-head, inlaid with silver

A. Danish iron spur,
inlaid with silver

B. Danish iron stirrup,
inlaid with silver

C. Richly ornamented Danish horse-collar

3

A. Bronze gilt heads on ornamented Danish harness

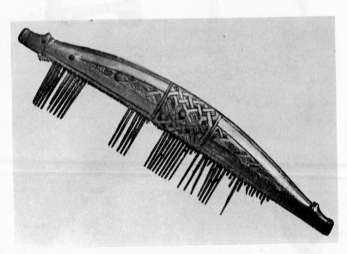

B. A horn comb from Hedeby in Slesvig

4

A. Glass imported into Sweden from the Rhineland

B. Danish gold brooch

A

B

C

A. Danish silver ring

B. Gold jewellery
from Hedeby

C. Danish silver brooch

D. Danish plaited
silver necklace

D

6

A. Gold jewellery from Hornelund, Jutland

B. Silver brooch from Lindholm

C. Norwegian bronze brooch

B

C

The Gokstad ship, Norway

The Oseberg cart, Norway

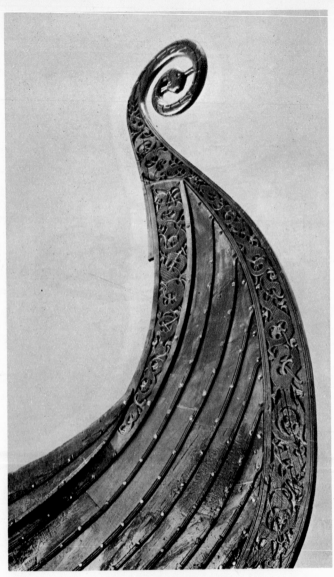

Prow of the Oseberg ship

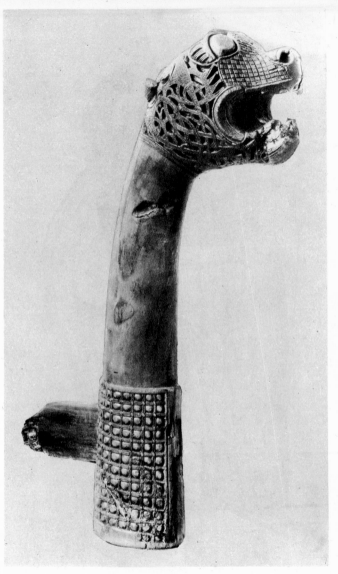

Wood-carving from Oseberg

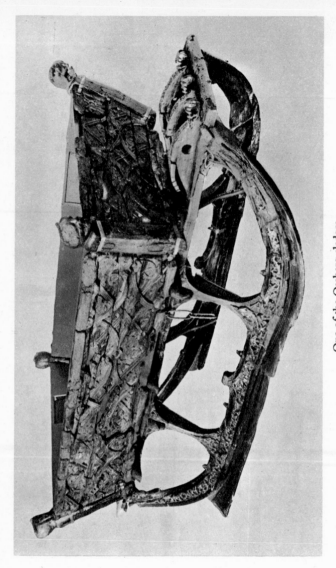

One of the Oseberg sledges

Excavations at Hedeby

13

A. Part of the main earthwork of the Danevirke

B. Part of the walls of Hedeby

A. The military camp at Trelleborg in Denmark

B. A common grave at Trelleborg

B. Runic stone at Turinge in Sweden

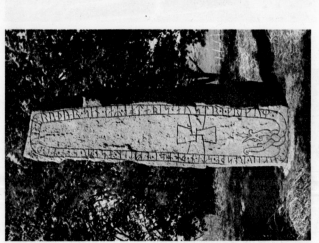

A. Runic stone at Högby in Sweden

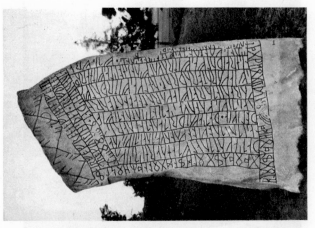

A. Runic stone at Sparlösa in Sweden

B. Runic stone at Rök in Sweden

17

A. Runic stones at Jelling in Denmark

B. Picture of Christ on the great runic stone at Jelling

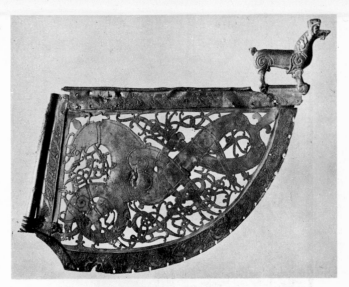

A. Ornamental Swedish bronze vane

B. Carvings on the Ramsund rock in Sweden

A. Irish bronze ornament imported into Norway

B. English silver bowl found at Fejø in Denmark

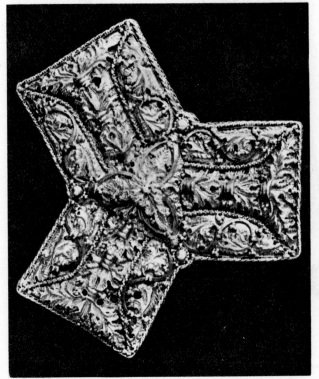

Carolingian gold ornament found in Norway

A. Carved and painted tomb-stone from Lärbro, on the isle of Gotland

B. Runic stone from Dynna in Norway

A. A Norwegian Viking head, from the Oseberg cart

B. A Swedish Viking head: the top of a bone stick from Sigtuna

23

A. A Danish Viking head: the head of a bronze pin

B. Bronze statuette of the god Frey

24

foreign power. The Danevirke was the protective bulwark of the north against the Frankish and Saxon powers of the south. The construction of similar defences in the northern countries was unnecessary, not because the Vikings were at peace with each other – far from it – but because militarily they were maritime powers and, for preference, waged their wars by sea. There are, then, no other known Danevirkes in Scandinavia; but there are, of course, many dykes and ramparts to be found which are associated with ribal conflicts in pre-Viking times.

It might be expected that the Viking colonies in England and France would employ earthworks as a defence against attacks by the natives, but there is no certain evidence that they did so. It is difficult to put a date to any walls or ramparts unless dateable objects are found within them, and corresponding literary evidence exists. There are in England many 'burhs' and 'camps' and 'dykes' associated philologically with 'the Danes', but we have no positive knowledge of their origin. The same is broadly true of northern France. Mention may be made, in this connexion, of the Swedish-Danish excavations of the strange earthwork which appears to cut off the northern end of the Cotentin Peninsula in Normandy from attacks from the south. It includes in its traverse from sea to sea two small harbours, and was apparently built by sea warriors against land assaults from the south. Its name, Hague Dike ('Hagedige') means the wall (*dige*) which cuts off a chin (*hage,* i.e. tongue of land) – a place-name of unquestionably Nordic origin. This defence may very well have been constructed by the Vikings in the ninth or tenth centuries, and the excavations have proved its military character. On the top of the earthwork, for example, were found extensive traces of fire of a kind which indicate that long ditches filled with fierce flames were employed as a means of repelling invaders. But no dateable objects have yet been discovered on the place, and Hague Dike is so far undated. It is possible that the date might be determined by using the method now employed for dating radio-active carbon (C 14).

MILITARY CAMPS

Special attention must be given to one kind of Viking monument so far found only in Denmark: military camps. Of these four have now come to light on Danish soil – one in Zeeland, one in Fyn, and two in Jutland. The earliest of them to be found, and the only one fully excavated (between 1934 and 1941) is the one on Zeeland called Trelleborg (Pl. 15A).

Trelleborg

Trelleborg was excavated by Dr Poul Nørlund, who in 1948 published a detailed narrative of the work. It lies in western Zeeland, two and a half miles west of the town of Slagelse, between the town and the sea (the Storebælt). The site is in a fork made by two streams which there join and run into the Storebælt north of Korsør. Here in the later part of the Viking period the camp was built, apparently on top of an old sacrificial place containing pits and remains of houses. The job seems to have been very thoroughly carried out: the site was levelled and filled in, and the camp was built on carefully-made plans by experienced engineers who evidently possessed exact mathematical knowledge. The fortified camp was constructed in two sections, a main and an outer camp.

The main camp is circular in shape. It is ringed by a strong wall which still exists, and on its landward side – south and east – is further protected by a broad deep moat. In the circular wall there are four gates, one in each quadrant, and the gates have been transversely linked by streets of paved wood which thus divide the circular area into four distinct quadrants. In each of these four sections of the camp there stood four houses of equal size, arranged in squares making sixteen in all. The design of these buildings – long curving walls with truncated ends – makes them look like ships with their bows cut off. Each of the houses is divided into three sections, the middle one being the largest (54 ft long). Although the timber of which these buildings was made has all vanished, the design of the houses can be readily traced from what is left of the post-holes in the ground. As a rule the houses had doors at both gables, with corresponding doors between the three inner rooms. The large central room also had side doors diagonally placed in each of its other walls. The end rooms sometimes had cellars underneath them, for stores, lumber, or even prisoners. The floor of the middle room was made of planks or clay, and had its fireplace in the middle – flanked, one likes to think, by broad settles on which the Vikings used to sit or lie. In the roof there was presumably a smoke-vent (Nordic: *lyre*). Besides the sixteen houses there were a number of small detached ones: guard-houses at two of the gates, chiefs' houses inside two of the squares, and a ship-shaped house of smaller dimensions to the north of the north-eastern square. There appears also to have been a street or footway running inside the whole length of the ring-wall. This circular wall round the main camp was fortified on both sides with palisades and inwardly strengthened with transverse timber sticks. Its four gates, protected by palisades and heavy stone-work, had wooden ceilings and were in effect tunnels. They barred entry from outside by two folding doors: iron rings and massive keys were found near the gates. The outer surface of the ring-wall facing the land was covered with a coating of thick clay held together by stout sticks and branches, and, facing the swampy areas to the north-west and south-west, the wall was built on a foundation of stones and piling and was, higher up, well protected by vertical palisades.

The outer camp served as a reinforcement on the landward side. Its southerly section was curved, to follow the shape of the main camp, but its northern section was a square; both were fortified by the same low wall and flat moat. On the curved section there were built, in a radial pattern, thirteen long-houses of similar design to the sixteen in the main camp, but slightly smaller. Within the square end of this outer camp, near the eastern gate of the main camp, were two similar houses set parallel to each other; and farther east in the same square was the burial-place of the camp (containing about 150 graves), probably an extension of the ancient burial ground which had belonged to the above-mentioned sacrificial place existing before Trelleborg was built. Dr Nørlund surmises that the two parallel houses indicate that the engineers' original intention was to build a row of house-squares in the outer camp, but, in view of the curved shape of the camp, they altered their plan to the radial design now disclosed on the site. The main approach to the main camp and the outer camp was from the south.

It is right and proper to describe the men who built Trelleborg as engineers, so mathematically precise were their methods of construction. Their standard unit of measurement was a modification of the Roman foot: that is, 29·33 cm. compared with the Roman 29·57 cm. On this scale the houses of the squares are 100 ft long, the houses in the outer camp 90 ft, the circular wall 60 ft wide. The small houses in the middle of two of the squares are 30 by 15 ft. The radius from the centre of the camp to the inner side of the circular wall is 234 ft, the distance between the two moats is also 234 ft, and the distance between the centre of the main camp and the nearest gables of the houses in the outer camp is double this: 468 ft. The engineers began by marking the centre of the camp and thence defining the circumference of the walls and moats. This centre is also the point of intersection of the two transverse axes at right angles to each other, which divide the area of the main camp into its four quadrants linking the gates and continuing through them outwards. The constructors' exactitude is everywhere apparent. Dr Nørlund points out that the curved sides of the long houses are always symmetrical about central axes and that their construction was based on ellipses. Two houses at right angles to each other had the same focus and to construct the four ellipses of a house-square the engineer only had to fix four foci constituting the corners of a square whose side was about 3,670 cm., or 127 Roman feet. The construction of the whole house-system within the circular wall of the main camp is therefore based upon squares.

Trelleborg is grandly sited in its flat meadows with its back to higher land. The holes in the ground left by the perished timber have been clearly marked by the excavators with cement, walls and moats have been cleared and partly reconstructed, so that the visitor nowadays gets a graphic impression of what a Viking base looked like.

The Trelleborg burial-place reveals, as we would expect in a military garrison, that most of those buried there were youngish men – between twenty and forty years old. There were also a number of women, but few children or old people. Funerary gifts were relatively few. Nothing particularly points to Christian rites, for even long before Christianity it was not uncommon in Denmark to bury corpses unburned and in the east-west position. Three mass graves were found, the largest containing ten bodies (Pl. 15B). The objects from the graves included few weapons, although one notable find was an exceptionally wide battle-axe inlaid with silver. There was a quantity of tools, such as scythe blades and a plough-share, ornaments, earthenware, and bits of equipment for spinning and weaving. From these discoveries it is possible to give an approximate dating to Trelleborg: i.e. the period from the latter part of the tenth century to the first half of the eleventh, say 975–1050. The camp did not have a very long life, therefore, but it evidently existed at the time when Sven Forkbeard conquered England and when Knud the Great fought the 'battle of the Three Kings' at the Helge in 1026.

Trelleborg was manifestly a military and naval base. Its situation for its purpose was the classical one, providing easy access to the sea and yet protected against attacks and storms. It is presumed that vessels were towed up the river to the camp, and that each of the ship-shaped houses afforded quarters for a ship's crew. The grave-discoveries (ploughshares, scythe blades) hint that the garrison were able to keep themselves supplied with staple commodities, so that foraging raids upon adjacent farms were not too frequent. The building of the Trelleborg houses must have made heavy demands upon the forests of the district.

It has been suggested by some scholars that each house at Trelleborg had as its roof a ship turned upside down, and that in this way the camp provided winter quarters for the fleet. This thesis, however, is scarcely tenable. Another supposition, popular as long as Trelleborg was the only such camp known, was that there, at last, was the elusive and perhaps mythical Jomsborg, for the ground plan did indeed conform to the legends about Jomsborg. But this theory was wholly discounted once four Trelleborg-type camps were found in Denmark alone, and was invalidated also by the fact that (as the graves prove) there had been women in the camp, whereas women were prohibited from entering Jomsborg. One thing is certain: Trelleborg betokens a powerful organization behind it; only the king would have had the means and power to construct such large establishments. That Trelleborg (and its equals in Denmark) should have been built by enemy invaders is very unlikely; it is not proved by the archaeological discoveries, and still less by the historical records which show that Danish power was at its height during this period. Dr Nørlund contends, with great justification, that Trelleborg seems to point to Sven Forkbeard's and Knud the Great's famous military organization called the House-carles, the *hird*. Such conquering monarchs as these would be likely to use effective garrisons to maintain peace in the homeland.

Trelleborg must have provided accommodation for about 1200 men. How and when it ceased to be a base is not known: there are certainly no signs of destruction by fire.

Aggersborg

The next military camp of the Trelleborg type is at Aggersborg in North Jutland, and it was partly excavated by C. G. Schultz between 1945 and 1949. It is situated almost in the middle of Denmark's largest fiord system, the Limfjord, a long fairway which cuts across North Jutland from sea to sea, and was in early Viking times the zone of departure for fleets sailing against England. It is a site as militarily advantageous as Trelleborg. The camp itself is between the Aggersborg estate on the coast and the church and churchyard on a hill; it lies on sloping ground, therefore, and commands an extensive view of the fiord. Nothing of the old camp is visible on the ground, which is now just an ordinary cultivated field; but anyone who knows what was once there can just trace the outline of the circular wall which surrounded the camp. It was similar in lay-out to Trelleborg, but much bigger. The date of its destruction is exactly known – in the year 1086 when the rebellious peasants rose against King Knud the Saint and sacked the place; the revolt ended with the killing of the king in St Alban's church at Odense in the same year. The Odense monk, Elnoth, wrote a graphic account of the destruction of Aggersborg. Meanwhile the archaeologists have been able to give a detailed picture of what it looked like.

The site has not been completely excavated, but enough has been done to establish the shape and size of the camp. Unlike Trelleborg there was no outer camp at Aggersborg; it consisted simply of one large circular area. But within the ring-wall there were 48 houses in 12 squares – compared with 16 houses (in 4 squares) at Trelleborg. Moreover, the houses are one-tenth longer (that is, 110 Roman feet) than those at

Trelleborg. The two axial roads across the camp had on each side a shorter parallel road, an upper and a lower. The inside radius of the Aggersborg camp was 407 Roman feet (cf. Trelleborg's 234), its extreme diameter no less than 960 feet. It had a central square 72 by 72, and there seems to have been wooden towers over its gates. The encircling wall was dressed with timbers inside and out – more strongly on the outside – and was, presumably, topped with a timber parapet and strengthened invariably with transverse timber sticks. The houses at Aggersborg had walls not so curved as those at Trelleborg, but their gable ends were broader. It is supposed by the excavator that the walls were not constructed of perpendicular close-fitting planks ('staves'), but of heavy upright beams with a 'filling' of wattle and daub between the beams; and that the ends of the houses were built of horizontal planks.

A most interesting discovery was that the camp had been built on top of an earlier village, a village moreover of boat-shaped houses, much smaller than those of the camp but built on the same pattern. The village also contained many out-houses filled with rubbish, facing east-west, without fire-places but with a large post-hole at one end whose post must have carried a horizontal plank, maybe a roof ridge. According to finds made on the site this village must have been there a couple of centuries before the camp was constructed in the middle of the eleventh century, and the boat-shaped type of house was evidently, therefore, a much-used design throughout the Viking period, in Denmark certainly and probably throughout the North. It is likely, indeed, that the design originated from the primitive shelter made by dragging a boat ashore and upending it across vertical beams either to repair or preserve it. This explanation is more likely than the somewhat fanciful theory that the early builders had made the technical discovery that a curved wall resists the wind better than a flat one!

Fyrkat

The third Viking camp of the Trelleborg type was found in east Jutland at the bottom of the narrow Mariager-Hobro fiord, a few miles west of the present town of Hobro. This one is called Fyrkat, a strange name which has been explained by the excavator of the camp, C. G. Schultz, as follows: the word *kat* is a seventeenth-century term for an earthwork built on top of an original wall, and when during the Renaissance there was nothing visible of this old camp except the remnants of four walls between four collapsed gateways, it was known as *de fire katte* – the Four Kats. This Fyrkat, not yet fully excavated by the archaeologist-architect Schultz, who is fully familiar with Trelleborg and Aggersborg, closely resembles Trelleborg, although it has no outer camp. It stand on a low promontory, and it is fair to suppose that vessels could have been towed to the camp from the fiord, up the little river Onsild. The site, once more, is militarily correct – providing access to the sea, and protected by geography from attack. The encircling wall was about 9 ft high: a solid wooden affair filled with earth, reinforced on the inside with timbers, and doubtless crowned with an upper parapet. Its four gates were, like those of Trelleborg, elaborate timber-lined tunnels; and within the circle of the camp were sixteen houses arranged in four squares. The ship-formed houses were rather shorter (96 ft) than those at Trelleborg; they had double clay-built walls and were even equipped with tambours. The streets of Fyrkat were wood-paved, and there seems to have been a road round the inside of the circular wall. In one of the gateways there are in the post-holes remains of the heavy oak timbers which supported the gate. Various objects have been found on the site – fragments of a gold filigree brooch, a pair of silver bracelets, a silver finger-ring, an iron axe, a couple of whetstones, some soap-stone utensils – and from these finds the camp has been dated, like Trelleborg, to about the end of the tenth century. Fyrkat appears to have been destroyed by fire during a south-westerly storm, but it is not known when. It may well be that it was sacked and burnt during the same rising of peasants in 1086 which brought about the fall of Aggersborg, but we do not know. The plan is to reconstruct the circular wall at Fyrkat and mark out its pattern of houses, as was done at Trelleborg. It will provide another remarkable picture of Viking times.

Odense

Finally we come to the fourth and, for the time being at any rate, the last of these Viking camps in Denmark. This one was situated right in the middle of the present town of Odense, capital of Fyn, on a height called the Nun's Mountain. Schultz's sharp eye discovered it by comparing an old map with experimental diggings on the spot. Further excavations are at present impossible because of buildings on the site, but enough has been done to establish the fact that there was a camp of the now familiar type in the middle of Odense, and to date it (by several hoards) to around the end of the tenth century – like Trelleborg and Fyrkat. It is not unreasonable, moreover, to surmise that this camp on the Nun's Mountain, which lay quite close to the church where King Knud met his end in 1086, was destroyed on that very occasion. All that need be added is that this camp, like the other three, was built to the classic pattern (here at the bottom of the long Odense Fiord).

Foreign Influence in Camp Building

The future may bring to light more Viking camps in Denmark and reinforce the belief that Sven Forkbeard and Knud the Great safeguarded the country by a network of forts manned by the royal house-carles, the mercenaries, the *hird*. The camps are shrewdly placed in relation to communications by land and water, and could serve an army no less than a fleet. But where did the Vikings learn the science of constructing such camps? The question is not easy to answer. To some extent this mastery of the science of fortification might be said to have a native origin in the north, for even before Viking times the northerners knew how to build forts and refuges of earth and stone: such as, for example, the rounded fort at Ismantorp, on Øland, Sweden, dating from the fifth century, with its nine gates and its houses radially placed on the inner area. Yet even this affords no effective comparison with the engineering feats of the Vikings; nor do the ringed camps of a later date found in north-west Germany and England assist our inquiry. What we need is to find real Trelleborgs in other countries, not merely primitive forts, and if they were pointed out we should still have to determine whether they preceded the Danish ones or whether they were imitations of Danish originals. The Anglo-Saxons for instance, had no more native technical or traditional basis for trying to construct a Trelleborg camp than had the Danes, and a Trelleborg in England would be just as foreign a phenomenon as are the Danish ones in Denmark. If we inquire which of the two peoples, the Anglo-Saxons or the Danes, would have been the more likely, around the year 1000, to learn the science of engineering from some foreign source, the answer must be the Danes – because of the wider horizon of experience provided them by the Viking raids. Engineering as skilled as that revealed at Trelleborg was not native: it must have originated either in the Roman tradition, diffused through the West Roman Empire: or in Byzantium whence it could have reached Denmark via the routes through Russia; or else in the Near East, derived, perhaps, from the Arab empire and spread, along the eastern or the western ways (Russia or Spain), finally on to Denmark.

If, however, we assume that military engineering of this order began in Rome, and penetrated north through the land of the Franks, we at once run into a problem: for Roman camps, forts, and castles are invariably rectangular, not round; the Frankish forts or *mottes*, too, were never circular. The unit of measurement, the Roman foot, is the only link between the Trelleborg and the Frankish camps; but this has no significance in relation to the radically different building-designs of the two types. My own belief is that the engineering of Trelleborg derives from Byzantium, but before enlarging on this I must mention the opinion which sees resemblances between Trelleborg and the Arab and Oriental Persian-Sassanid circular towns, forts, and holy places. I find these resemblances and comparisons too vague, too tenuous and remote; the likenesses are no more conclusive or significant than certain similarities to be found between Viking ornaments and some Chinese decorative art. The significant links in both cases are missing.

The Byzantine world, as we know, was not so remote from the Nordic countries, especially Sweden. Without repeating what has been said earlier on this matter, I may refer to the salient elements of the connexion. It was at the end of the tenth century that the Greek emperor in Constantinople engaged Vikings as mercenaries in his household guard. The contact with the North was active in many other ways as well, and about half-way between the Greek and the Nordic worlds lay the important junction of Kiev. The nineteenth-century Danish historian, Johannes Steenstrup, who had no knowledge whatever of Trelleborg camps when he wrote about the Northmen in 1876, cited the book called *De administrando imperio* in which its author, the emperor Constantine Porphyrogennetos, describes the way of life of the Rus folk in the region of Kiev. Every November, says the emperor, they move out from Kiev to 'towns called Gyra' where they spend the entire winter, returning to Kiev in April when the ice breaks up in the river. Now the Greek *gyros* means a circle, and a possible interpretation of this bit of information about the Swedish Rus folk in Kiev in the tenth century is that they used circular camps as their winter-quarters, and these would naturally be fortified. The Swedish archaeologist, Oscar Almgren, has also mentioned Gyra as a possible clue to Trelleborg. Other archaeologists have called attention to the similarities between the huge defences of Hedeby and the famous wall which defended Constantinople. It seems to me very possible that the highly-developed mathematical skill revealed in the construction of the four Danish Trelleborg camps was brought to the north from Byzantium: by Byzantine engineers, perhaps, who had been taken prisoner and who applied the science they had practised in stone to similar constructional tasks in wood. But this Byzantine skill did not endure long in the North. It could be employed only in the service of a powerful employer – that is to say, a king, for no minor chieftain could build himself these strong and elaborate military bases. For that reason it seems unlikely that other Trelleborgs will be found in Denmark. The four we know of would amply suffice for the security of the kingdom, except perhaps that a further one in the south, in south Jutland, would have been warranted. (On this point the Danish writer Palle Lauring has ventured the suggestion that there was, in fact, a fifth camp – at the mouth of the Slie fiord.) If a Trelleborg should ever be found in England it seems to me highly probable that it would be a camp owing its existence to Danish influence. The idea would have come from east to west, in this case, not the other way round. One Danish province which might have required a Trelleborg in the first half of the eleventh century is Skaane. There is a town called Trälleborg in Skaane, and a circular camp may possibly one day come to light there.

In the feudal times of the early Middle Ages there was developed in central and western Europe a new type of defence work, one that was adopted in the Northern countries, too, after Viking times. The old-style defences constructed of earth and timber gave place to fortifications made of brick, reinforced by earthworks and moats. This new type of defence was the *motte*. The timber which was so extensively used in the Viking camps was an evident fire-risk, and so the Byzantine wooden fortress of the Trelleborg type proved a short-lived feature of Nordic history: from the time (1000) when Byzantine influences and possibilities in Denmark were at their strongest, until the advent of brick-making and the adoption of designs from centres nearer than Byzantium.

Though scholars are generally agreed that Trelleborg, Fyrkat, and the Nun's Mountain were built in the late tenth century, there is some doubt about Aggersborg. The supposition most in favour is that it dates from about the middle of the eleventh century, in the periods of Kings Hardeknud (1035–42), Magnus the Good (1042–7), and Sven Estridson (1047–76). It is relevant in this connexion to point out an evident Byzantine influence in Danish coins minted in this period, an influence which began with Hardeknud and was developed further in the reigns of his two successors. Coins from Lund, for example, display Sven Estridson in the style of a Byzantine emperor, at full length, holding the sceptre and orb. This phenomenon is generally explained by the fact that the Værings (and not least Hardrade) brought back coins from their journeys to the Byzantines, and that these coins were then copied by the local minters. It is noteworthy that, at the same time this Byzantine example was being copied in coins, there was being constructed the last, and the largest, of the four Trelleborg camps which seem also to be designed on Byzantine models. Supposing that the three older camps were built by imported Byzantine experts, we shall feel no difficulty in accepting the further likelihood that the fourth, half a century later, was built at a time when Byzantine influences and traditions were asserting themselves in such other spheres as coinage.

CHAPTER 10

COINS, AND WEIGHTS AND MEASURES

COINS

DURING the greater part of the Viking period a coin was esteemed not *qua* coin but as a piece of metal valued according to its weight. Archaeological finds have often revealed, for example, silver coins cut into pieces of a certain weight or pierced for stringing in a row like an amulet. But although the northerners seem to have had little use for coins as such, it was in Viking times that the first Nordic coins were made. This action can be divided into two periods: first, the middle and late ninth century; second, around 960–80. The model for coins of both these groups was the emperor Charlemagne's Dorestad coin, dating from the early ninth century before the destruction of the town. The front of this well-known and much used Dorestad silver coin was inscribed:

CARO
LUS   and the back   DOR
STAT

This model was copied more or less exactly by the earliest Nordic mint masters. Where they worked is not certain; some say Birka in Sweden, others suggest Jumne in Wendland and Hedeby in Denmark. The latter place is perhaps the likeliest, lying nearest to Dorestad. This oldest Nordic coinage shows how a design can continue long after the disappearance of the place where it was originally made. The Dorestad coin was known and appreciated on the great trade routes between Friesland and the North, and after the destruction of Dorestad in 830 the Northmen tried to copy the coin. But through lack of familiarity with the craft of coining they soon misunderstood the inscriptions on the prototype, for these became unrecognizable in the new imitations, and were therefore dropped in favour of fresh inventions such as human masks, animals, birds, ships, etc. Coins of the second period, dating from the later tenth century, are as rule light and thin, sometimes struck or embossed on one side only: hence the name 'half bracteates'.

The first Danish Viking monarch known to have had his own coins made abroad was Halvdan Lodbrogson in London in 872. Other Danish kings, Knud and Siefred, made their coins at Quentovic on the Continent at the end of the ninth century, and Norman princes did the same at Rouen from the 930s. From around 900 to the middle of the tenth century the Danish and Norwegian kings of Northumberland produced coins bearing their own names – Sitric, Regnald, Anlaf, Eric (doubtless Bloody Axe, son of Harald Fairhair). Some of these Nordic coins made in England bear martial designs – a sword, a banner, or a bow and arrow – others Christian symbols and words – crosses, the Hand of God, the monogram of Charlemagne, or letters like D(omi)-N(v)S D(ev)S – Rex (Lord God the King) or MIRABILIA FECIT – 'He did miracles'. There are other coins decorated with a bird, a triangular design, a hammer, of which it is difficult to say whether they were heathen or Christian. The bird may be Odin's raven or the dove of the Trinity; the hammer may be Thor's celebrated weapon or the pall or the Tau cross. One might not expect the latter two were it not that coins deriving from ecclesiastical sources such as St Peter's at York and St Martin's at Lincoln have the same hammer design. This group of differently stamped coins illustrates the conflict between paganism and Christianity among the Danish and Norwegian immigrant Vikings at a time when both their homelands were still heathen. The three kings named above, Halvdan, Knud, and Siefred, introduced the Anglo-Saxon penny to Northumberland at the end of the ninth century, and a hundred years later the Norwegians did the same in Ireland (Sigtrygg Silkbeard in Dublin).

This whole Anglo-Saxon world of coins served as a model for the earliest regular and native production of coins in the Nordic countries – except for the copies of Dorestad coins made, as noted earlier, in the ninth century. This native production on the Anglo-Saxon pattern began about the same time in all three countries: in Denmark, about 1000, under Sven Forkbeard (988–1014); in Sweden, under Skotking (994 to 1022); and in Norway under St Olav (1016–30). It is only during the last third of the Viking period, therefore, that the Northmen produced their own native currencies.

The first Danish (and the first Nordic) coin bearing a king's effigy is a very rare silver one showing Sven Forkbeard in half length holding his sceptre vertically before his face. He has a fierce aspect, though one can hardly expect an exact likeness. The coin's legend is 'Sven, King of the Danes', this title being formulated half in Latin (*Rex*) and half in inaccurate Anglo-Saxon (*Addener*). The back of the coin bears a cross with the Latin word *crux* and the Anglo-Saxon legend 'Godvine, *danernes*' (sc. mint master). The place of origin is not mentioned on this oldest of Northern royal coins. Knud the Great's coins, on the other hand, frequently bear the names of their places of origin: Lund in Skaane; Roskilde, Ringsted, and Slagelse in Zeeland; Odense in Fyn; and Ribe, Viborg, and Ørbæk in Jutland. Later coins add several places in Jutland – Hedeby, Aarhus, Randers, and Aalborg. It was customary to give not only the town where the coin was struck but the mint master's name as well, so that we now know the names of many hundreds of these *monetarii*. What their status was, however, is not known: whether they were civil servants in the king's employment, or persons licensed to make coins. On Knud's coins, apart from the royal effigy, there are several Christian symbols – the Lamb of God with the Gospel book, God's Hand, and the Dove of the Holy Ghost, these three together simplified into the sign of the Trinity; the three shields; a cross bearing the magic inscription (light, law, peace, king). Occasionally, too, heathen symbols appear, such as the six-footed dragon guarding the treasure, or the man's mask for warding off evil, or the distorted classic (Carolingian) temple-gable. As mentioned above, a distinct Byzantine influence is marked in the coins of Knud's successors Hardeknud, Magnus the Good, and Sven Estridson (the period 1035–75); here we can see motifs such as the full figure of the monarch with orb and sceptre, or two angels, or an angel presenting a banner to the king, or Christ enthroned

In the last quarter of the eleventh century Danish coinage becomes stabilized: that is to say, the royal monopoly in making coins seems to have been confirmed; the number of mints is reduced to five – Lund and Tumatorp in Skaane, Roskilde and Slagelse in Zeeland, and Viborg in Jutland; and the number of coins to two – the King and the Holy Bishop, both of which weighed 0.9 grams. The east Danish penning maintained its quality, but in Jutland it deteriorated during the reign of St Knud (1080–87) and became not only deficient in weight but also mixed with copper. (This may well have been caused by Knud's rearmament programme in his plans for conquering England.) The deterioration continued under Knud's successor, Oluf Hunger (1087–95), and it was probably German influence which produced coins of the same weight as before but on a larger and thinner planchet – and, therefore, more crudely stamped. At this time, too, also under German influence, the bishops began making coins; but by this time the Viking period was over.

The coinage situation in Sweden during Viking times was rather complicated. To begin with, in the ninth century, there were the Dorestad coins; these may well have originated in Birka, but in any case they represent an isolated event in Swedish numismatics. Native Swedish coins reappear under King Olav Skotking (994–1022) and King Anund Jacob

(1022–50), both of whose coins were designed on Anglo-Saxon models. They were minted at Sigtuna, and most of the mint masters were already known for their work in England, where they had made coins for Ethelred II and Knud the Great at Lincoln. It is reasonable to surmise that a team of mint masters from Lincoln was brought to Sweden by King Olav Skotking in order to turn out the native Swedish product. One of King Anund Jacob's coins stamped by Thormod in Sigtuna is remarkable for bearing the legend 'Knud, King of the Swedes'. This Knud can be none other than Knud the Great; but this oddity may be of no significance. At the death of Anund Jacob in the middle of the eleventh century coin-making in Sweden was broken off, not to be resumed for a hundred years. The reason for this can only be the powerful heathen reaction which occurred in the turbulent latter half of the eleventh century when, after the banishment of the bishop of Sigtuna, Christianity was forced on the defensive, almost to the point of dissolution for a long time.

Greater continuity in coin-making can be seen in Norway. It has been much debated whether Norwegian coinage first began under Olav Tryggvason or under St Olav. Probably it was under the latter. The Norwegians, too, followed Anglo-Saxon models, the pennies of Ethelred II; the owner of the privilege is called the Norwegians' king, the mint masters' names are all Anglo-Saxon, no Norwegian mints appear. Harald Hardrade (1066) had much to do with coining from the middle of the century. He had brought much treasure back with him from Byzantium, and must have been largely responsible for the Byzantine influence on Danish and Norwegian coins. He frequently used the sign of the Trinity on his penning, but he did not scruple, it seems, to produce two very different kinds of currency; one a coin of solid silver, the other a debased coin containing half or less than half silver. The latter was scarcely accepted outside his own domains. This situation was to some extent amended by King Olav Kyrre (1066–93), whose coins, though only half the weight of their predecessors, were at least made of fine silver. In the second half of the century Norwegian mints begin to be mentioned – at Nidarnes, Hamar, and Kaupangr (in Trøndelag); and, after Hardrade's death, coins begin to appear with inscriptions in runes and in the Norwegian language, doubtless as a reaction against Latin and Anglo-Saxon inscriptions.

WEIGHTS AND MEASURES

We now turn to the Viking system of weights and measures. As we know from archaeological finds, their weights (made of lead, bronze, or iron) were spherical and often stamped with signs on the flat base. There have also been found elegant little collapsible scales in round bronze containers. Extensive researches have been made into the Viking system of weights and measures, especially by those scholars, Swedish and Norwegian, in whose countries most of these finds have been made. Foremost in these researches have been the Norwegian, A. W. Brøgger, and the Swede, T. J. Arne. Although final answers have not yet been achieved, much has already been settled: such as the conclusion that the early Vikings employed a system based on the formula:

$$1 \; mark = 8 \; ører = 24 \; ørtuge = 240 \; penninge$$

The latest of these constituents, which developed at different periods, was the *mark,* and the word itself probably derives from the 'mark' on the bar of the yard weight. It appears in literature for the first time as a unit of weight in a treaty between the English king Alfred and the Danish (east English) king Gudrum at the end of the ninth century. It seems to have spread from Scandinavia to England, and towards the close of the Viking period it spread also across western Europe and Germany. It has been suggested that this *mark,* with its equivalent of eight *ører,* constituted an arithmetical unit related to the Carolingian *libra,* the pound with its 12 *unciae,* in the proportions of two to three, and that the mark bore a relationship to silver (as the *libra* did to gold) which facilitated the transition from reckoning in gold to reckoning in silver.

The oldest element in the system is the *øre* (derived from the Latin *aureus* (=of gold), as applied to the Roman *solidus*). It originated in the days of the Roman emperors and was, as the name implies, based on gold and not silver. Examination of Nordic gold hoards of the time of the migrations has brought to light gold rings which are multiples of a gold *øre* weighing about 26·4 grams: a correspondence resembling the relationship of the *uncia* to the Roman pound or *libra.* As the Viking period developed, the *øre* was reduced in weight to 24·5 grams, corresponding approximately to about 3 *ørtuge* of 8 grams each.

The third component in the system was the *ortug* which is younger than the *øre.* The derivation of the word is doubtful. Marstrander suggests it may have come from the Latin *denarius* (*argenteus* = of silver) and a Germanic word for a weight. The *ørtug* was based on silver, the basic precious metal of the Vikings, as the *øre* was based on gold. Brøgger believes that the model for the *ørtug* as a unit of weight was the emperor Valentinian's silver coin called the *tremissis* (=⅓ of a *solidus*) which became the basis also of the Anglo-Saxon pennyweight.

The fourth and last element in the Viking system of weights, the penning, coincided with the silver coin of the same name which was (or should have been) of the same weight. The existence of underweight coins led to the practice of differentiating between weighed pennings and counted pennings.

T. J. Arne, after examining Viking scales and weights found

in Sweden, has determined a basic weight unit equal to a little more than 4 grams. He relates this to the Sassanid drachm, a unit equal to 4.25 grams, and suggests – considering various kinds of weight reductions – somewhat doubtfully, a connexion between the two systems.

As far as Viking linear and cubic measures are concerned, very little is known. It was noted in an earlier chapter that the construction of the Trelleborg camp in Denmark was based upon a measure roughly equivalent to the Roman foot (about 29.5 cm); but that is about all we know. No yard-stick of any sort has been found. As to measures of volume, the Viking trader no doubt knew the accepted rules when buying or selling: the exact sizes of the pot, the mug, or the bushel – but we cannot be sure of this. No clues survive on which we can measure a scale of volumes.

CHAPTER 11

RUNIC INSCRIPTIONS

I T is through their runic writings that the Vikings communicate to us in their own tongue. These are our most important primary sources, and as such as they are regrettably brief and very frequently stereotyped in form. Yet they do tell us something, if only in snatches, about the ideas, beliefs, and social conditions of the time.

ORIGINS AND PURPOSE

When the Viking period began runes had already existed in the North for many hundreds of years. I shall not elaborate on the numerous theories of the origin of runes, but will mention only the one interpretation which to me seems the most likely. It is that the oldest Germanic runic alphabet of twenty-four signs, now called *futhark* from its first six, was created by the Germans, under direct or indirect Roman influence, from one or more southern European alphabets somewhere around the year A.D. 200 or soon after. These twenty-four signs – the 'longer row of runes', as it is called, to distinguish it from the later runic alphabet of sixteen signs used in the Viking period – have curious angular shapes which suggest they emerged from the technique of wood-carving.

They must have made a compelling and mysterious impression, these signs bearing meanings fathomable to none but the elect; their magic was not something invented by the men who carved them on stone or in wood; the secret powers existed beforehand in the runes themselves, powers which could be released and disclosed only by the initiated. This conception is reflected in the Nordic myth about Odin, wisest of the gods: even he is not credited with *inventing* the runic signs, but rather with finding them and releasing from them their magic potency.

A further confirmation of this attitude is provided by the practice, common in the centuries next before the Viking period, of putting short runic inscriptions on arms, ornaments, and implements, often some few words or nothing but a name (the owner's), and sometimes on the back only of the object where they would not be exposed to general view but where their spell could work in secret. On a ferrule, for instance, there is engraved '*Gid Marr ikke maa skaane*' meaning 'May Marr (the name of the sword) spare nobody'; these runes would invest the sword with irresistible potency. And on another ferrule: 'I, Alla, own the sword Marr', a formula designed to enhance the value of the weapon. Such hidden magic runes can equally be found inside a woman's ornaments or on the inner side of a shield-boss. Similar trust in the secret magic of the runes is shown in the carving of the entire runic alphabet on one of the stones inside a fourth-century subterranean grave at Kylver in Gotland: the dead alone were to benefit by their power. And another runic inscription, this time inside a Norwegian grave of about a century before the Vikings at Eggjum, in Sogn, Fjordane, declares that the stone on the underside of which it is carved has never been exposed to the rays of the sun, and that the runes are not carved with an iron knife. In other words: the stone and the runes as well are secretly to benefit the dead man and none other. This is the longest of all the early runic inscriptions, and it says about the stone that it shall never, by sorcerers, be brought out into the light of day. To begin with, then, these early runes of the Germanic peoples were not a literature or even a language of communication; they were simply symbols of magic which the initiated could employ for good or evil.

But in the period before the Vikings, the runes were already developing into something else; they were being employed as a form of commemoration. Runes of this kind are found in Sweden and Norway, though not in Denmark. At Møjebro, in Uppland, for instance, there is a stone bearing a portrait of a horseman under a runic inscription; and the runic stone from Tune, in Østfold (Norway), is also without doubt a monument. In these cases magic or secret sorcery are out of the question. In Denmark no runic stones of the pre-Viking period are known, either secreted in graves or raised as monuments. The practice of adapting runes to the latter purpose probably came to Norway from western Germany, in the late Roman period, by the sea-route (i.e. from the mouth of the Rhine and around Denmark); and from Norway the practice may have been communicated to Sweden by the ancient route via Trøndelag to Zämtlant and southward to Uppland.

This double use of runic inscriptions as magic and memorials continued during the Viking period. The two uses were not invariably differentiated, and a stone erected primarily as a memorial might also bear upon it some incantation such as a threatening curse upon anyone who might deface or demolish the monument. The inscriptions sometimes went further than that, and they include many which have so far baffled scholars and appear to be based on shifting varieties of some secret and elusive number magic. There can be no doubt that this secret language or algebra of witchcraft existed in the north, though some philologists have developed such fanciful notions about it as to have promoted a strong reaction against their theories on the part of more sober scholars.

THE RUNIC ALPHABET

At the time of transition to the Viking period the twenty-four signs of the older runic alphabet were replaced by a shorter row of only sixteen runes, the younger *futhark*. Why this transformation occurred is a matter which has evoked considerable discussion. Bearing in mind that the number of transitional runic inscriptions which have survived is relatively small, it is easy to see why this question is difficult to answer. What can be said is that the change was a simplification of the runic system, and that there may well have been practical reasons for the reform. But the use of fewer runic signs must evidently imply that one rune must sustain more phonetic varieties than before – a factor which in itself presents the interpreter of the latter inscriptions with more difficulties.

Three types of script are found among these later runic writings: first, the Danish, or 'ordinary', runic forms which are encountered throughout Denmark, including Skaane, western (later the whole of) Sweden and Norway; second, the Swedish-Norwegian runes of eastern Sweden, south and western Norway – which also appear in the western Norwegian colonies, especially the Isle of Man; and, thirdly, the so-called Helsinge Runes, a kind of code-writing or system of shorthand prevalent in north Sweden, produced by leaving blanks so to speak, in the rune, chiefly by omitting the main stroke.

DISTRIBUTION

In Denmark most of the runic stones belong to the period 950–1050, and they are fairly evenly distributed throughout the country but with special concentrations in south-west Skaane and east Jutland (e.g. at Randers, Aarhus, Slesvig). The island of Bornholm has, as a late group of its own, some runic stones of the eleventh century. In Norway there is a concentration of runic stones in the region of Jæren, south of Stavanger, and 'Østlandet' has some specially interesting decorated stones. (The Isle of Man has runic stone crosses of the tenth and eleventh centuries.) In Sweden runic stones occur throughout the south and middle of the country; the province in which they are most abundant is Uppland, with a total of about 1000 stones. This Uppland group is dated mainly from the eleventh century and is distinguished by its abundance of ornament. Of all the Nordic countries Sweden can claim by far the most runic stones, some 2,500 in all.

HISTORICAL VALUE

What do the runic stones reveal? First of all they briefly disclose something about leading personalities in the aristocratic part of the community: the kings, chieftains, and warriors. The man who erected the stone often mentions himself and always, of course, the one in whose memory the stone is raised; on him a shorthand comment is sometimes made. Now and then the rune carver gets a mention, and not infrequently the stone records the circumstance that it has been raised in honour of someone who fell in battle in a foreign land, east or west, far away, or within the Nordic homelands. Occasionally the social position of the dead man is recorded, his post in the hierarchy of the house-carles (the *hird*), or his standing with the heathen priesthood. Seldom does a runic stone mention that the man it commemorates followed a peaceful occupation, such as road-maker ('bridge-builder'). Another item sometimes included on the stone is the expression of a hope of some kind – such as that the stone will stay long in its place, that the dead man may enjoy his grave, that the god Thor will sanctify the runes, or that the Christian God will help the soul of the dead. Many of the later runic stones have a Christian stamp.

It may be well, at this point, to describe these themes in some detail through examples of runic inscriptions: we will hear the very voices of the old stones.

References to Kings and Princes

The most frequent runic references in this category apply to the Danish royal house of Jelling. The two Jelling stones have already been mentioned – the stone set up by King Gorm for his wife, Queen Tyre, calling her the 'ornament (jewel) of Denmark'; and the stone erected by Harald Bluetooth to his parents, King Gorm and Queen Tyre. The latter is the most impressive runic stone in the whole Nordic sphere, including in its inscription a summary of Harald's own achievements – the sonorous reminder that he was 'the Harald who conquered all Denmark and Norway and christianized the Danes'. There are three other Jutish stones in this category, one from Sønder Vissing, one from Læborg, and one from Bække, all of which refer, as it seems, to King Harald and his mother Queen Tyre. The Swedish royal house in Hedeby is commemorated in a pair of runic stones from Hedeby, both raised by Queen Astrid and dedicated to Sigtryg, her son by King Gnupa. Two other stones from Hedeby probably refer to Sven Forkbeard: one erected by Sven's house-carle Thorulv for his comrade Eric, a warrior of high degree who 'found his death while men sat around (besieged) Hedeby'; the other put up by King Sven himself and inscribed: 'King Sven raised this stone for his house-carle, Skarde, who had sailed in the west but now has met with death at Hedeby.'

Reference to Chiefs and Nobles

A Danish runic stone from Snoldelev is carved with various heathen symbols – a swastika, a sun-wheel, a tricorn – and its inscription says: 'Gunwald's stone, son of Roald, Thul in Salløv.' A *Thul* was probably the head of a religious order, but the wording is so terse as to leave it uncertain whether Gunwald or his father Roald was the *Thul*.

Two Danish chieftains were married in turn to Ragnhild, presumably one and the same woman. The first was Gunnulv, from Zeeland, 'a baying man' (that is to say, a heathen priest), the second a temple-priest from Eyn called Alle Sølve. The first to die was Gunnulv, and his runic stone (at Tryggevælde in Zeeland) says, 'Ragnhild, Ulv's sister, raised this stone and constructed this mound and ship-burial for her husband, Gunnulv, a baying man, the son of Nærve. Few men nowadays are more high-born than he. A *ræte* be the one who defaces this stone or removes it from here.' Next, Alle Sølve dies, having had several sons by Ragnhild; and his stone (at Glavendrup in Fyn) declares: 'Ragnhild raised this stone over Alle Sølve, priest of the *vier,* most worthy *thegn* of the *lid.* The sons of Alle made this monument for their father, and his wife for her husband. Sote carved these runes for his master. May Thor consecrate these runes. A *ræte* be the one who defaces this stone or removes it to another.' What the word *ræte* meant can only be surmised: an outcast spirit, perhaps. *Vier* means holy shrines, *thegn* means chief, *lid* house-carles (*hird*). The reference to removing the stone to another refers to the possibility of using it to commemorate some other dead man – a form of thrift which is evidenced by stones thus used at Tillitse in Lolland, and Alstad in Norway. Another stone, at Rønninge in Fyn, also refers to its carver Sote, and describes him as 'son of Asgøt with the Red Shield'.

The inscriptions frequently emphasize the honourable lineage of the person they commemorate – 'a highly born chieftain', 'a chieftain of noble lineage', 'a most noble warrior', 'a warrior of very good descent', 'a woman of noble birth', 'a man of noble birth', and so on. Still better, of course, if the stone embodies the family tree, or a portion of it – as on the north Swedish stone from Malsta which proclaims, 'Frømund raised this stone for Rige-Gylfe, the son of Bræse; and Bræse was the son of Line and Line the son of Øn and Øn the son of Ufejg, and Ufejg the son of Ture'.

References to Viking Life

Two qualities especially appreciated by the Vikings were hospitality and generosity, and these are sometimes specifically referred to on memorial stones; the runic stone from Sövestad in Skaane declares, 'Tonne raised this stone over her husband Bram and (i.e. together with) Asgøt his son. He was best among the landowners and the most generous in food'. Bram was evidently a large farmer who kept a good table.

Another merit much esteemed by the Vikings was a landowner's readiness to employ his men on such public utilities as making roads across marshes, filling up swampy patches, and building bridges over rivers. It seems probable that it was the clerics who persuaded noblemen to act in this way, because it is often Christian runic inscriptions which praise a man for 'making bridge', as this kind of public-spirited action was called. A classic example is provided in Uppland, where Tarlabanke, great landowner, mentions this himself on several runic stones, two of which are still standing on the road through the village (Täby) where he lived, and where he filled in swamps and made paths. These two stones testify that 'Jarlebanke raised these stones in his own honour, while he was still alive, and made this bridge for the good of his soul. He was the sole owner of Täby. May God help his soul'. It may well have been in his mind that these beneficent actions would assist his passage through purgatory. Three other similar stones are still in the vicinity. Farther north in Sweden, on the hold island 'Frøsøn' (Frøj's Island) in the Storsjøn (Great Lake) of Jæmtland, mentioned above, lived another great Christian landowner, Østmand Gudfastsen, who commemorated himself on a stone inscribed: 'Østmand, son of Gudfast, had this stone raised and this bridge made, and he made Jæmtland Christian. Asbjørn made the bridge, Tryn and Sten carved the runes.' The Källstorp stone in Skaane says, 'Thorkil, son of Thord, made this bridge after his brother

Vrage' – the word 'after' probably signifying that by building the bridge he will benefit his brother in the beyond. Similarly, an inscription on a rock at Södertälje, near Stockholm, reads: 'Holmfast had the ground cleared and a bridge built in memory of his father, Geir, who lived in Näsby. May God help his soul. Holmfast (also) had the ground cleared and a bridge made in memory of his good mother, Ingegärd.'

There are rune-stones of this type, too, in Denmark. One which now stands in Fjenneslev church on Zeeland reads: 'Sasser raised the stone and made the bridge'; and in a swamp near by there is actually a little bridge crossing a rivulet, and to our days this bridge bears the name: 'Sassbvo' (Sasse's bridge).

In Norway only one example exists of this type, but it is one of the few which, like the Källstorp stone already mentioned, declares that the bridge was made to safeguard the soul of the dead. This is the high, pointed picture-stone, belonging to the mid eleventh century, which originally stood at Bynna in Hadeland, and is now in Oslo. The pictures show God the Father and the Star of Bethlehem, and below, on horses, the Three Wise Men; the inscription says: 'Gunvør made the bridge Thrirek's daughter, after Asred her daughter. She was the most skilful maiden on Hadeland.' This good deed performed by a woman landowner for her dead daughter is one of many reminders that women enjoyed a high degree of freedom and status among the Vikings.

One more Norwegian picture-stone, this too erected by a woman, deserves a mention. This is the splendid stone (now in Oslo) from Alstad in Ringerike which mentions the journey of a bride: 'Jorun raised this stone after Øl-Arnir who took her by the hand (i.e. married her) and took her from west of Ringerike from Ve to Ølvestad. Øgmund's stone records it.' The stone is a work of art on which there are handsome pictures of a hunt, with horses, hounds, falcons, and people. No wonder Øgmund wanted his name on it. But there is a later and very significant further inscription on the foot of the stone: 'Igle raised this stone over Thorval, his son, who found death in —' This then, is a clear case of pilfering someone else's stone; but as the stone was not protected by the runic curse upon defacers and thieves, Igle evidently was willing to take a risk. Another example (Danish, this time) of the same kind is the runic stone from Tillitse, on Lolland, which reads: 'Eskil the son of Sulke had this stone raised for himself. While the stone lives, this monument which Eskil won will always stand. May Christ and St Michael help his soul.' But elsewhere on the stone is the further inscription: 'Toke carved the runes for his stepmother, Thora, a woman of good lineage.'

Reference to Warriors

One would expect the main theme recorded on runic stones of Viking times to be tributes to the prowess of warriors killed on raids to the west or east. Nearly all the ones which do so, however, are Swedish and belong to the younger part of the Viking period. There are, indeed, stones set up to Norwegian and Danish warriors; there is the Stangeland stone from Jæren, south of Stavanger, in Norway, inscribed to Stenthore 'who fell in Denmark', and in Denmark there is the Kolind stone in Jutland in memory of Tue 'who met his death in the east', and the Scanian Uppakra stone to Toke, 'who met his death out in the west'. But these are rarities, and it is central and eastern Sweden which provides the real source of this kind of stone, the kind which records the great Viking raids to the east and the west.

Let us consider a few examples. Of western raids there is a commemoration in the stone at Grinda in Södermanland raised by two sons 'over brave father. Gudvir went to the west, to England, and received a share of the *geld*. Fortresses in Saxland he bravely stormed.' The brave father, then, is Gudvir. Danegeld is mentioned again on the stone at Orkesta in Uppland – 'But Ulv has taken three danegeld in England. The first was that which Tost gave. Then gave Thorkild. Then gave Knud.' These men were undoubtedly the famous historical personages Torkil the Tall and Knud the Great. Another runic stone in Uppland is dedicated to 'Geire who belonged to the *tinglid* (house-carles) in the west' – that is to Knud the Great's celebrated *hird*. Another Swedish Viking with similar name is mentioned on the Harlingtorp stone in Västergötland: 'Tola raised this stone for his son Geir, a very good man. He died on the western road during a Viking raid.'

Most of the Swedish Viking stones, however, naturally refer to raids in the east rather than in the west, and Uppland and other eastern provinces of Sweden are prolific in stones of the tenth and eleventh centuries when such runic carvers and artists as Asmund Kareson, Livsten, Balle, and Øpir carved and decorated an immense number of runic inscriptions for brave Vikings who had perished in the east. 'Østerled' and 'Øster-færd' and 'Østervy' were general names for 'Great Sweden' in the east, but eastern countries and localities are specifically mentioned on the Swedish stones: 'Semgallen' is a part of Latvia, 'Domesnæs' is in Courland, 'Virland' in Estonia (all three in the Baltic); 'Holmegaard' is Novgorod, 'Gardarike' is Russia, 'Grækenland' is either Hellas or Byzantium, 'Särkland' (which means the Silk Land) is farther away: south and south-west of the Caspian Sea. 'Jerusalem', finally, is just what it says. Let us hear some of these eastern Swedish voices!

Both sides of a rock at Ed in Uppland have runes made by the Viking Ragnvald. One side says 'Ragnvald had runes carved for Fastvi, his mother, Onem's daughter. She died in Ed. May god help her spirit'. The other says, 'Ragnvald had runes carved he who in Grækenland was commander of the *lid* (the carles)'. This latter may refer to the Byzantine life-guards, the Værings of Constantinople; and, if so, Ragnvald was a very important commander indeed. Two inscriptions are found on a large stone at Högby in Östergötland (Pl. 16A); the first says, 'Torgerd set up this stone for Assur, his mother's brother, who died in the east, in Grækenland'; on the second we are further told of this same Assur and his brothers: 'Gulle the Good had five sons. The brave man Asmund fell at Fyris. Assur ended in the east, in Grækenland. Halfdan was slain in duel. Kare died at home. Dead too is Bue.' Thus could a Viking family lose all its men. The stone at Ängeby in Uppland records that Bjørn fell in Virland (in Estonia) and that Asmund (Kareson) carved the runes. The Broby stone in Uppland tells of a Viking Østen who went to Jerusalem and died in Grækenland. One stone of special interest is that from Sjusta, in Uppland, which declares of the warrior Spjallbode: 'He was brought to death in Holmegaard (Novgorod) in 'Olav's Church'. Øpir carved the runes. A stone from Turinge in Södermanland (Pl. 16B) first describes in prose how the stone is a memorial to the warrior Torsten, erected by his sons Kettil and Bjørn, his brother Anund, his house-carles and his wife Kettilløg, and then breaks into poetic praise of both brothers – the dead Torsten and the still-living Anund – so: 'Kettil and Bjørn erected this stone for Torsten, their father, and Anund for his brother, and the carles for their equal, and Kettilløg for her husband. Brothers they were – the best of men in their homeland and away at the wars. Looked after their house-carles as well. He fell in battle – in the east, in Garda – the guard's commander – best of country-men.' Finally we cite the runic stone from Gripsholm Castle: 'Tola had this stone raised for his son Harald, Ingvar's brother. They went away on manly pursuits – far away, in search of gold and in the east they gave to the eagles – Died in the south – in Särkland.' To give (food) to the eagles, means to be killed. In such words the Nordic homeland commemorates her wild sons.

The Ingvar of this stone is a strange figure, part real and

part mythical, belonging to the later Viking times of Sweden: Ingrar Vidfarne appears in a late Icelandic saga as a Swedish royal prince who went with many companions on a difficult and disastrous raid to Särkland in the far east. And in fact no fewer than twenty-five runic stones from eastern Sweden, dating, as it seems, from about the mid eleventh century, refer to a certain Ingvar (and his four brothers). Ingvar himself was killed on his great enterprise, and 'the Ingvarstones' at home, set up as memorials to the many highborn companions, commemorate this in such phrases as: 'He fell on the eastern road with Ingvar. May God help his soul'; or 'He was brought to death in Ingvar's guard'; or 'He went east with Ingvar'.

Other Swedish Viking stones are bound together by one great event namely those which record the celebrated battle at the Fyris Plain at Uppsala, when the Swedish king Erik Sejrsæl defeated his dangerous and turbulent nephew Styrbjørn who commanded a force including Danish warriors and Joms-Vikings. There are two such stones in Skaane, one from Hällestad, one from Sjörup, raised to Toke ('He did not flee at Uppsala') and Esbjørn ('He did not flee at Uppsala but slew as long as he had a weapon'). Another such stone is the one mentioned above from Högby celebrating, among five brothers, the brave Asmund, Gulle's son, who also 'fell at Fyris'.

References to Peaceful Pursuits

Nordic runic stones seldom mention peaceful activities, except for the occasional references, already noted, to road-making or bridge-building. Yet there is one, now badly defaced, from Mervalla in Södermanland which records that 'Sigrid had this stone raised for her husband Sven. He often sailed to Semgallen (Latvia) with his precious ship round Domesnæs (Courland)'. This Sven apparently was a peaceful trader who followed a regular route in the Baltic.

Not infrequently the inscriptions on runic stones are cast in metrical form, and the phrases, put up in powerful splendour, come to life in rhythmic waves. Here, as a matter of interest, are the texts of two of the runic stones mentioned already. Turinge says:

> Brøðr váru þeir – bestra manna – á landi ok –
> i liði úti – Heldu sina – húskarla vel – Hann fell í
> orrustu – austr i Gorðum – liðs foringi –
> landmanna bestr.

Gripsholm says:

> þeir fóru drengila – fiarri at gulli – ok austarla –
> erni gáfu – Dóu sunnarla – í Serklandi.

Apart from the metrical pleasures which the runic stones can give to the ear, they are sometimes a joy to the eye as well. The runic craftsmen in Uppland in the eleventh century devised a whole system of decoration involving scrolls and animals. One recurrent motif, doubtless intended to ward off evil as well as to look decorative, is the large human mask with braided beard and round eyes. Ships are used entirely for ornamental effect. Significant symbols as well as illustrations of Christian or pagan myths occur on stones of all three Nordic countries: at Dynna in Norway (Pl. 22B), Jelling in Denmark (Pl. 18B), Sparlösa (Pl. 17A), Altuna, Hunnestad in Sweden – and on the carved stones from Gotland. The Ramsund rock in Södermanland depicts the myth of Sigurd Fafnesbane. From traces of paint which have occasionally been found on runic stones, it may fairly be concluded that colour was used for decorative effects – notably yellows, reds, and blues.

Not all the runic stones which survive can be deciphered; there are some inscribed in codes which may never be solved. The classic example is the famous stone from Rök in Öster-götland (Pl. 17B) containing the longest runic inscription in the North – about 800 signs – which begins, 'Over Væmod stand these runes. But Varen carved them, the father to his doomed son.' This mammoth inscription, full of secret runes, number magic, and puzzling and inscrutable passages, has provoked a large controversial literature among specialists, one of whom has claimed a connexion between it and the Trelleborg camp on Zeeland.

RUNIC STONES OUTSIDE SCANDINAVIA

Are there any runic stones outside the North? The question is really a double one: (a) Did the Vikings erect stones over their families in the lands they colonized? and (b) Did they set up stones to their fallen dead on raids into foreign countries? To both these questions the answer is yes. Examples of the first kind are the richly decorated Danish–Anglo–Saxon stone crosses found in northern England, many with runic inscriptions and animal decorations in Nordic style. There are also the Norwegian–Celtic runic crosses on the Isle of Man (some of them the work of the runic master-craftsman, Gaut). The latter have been described by the Norwegian scholar Haakon Shetelig as 'Christian funerary monuments inspired by the Celtic culture but Norwegian in their language and runes and showing conspicuously the survival of pagan traditions'. These Manx grave-stones are often decorated with a great Celtic cross in relief, filled up with Celtic interlace but frequently surrounded by effigies illustrating Nordic pagan myths such as Odin and Fenris, Sigurd Fafnesbane, etc., and their ornamental pattern is sometimes of a Norwegian stamp. A similar relic is the fragment of a stone cross found in the churchyard of Killaloe in Ireland with a Norwegian runic inscription, 'Torgrim erected this cross.'

Runic stones raised over a fallen comrade by Vikings on a foreign raid or journey are rare, but they do exist. In the London Guildhall Museum is a runic stone – apparently the side of a stone coffin – decorated with the figure of a lion in the early eleventh-century style, and bearing a defective runic inscription: 'Ginne had this stone laid and Toke . . .' The remainder of the text, containing the name of the buried person, was probably on another side of the coffin, which has now disappeared. The stone, probably Danish and found in 1852, at that time clearly showed traces of blue colour. Another such stone, Swedish in origin, is a small one (now in Odessa) found on the island of Berezanj in the Dnieper Delta. There apparently the Swedish Viking, Grane, lost his friend, for the stone records, 'Grane made this grave for his comrade Karl.' In this connexion mention must be made, too, of the celebrated marble lion which now stands off Venice's old naval arsenal, where it was brought long ago by Venetians who found it in the Greek harbour of Piraeus. This lion is not a burial monument, at least not a Nordic one, but it is incontestably a Nordic (Swedish) runic memorial for the left shoulder of the lion still bears the dim remains of a runic scroll or ribbon of the same kind as those shown on runic stones of the tenth and eleventh centuries from Uppland. The inscription unfortunately is so weathered as to be no longer decipherable: the imagination is teased by speculating on what a Swedish Viking confided to a Greek lion.

Finally, before leaving the Vikings' runic stones, let us return to Sweden and note the stone from Skarpåker, Södermanland. The whole of its broad front side is taken up by a rich flowery Christian ring-cross, the arms and top of which, however, are entwined with pagan ornamentation, while the foot of the cross is planted as a mast in a ship picture, the well-known Viking ship. In the surrounding runic scroll, which bears a heathen animal's head, is carved: 'Gunnar raised this stone for Lydbjørn his son' – and then partly in shorthand runes: 'the earth shall split and high heaven.' In other words: Ragnarok (p. 253). Were these two, father and son, pagan or Christian? No man can tell. But this they knew: all things shall perish!

CHAPTER 12

ART

DECORATIVE ART

IN the three centuries of the Viking period the Nordic countries developed a rich and varied decorative art. Its native basis was that of animal designs, but from the ninth to the eleventh centuries it was stimulated by influences derived from the many lands, both east and west, with which the Vikings made contact. There were three principal spheres of art in western Europe able to act on the North: the Irish, the Anglo-Saxon, and the Frankish (Carolingian–Ottonian). The influence from the Orient was much less, some eastern motifs reached the Nordic countries directly by way of the links between Russia and Sweden, and indirectly by infiltration through western Europe. However, the animal motifs were always predominant in Viking art, whereas the floral elements were less popular.

The Pre-Viking Period

Before considering the development of the decorative art of the Vikings, in each of the ninth, tenth, and eleventh centuries, we should look briefly at its origins in the pre-Viking period. All the Germanic peoples shared a preference for animal designs in their forms of decoration; so too, indeed, did other races such as the Irish and the Scythians. The southern Germans were never entirely dominated by this fashion, but the northern Germanic tribes practised it intensely and constantly for a very long time. Around the year 700 animal ornament was declining on the Germanic continent, but in Scandinavia it continued to flourish through the whole eighth century. When the Viking period was about to begin (about 800) the Nordic artist had achieved an extreme refinement in the depiction of animal forms. This decorative art, common to all three Nordic countries, had then reached its fullest development. It had gone far since its beginnings in the sixth century, and now revealed an intimacy and dexterity of design as notable as that of contemporary Irish art. So far had this evolution gone, indeed, that it was now liable to reach a dead end. Although the animal forms themselves were still discernible the artists were practising all sorts of fanciful elaboration of detail and thereby allowing some disintegration of the decorative patterns to appear. This incipient decadence was plainly evident at the end of the eighth century, and if it had not been counteracted by some new positive impulse would have reduced Nordic art to rapid degeneration. This was the position when the Viking period began.

Of the three spheres of west European art with which, as mentioned, the Vikings came into contact, the following characteristics must be noted. The Irish had been developing animal patterns for as long as the Germanic peoples and had not allowed their designs, however intricate, to degenerate. Anglo-Saxon decorative art was partly derived with little sign of originality from the Irish and partly from a motif borrowed from Syria and subsequently developed in North England – namely, a vine-scroll decoration, its branches inhabited by animals in motion – leaping, climbing, and flying. In adopting this Syrian formula the Anglo-Saxons stressed the animals more than the vine, and the new pattern became a popular form of decoration in the eighth and ninth centuries, on stone crosses and other burial monuments in the north of England. The third influence the Vikings encountered was the Frankish–Merovingian–Carolingian of the eighth century: animal motifs, again, partly oriental in origin, such as lions and bears, with copious plant and leaf conglomeration, especially acanthus. Against this background of influences let us now look at the progress of Nordic decorative art during the Viking period, century by century.

The Ninth Century

The century began with that infusion of a new element which, as we have seen, was badly needed if Nordic animal designs were to be preserved from decadence. The renewal which emerged was, in fact, a new animal. During the ninth century there appeared everywhere in the decorative art of the North this new and invigorating animal figure, surprisingly varied in treatment, in the famous Norwegian wood-carvings of Oseberg. It may be asked how such an invention could within a century transform the decorative traditions of three hundred years. Yet that is precisely what happened. The invention which achieved this result was the 'Gribedyr', a word which means the clutching animal. This 'gripping beast' was a composite fantastic creature, a mixture of bear, lion, dog, and what not, a sort of comprehensive goblin, full of vigour and animation. It was never still: always clutching either itself or a neighbouring animal in the next cage. Its head was large, its eyes as round and solemn as a giant panda's, seeming almost to wear spectacles; the wide forehead was bald, and there was a long tuft of hair at the back of the head. The body of the beast was often elongated. This fantastic invention seems to have captured the Viking fancy immensely, for it dominated their decorative art in the ninth century. The restless energy and mobility of the 'gripping beast', expressed in its ever-clutching limbs, invested it with endless possibilities from the designer's point of view as he drew its image inside frames or cages of various shapes, and its wildness and virility were evidently qualities which keenly appealed to the Vikings. The 'gripping beast', then, was a versatile and regenerating force in transforming the traditional Nordic animal-art. It is important to stress the fact that it was an invention, rather than a variation of existing forms;

this is shown by the fact that on some early ninth century bronze tibulas from Gotland the new animal is placed in its own special sections side by side – but never intermixed – with the old familiar designs.

Whence did this potent beast derive? What seems to me a sound answer to this question was offered in 1880 by the Danish scholar, Sophus Müller, and subsequently endorsed by the Norwegian Haakon Shetelig and others. It is that the animal is a composite invention resulting from the impact upon Viking artists of the realistic pictures of the Frankish–Carolingian lions and other creatures unfamiliar to them. The ferocity and power of these figures took the fancy of the Northerners who liked animals, and they proceeded to evolve a new motif from the experience. Shetelig has pointed out that the characteristic frames or cages in which the 'gripping beasts' are presented are also found in Carolingian ornamental art. Although, as we noted above, the Gotland bronzes show the new motif in isolation from the previous tradition, yet by the middle of the ninth century a fusion of styles occurs, named by archaeologists after a place called Borre near Oslo-fiord. This Borre 'animal' retains from the old tradition the elongated animal body, though somewhat thickened, and from the 'gripping beast' it has borrowed the clutching paws and the mask-like face and head. What is very significant about the new style is its vigour and savagery, which is partly revealed in rough surfaces; the former refinement of design and composition is abandoned in favour of a robust and bar-baric representation. Thus did the 'gripping beast' play havoc with the decorative fauna of Nordic art.

Viking artists were rather unresponsive to plants and flowers as a basis of decoration – not yet aware of their beauties. They went for animals almost every time. Never-theless they do appear to have seen possibilities in the Caro-lingian handling of Classical plant-forms, especially the acanthus. The three-foiled golden buckle from Hon in

Norway, brought home no doubt by a Norwegian Viking, was a masterpiece of Carolingian jewellery – and it was wholly adorned with luxuriant acanthus. Such revelations as this persuaded Viking craftsmen to try their hand at similar shapes and decorations, but with little success. Their stiff and clumsy depictions of vegetable motifs soon gave way again to their old favourites the animals. They did better in their efforts to copy the Carolingian vine-pattern designs in filigree, usually silver – but here, too, the animals finally prevailed again.

The Tenth Century

The Borre style continued in the tenth century, but new manifestations of it appear. The dominant motif becomes a ribbon-shaped animal figure, harmoniously drawn in the shape of an S, often symmetrically crossing another design of the same shape. The head with the tuft at the back (and looking like a dog's) is displayed in profile. This innovation is known as the 'Jelling animal', after the little silver cup found at Jelling in Jutland. The cup bears signs of Irish influence in its ornament, and it is fair to conclude that the Jelling style arose from the long and intimate association of the Nor-wegians with Ireland. I do not accept the theory, sometimes advanced, that this style is a revival of eighth-century Nordic art, for it bears no resemblance to the old pattern. This 'Jelling style' with its ribbon-shaped animal must not be confused with the design found on the great runic stone mentioned earlier, the noble monument which King Harald Bluetooth raised in Jelling over his parents and to his own honour as well. This famous runic stone is triangular. Most of the inscription is carved on its largest side, in horizontal lines (as, later, on manuscripts); one side bears a picture of Christ, and one a large animal – a fine ornamental lion, its mane and tail adorned with leaves and a snake coiled about its loins and throat. This great Jelling lion – related to lions on Swedish runic stones of around 1000 – is evidently inspired by English ornament (as are the plant-motifs of the same stone). 'The great animal' festooned with plaited work or vines is a common figure in Anglo-Saxon art, frequently used as decoration on the stone crosses of northern England ('The Anglian beast').

The Eleventh Century

The great lion of Jelling seems to have established the predominant design for decorative art throughout the remainder of the Viking period. It appears again and again in various sizes: on runic stones in eastern Sweden, on a wooden church in western Norway (Urnes), on Swedish and Norwegian bronze vanes, on bone-carvings decorating treasure-chests, on silver and bronze jewellery. It is a typical motif of eleventh-century Nordic art. During this century the Viking artists seem more sympathetic than before to vegetable ornamentation, as the beautiful Norwegian runic stones of the 'Ringerike group' reveal. On these the decorations are acanthus and long narrow leaves rolled up at the points and arranged in rays radiating from a central pattern. This design came from southern English art, as is proved by the illuminated manuscripts of the Winchester School. Elsewhere in the North there are to be found other English influences upon Viking art in the eleventh century, a phenomenon probably due (as Holmqvist suggests) to the extensive English missionary activities in Scandinavia at this time. The decorative art of the Vikings, then, reached its native fulfilment in the eleventh century. Two of the items mentioned above are typical of it during its last phase, before it gave way to Romanesque art – the great lion, in its network of lines and vines carved on the late east Swedish runic stones, or the similar beast on the fine wooden door now installed in the little stave church at Urnes in western Norway.

PICTORIAL ART

Apart from decorative art the Viking period also produced figure-paintings. The themes of these were taken largely from myths and sagas, and sometimes even from recent history. The following examples are derived partly from the three northern countries, partly from their foreign colonies.

Very important is the group of large carved and painted memorial stones from Gotland. One of them, the Lillbjärs stone, depicts a large horseman, the deceased no doubt, riding to Valhalla: a very fine painting in which the proud motion of the horse is particularly well composed. The Lärbro stone is another good example (Pl. 22A). At the base of the picture is the dead warrior's long-ship, its crew manning the rails and holding the hanging ropes, and its steersman on the high poop handling the long steering oar. The sail is taut as the vessel breasts the waves, and the latter are skilfully drawn in an ingenuous spiral pattern. Many of the Gotland carved stones of the Viking period bear this vivid marine picture upon them; it is as typical of these later stones as is the circular ornament on top of the older pre-Viking Gotland stones. The ship on the Lärbro stone has, in fact, nothing to do with the actions depicted on the three upper sections of that stone. The uppermost section shows a battle in progress; the sky is full of eagles and men. On the right a warrior is pitching off his horse, and on the left two men seem to be pledging an oath together. The middle section shows Odin's eight-legged horse, Sleipner, above it the figure of a man lying down; and to the left walk three men each bearing a sword which points downwards to the ground. The third section displays a proud horseman (the deceased evidently) followed by his men, arriving at the gates of Valhalla where he is welcomed by a figure bearing a drinking-horn. The purport of the Lärbro picture stone is, then, to show, first of all, at the bottom, the customary emblem of nobility, the long-ship; and above it to sum up in pictorial form the dead hero's end on the battle-field, where Odin is assisting him, and his final happy arrival at Valhalla.

Other Gotland picture stones portray mythical scenes and episodes such as those we know from the Edda, and other Norse literature: Odin riding Sleipner; Thor fishing for the Midgaard serpent with a bait consisting of a bull's head; Vølund's smithy, and Vølund himself transformed into a bird; Loke and his wife Sigyn. But not all the picture stones can be made out by any means, partly because some of the myths they seek to portray are not known to us at all from literary sources, partly because it is not always possible to say whether the scenes and persons shown were not myths at all but were really related to the life and times of the man to whom the stone is the memorial. Another group of picture stones are those, already mentioned, from the Isle of Man, mainly crosses on which Celtic and Norwegian, pagan and Christian influences are combined.

There are here and there in the Nordic countries other sur-vivals of their pictorial art, not only on stone but on wood and textiles as well. Reference to some of these examples has already been made, but nevertheless I shall enumerate the following specimens. First there is the Fafne's saga carved on the Ramsund Rock in Södermanland, Sweden (Pl. 19B). Within the great oval ribbon – which at the same time represents the dragon Fafne and contains the runes – the whole story is depicted. From left to right we see: the dead smith Regin, his decapitated head lying among his blacksmith's tools (hammer, tongs, anvil, bellows); the hero Sigurd frying Fafne's heart and putting his finger in his mouth (turning at the same time to the birds in the tree, for he now under-stands their language); Sigurd's horse tethered to the tree, with the two birds on the top; and, finally, the great deed itself – Sigurd thrusting his sword through the body of the dragon. Many similar examples of Viking pictorial art are known. Then there are the Alstad and Dynna stones (Pl. 22B) in south Norway showing a chieftain hawking, and the Three Wise Men respectively. The Altuna runic stone in Uppland, the Hørdum stone in north Jutland, the fragments of crosses from Gosforth in Cumberland, all bearing (though in different styles) pictures of Thor fishing for the Midgaard serpent. There are the carvings on the famous carriage from Oseberg bearing two versions of the saga of Gunnar in the dragon's cave. The Oseberg tapestry, with its coloured pictures of warriors, carts, and weapons, and Odin's holy tree with its human sacrifices dangling from the branches.

We know from literature that it was the Nordic habit to paint figures on shields and to decorate the house-hall with tapestries and paintings. There is similar evidence about large sculptures in wood as well; e.g. Adam of Bremen's account of the statues of three gods in the heathen temple of Old Uppsala; and the statuettes of silver, bronze, and amber which have survived may well be reproductions in miniature of lost sculpture.

The favourite themes for pictorial art among the Vikings – whether in paint, carving, or weaving – seem to have been taken from the myths and sagas. Especially popular were such incidents as Odin's fight with the Fenris wolf and with the giant Tjasse; Thor's feats against the giants and his Midgaard fishing; the burning of Balder; Gefion ploughing with her oxen; the Vølund saga; Sigurd Fafne's killer; and Gunnar in the snake pit. And there remain many themes we cannot interpret. No doubt certain stylizations, certain types were well known: thus a man surrounded by serpents stands for Gunnar; a man spearing a dragon, for Sigurd; a man fishing with a bull's head as bait, for Thor.

Did the Vikings ever depict contemporary or recent events? Is it conceivable, for instance, that the scenes depicted on the Gotland stones represent the feats of the men to whom they are memorials? Some scholars declare that such action would be wholly alien to the Nordic mind. It seems to me, however, although I can produce no proof, that the supposition is not an untenable one. When I wrote, a little earlier, that the themes of Viking pictorial art included some 'recent history' I had in mind the Bayeux Tapestry made in the latter part of the eleventh century to commemorate the glories of the Norman Conquest of 1066. The Norman needlewomen were not Viking women, yet Normandy had been a Viking colony created only 150 years before the Norman Conquest. We therefore may dare to postulate the proposition that since the idea of celebrating in art the achievements of the time was operating in Normandy around 1070, it may not have been wholly foreign or unacceptable to the Vikings in their homeland at that time. It may be said that any such comparison is invalid, because the Bayeux Tapestry is the result of a foreign feudal system very different from the Nordic way of life. A Norman duke had more absolute power than a Nordic king; in Normandy the people were suppressed by a despotic duke who created round him a complaisant and obedient court. All this is true. The Nordic traditions of Normandy had indeed been transformed by an alien feudalism, and we had better pursue no further the hypothesis provoked by the Bayeux Tapestry. But if we turn from one kind of Viking art to another – from pictorial art to minstrelsy – we observe a remarkable phenomenon. It was very common indeed for a bard to sing the glories of a living king, earl, or chieftain; and it seems to me a short step from this practice to that of painting or carving the effigy of someone lately dead, or still alive, on a gravestone or inside the great hall.

CHAPTER 13

THE VIKING WAY OF LIFE

ADAM OF BREMEN'S ACCOUNT

O UR sources of information about the social life and habits of
the Vikings are scanty, and not always reliable; nevertheless,
it is possible to establish some facts on these matters. We
referred earlier to the description of the Nordic peoples and
countries given by Adam of Bremen at the end of the Viking
period, about 1075. He takes the three countries in turn,
beginning with Denmark.

Of the Danes he tells us that they amass gold by means of
piracy, and that the Vikings pay the Danish king a tax in
return for the privilege of pillaging barbarians living around
the Norwegian Sea (i.e. the Kattegat and Skagerak) but that
they sometimes abuse this privilege and turn treacherously
upon their own countrymen – 'As soon as such a man has
caught his neighbour, he sells him ruthlessly either to a friend
or a stranger.' There is a good deal in the laws and customs
of the Danes, says Adam, which conflicts with justice and
reason; for example,

If women have proved unchaste they are sold off at once, but if
men are found guilty of treason or other illegalities they prefer to be
beheaded rather than whipped. They know no other punishments
than the axe or slavery. Even when a man is condemned he retains
his good spirits, for the Danes detest tears and lamentations and all
other such expressions of grief to such a degree that no one weeps for
his sins or for the death of his dear ones.

The Swedes are characterized by Adam of Bremen in
terms which bring to mind the rather stereotyped praise
given in classical literature (from Tacitus onwards) to the

Germanic peoples; in this sense he speaks of their modesty of demeanour and their generous hospitality, in almost excessive terms. His commentary runs thus:

The Swedes lack nothing of what we revere except our arrogance. They have no acquisitive love of gold, silver, splendid chargers, the furs of beaver and marten, or any of the other possessions we pine for. It is only for women that they show no moderation; every man according to his means has two, three, or more wives at a time; the wealthy and the noble have numerous wives. The sons of all these unions are accepted as legitimate. But anyone who sleeps with his neighbour's wife or ravishes a maiden or plunders a neighbour's property is punished by death. All northern people are noted for their hospitality, but the Swedes excel. They consider it shameful to deny good cheer to a traveller, and there is keen competition among them for the privilege of entertaining the stranger. He is welcome in their midst for as long as he likes, and they take it in turns to look after his comfort during his sojourn among them.

The Swedes consist of several tribes, distinguished by their strength and their weapons; they fight as well on horseback as they do at sea, and have the warlike skill to keep the other Northern people in check. They are ruled by kings of ancient lineage, but the monarch's power is limited by the will of the people; what they are agreed about the king must ratify, and even if he proposes a course of action better than theirs they accept it only with reluctance. This is their mode of political equality in peace time – in war they develop complete obedience to the king or his appointed leaders; if they find themselves beset in battle they call upon one of their many gods, and if victory is secured they give him precedence in their thanksgiving.

We have already referred to Adam of Bremen's observations about the piratical practices of the Norwegians. His further comments run:

They manage to live off their cattle, using the milk for food and the skins for clothing. Their country breeds many brave warriors who attack more frequently than they are themselves attacked, for they have not been softened by rich harvests. They live harmoniously with the Swedes, but are sometimes attacked by the Danes (not without retaliation) who are as poor as they are. . . . The Norwegians are the most frugal people, they greatly appreciate simplicity and moderation in food and in habit too. . . . Their good habits, indeed, are marred only by the greed of the priests. In many parts of Norway, as of Sweden, shepherds are highly esteemed, for they live as patriarchs and by the effort of their own labour.

When Adam of Bremen was writing about them the Nordic peoples had been living in the three northern countries for more than 10,000 years, and during this long period of time there was probably only one wave of immigration, soon after 2000 B.C., an Indo-European renewal from the south and south-east. A good deal is known of the development of their material culture and ways of life during the Stone, Bronze, and Iron Ages. Although it is only during the Viking period that the three Nordic peoples really appear under the spotlight of history, they are archaeologically an ancient race. Although history in the north begins only with the Vikings, around 800, these peoples had then already many thousands of years behind them, and we have enough archaeological knowledge to correct even a contemporary source as, for instance, Master Adam himself when he declares that agriculture was unknown in Norway. The archaeological evidence is, in fact, that Norway had practised agriculture for long periods of its early history, although it is also true that its main activities, especially in the north, were cattle-breeding, hunting, and fishing.

In assessing the fertility of the three Nordic countries Adam graduates his expressions. He puts Norway very low. Norway, he says, is useless for agriculture (*sterilissima omnium regionum*). The soil of Jutland, too, he declares is barren (*ager sterilis*); but the islands of southern Denmark are fruitful (*frugibas opulentas*), and so are Skaane, Fyn, and the adjacent islands. Sweden is very fertile, but even more so apparently is Sjælland, which is widely acclaimed for its productivity. In speaking of Jutland's unfruitful soil Adam says:

Apart from the areas of land near the rivers the region looks a waste and desert land. Jutland is even worse than Germania with its impenetrable forests; people shun its land because of the poor crops it yields, and they shun its waters because of the hordes of pirates. Hardly anywhere is it cultivated or even habitable – except by the fiords where there are considerable towns.

These comments are distinguished by Adam's usual rhetorical excesses, yet there is no doubt much truth in his picture of Jutland – whose 'waste and desert land' is, of course, its great heaths – and in his assertion that travelling is so difficult by land in those parts that sea-journeys are much to be preferred – except for the pirates. This business of travelling in the wilder regions in Viking times is graphically described in the *Østerfareviser,* a poem which Sigvat Thordarsson, the Icelandic minstrel to St Olav, wrote after a journey to the Swedish chief, Ragnvald, somewhere in the province of Mälar. His route lay through the forest of Ed, on the borders of southern Norway and central Sweden – 'Hard it was for the men to penetrate the Ed forest', and later 'It was not for pleasure that I, in sombre mood, struggled the thirteen miles through the forest. God knows we suffered. Of the King's men none had unhurt feet – I had sores on both.'

Apart from the Danevirke in south Slesvig there were no artificial boundaries between the Nordic countries, and the natural frontiers were defined by sea and moorland. But towards the close of the Viking period (during Adam of Bremen's time) the Swedish king Emund and the Danish king Sven agreed to define the boundaries between their two territories. The line of demarcation ran from the northern end of the province of Halland (not far from the present Gothenburg), north of Skaane, along the southern border of Smaaland to the Baltic (now Karlskrona). At that time Halland, Skaane, and Blekinge belonged to Denmark and Øland to Sweden. The frontier was defined by a commission composed of six Swedes and six Danes who set up six stones. Gotland was an independent country at this period, and the province of Bohuslen was Norwegian. The river Göta was Sweden's narrow water-link to the Kattegat: throughout the whole of the Middle Ages the three Nordic countries linked up with each other at the mouth of this river Göta, and it was here (we learn from Icelandic literary sources) that the Nordic monarchs met on ceremonial occasions, either on the Bränn Islands, off the river's southern branch, or on Dana Island (Danaholm) in this branch. A whole series of such meetings is recorded. In the Older Västgöta Law (a Swedish source from the Middle Ages) a conference of three kings on Danaholm is mentioned, and we are told that this island was divided among the three monarchs – 'One section is owned by the Uppsala king, one by the Danish king, and the third belongs to the king of Norway. When the meeting took place the Danish king held the bridle of the Uppsala king, and the Norwegian king held his stirrup.' It seems, therefore, that the Swedish king was the highest in rank (though we must not overlook that the source is Swedish!).

OCCUPATIONS

The Nordic people of the Viking period had, as we have seen, many thousands of years of development behind them. Their principal peaceful activities were the ancient ones of hunting and fishing, the less ancient ones of agriculture and cattle breeding, and finally the practice of commerce. All five of these occupations were often simultaneously pursued in southern Scandinavia.

The most important agricultural implement was the plough, of which the Vikings had several varieties. There were two old types of *ard* (the *crook-ard* and the *bow-ard*) and there was the more elaborate and effective plough fitted with a soil-board, a front wheel, and a ploughshare which was made either of wood reinforced with iron, or entirely of iron. Some of the fields were flat and wide, others narrow and steep. We do not know which regions of the Nordic lands were cultivated in Viking times; but from the evidence we have of agriculture during the Iron Age (i.e. before Viking times) and during the Middle Ages (i.e. after the Vikings) it is possible at least to surmise which were the districts the Viking peasant preferred to till. In Sweden this was a broad strip, running from the present-day Gothenburg towards the northeast between the two big lakes to the Mälar country and the Uppsala plain. Towards the Baltic the region east of Vettern was also cultivated, as well as extensive areas of Gotland. In Norway, which in later Viking times stretched as far as the river Göta, the most fertile regions seem to have been in Bohuslen and Viken, from there north in the valleys of the Østlandet, and south-west in Rogaland and farther north in the Trøndelag. In Denmark the plough was in wide use in Skaane and Halland, in west and north Zeeland, on Fyn and the surrounding islands, and in north Jutland (mostly in the regions of Himmerland and Vendsyssel). These Nordic areas where agriculture was in all likelihood practised in Viking times are defined by our knowledge of Iron Age archaeology and the history of the Middle Ages, and they differ very much, as we have seen, especially in regard to Norway and Jutland, from the Latin descriptions left us by Adam of Bremen.

For the Nordic people, as for so many others, the practice of agriculture was closely related to religious beliefs and fertility rites. The evidence of this is very old. It is to be found, for example, in Bronze Age rock-carvings in southern Sweden, dating from about 1000 B.C.: the figures of the ploughman and his bulls are drawn with a strong phallic emphasis as they cut the first three furrows in the field, as they drive the ploughshare into the fertile womb of mother earth. This evidence occurs 2,000 years before the Viking period; and, indeed, a thousand years after the Vikings, in our own times, there are old-fashioned Swedish peasants who participate in old ceremonies at the season of the spring ploughing and practise rites devised long ago to bring fertility to their fields. At this season, for instance, a Swedish farmer and his wife may eat and drink in the company of their plough-horses, for it is vitally important at this fateful period of seed-sowing that all concerned in the process should be in harmony with each other. There is an element of renewal about this little rite, for the mother of the house brings out into the field carefully preserved symbols of the earth's bounty: drink, cake, and pork put by after the solstice feast at Christmas-time. The cake will very likely be fashioned in the shape of the sun-wheel. The ploughman and his beasts must all have a piece of it; the rest is crumbled into the seed trough, so that fragments of the cake, along with the new seed, will be ploughed into the freshly turned soil. The drink is divided into three portions: one the ploughman drinks himself, the second he throws over the horse, and the third over the plough. After this little ceremony the ploughing begins. From long before Viking times to long after them, this association of agriculture and religious magic has thus persisted.

Other agricultural implements of the Vikings were the sickle, the scythe, a sharp knife for cutting branches and leaves into cattle-fodder, the spade, and the hoe. All these tools have been found in Viking graves. Among Danish archaeological discoveries there have also been fragments of grain, and impressions of it in clay, which show that rye was gaining in Viking times, while the amount of barley and oats remained the same as in Roman days. The breeding of cattle was no less important in southern Scandinavia than agriculture, and in northern Scandinavia far more so. Adam of Bremen is indeed justified in saying that as we get into the far north agriculture ceases to exist.

The domestic animals of the Vikings were the horse, ox,

sheep, goat, and pig, and in addition, the dog and the cat. In the lower mountain regions of south-eastern Norway, the *Sæterbrug*, the method of cattle-raising employed nowadays is to move the animals in the summer up to higher ground – the *sæter* – and allow them to run wild there until the approach of autumn. Was this the practice in Viking times, too? It has been established that in Norway, from and including the fifth and sixth centuries, the *sæter* fields of our days were hunting regions, and that again in Merovingian times (the seventh and eighth centuries) farms and hunting areas moved still farther up to higher ground. The oldest burials in the *sæters* also date from this time. In Viking times this development continued, and it can be maintained that in these lower mountainous regions of south-eastern Norway the breeding of cattle on the *sæters* was one of the basic activities, the others being hunting and the excavation of iron ore.

Finally we must consider the fifth of the Viking methods of livelihood – their commerce. Their two principal commodities, furs and slaves, are both frequently mentioned in literary sources. There is Ottar's report to King Alfred on the fur trade; and of the slave trade there are many accounts. The Rimbert biography recounts how, on a visit to Hedeby, the saintly traveller gave away his horse to secure the liberation of a slave woman. Adam of Bremen makes frequent reference to the slave trade; and the narratives of the Rus folk make it plain that slaves were one of their more important trading commodities, if not the most important. The Laxdøla Saga (which deals, it is true, with the period after the Vikings) makes direct references to the slave trade. Most of the slaves seem to have been women, and those exported were the ones surplus to the domestic requirements of the Vikings. The Rus folk acquired their stocks of this human commodity to a large extent by raids on their Slav neighbours.

HOUSES

Domestic architecture was by no means of a uniform pattern among the Vikings. There were several types of house, some of them derived from old traditions of building, and some determined by climatic conditions, availability of materials, and so on. Countries which are well-wooded evidently show a preference for timber houses, while treeless regions go in for stone, clay, and turf. Where forests exist on a moderate scale the tendency is to varied types of houses.

Relics of Viking houses exist in Sweden, although they are few and widely scattered. At Levide in Gotland has been excavated the site of a house some 55 ft long and 22 ft wide. The roof was carried on free inner posts, and the walls were made of wattle-and-daub. Houses of this kind have been found on the Åland Islands also; and somewhat similar is the discovery at the Triangel in Sigtuna of a small square house with walls of close-set poles set into a foundation beam and held together by wattle-and-daub. In Lake Tingstäde on Gotland there stands an odd wooden fort, probably Viking, named the Bulverk, constructed in primitive carpentry partly recalling 'bul houses' and partly corner-timbered ones. Corner timbering has also been found in Sigtuna. These and other discoveries, then, have established the variety of Swedish Viking buildings. As one would expect in a well-forested country, there were several methods of building in wood – horizontal log-walls, jointed at the ends; walls built with vertical wooden posts, and horizontal planking between them ('bul houses'); and finally 'stave' walls composed of vertical staves or planks. Long before Viking times, in the Iron Age, the Swedes appear to have copied the 'long house' of the Danes and Norwegians – a building made with free inner posts and thick earth walls for the shelter of human beings and animals alike. They existed on Øland and Gotland at the time of the migrations. But during the Viking period the most typical Swedish farm probably comprised several small separate buildings, for timber is the most convenient material for such small units of construction, whereas the big 'long house' and the great hall are better adapted for the use of such materials as stone, clay, turf, and wood. Both types of house were known in Sweden during Viking times. In the towns, such as Sigtuna, small timbered houses were built close together in clusters.

Although archaeological discoveries tell us even less about Danish building than about Swedish, certain reasonable suppositions can be accepted provisionally until actual sites have been found and examined, as they doubtless will be sooner or later. It is likely that the Iron Age 'long house' mentioned above continued to be built in Denmark in the Viking period. There are relics of timber-built houses in Denmark, too: the large ones inside the military camp at Trelleborg, and partly in Fyrkat too, seem to have been built on the stave principle; Aggersborg, on the other hand, shows wattle-and-daub on the long sides of the house and horizontal planking on the ends. The very substantial houses in these camps were of course designed for garrison life, not for ordinary dwellings, but there is also some evidence available about the latter. Under Aggersborg was found a village the houses of which resembled those in the camps – with long curved sides – but were much smaller, and there were also small half-buried outhouses. On Lindholm, again, near Aalborg, rectangular 'long houses' and stables have been found. An example of primitive paling construction exists in the grave chamber of the northern mound at Jelling, and remains of a stave building have been established under St Maria Minor in Lund, Skaane. Finally, in Hedeby excavation has disclosed several types of dwelling house: wattle-and-daub houses; stave constructions; outhouses whose walls were double – that is to say made of two layers of planking made fast to each side of the structural upright posts.

It seems as if the Danish peasant's dwelling had developed, during the late Viking time, from one 'long house', common to man and cattle, into several buildings – either a couple of parallel ones or two or three lying at angles. In this way a barn and, if desired, another storehouse were added to the 'long house' as independent smaller units. The farm consisting of a group of houses, then, was growing up; and finally we see – as has recently been shown by the excavations at Lindholm Høje in north Jutland from the close of the Viking age – that even the four-winged peasant farm was fully developed before the Middle Ages in Denmark began.

In Norway the Danish 'long house', built east and west to cope with the prevailing winds, walled and roofed with turf, appeared in the south-westerly districts (Rogaland and Lista) during the times of the migration. Sites of Viking houses are known in Gudbrand's Valley, at Langest and Nygard. These were large rectangular buildings, some 50 ft by 20, and some 74 ft by 52, with stone foundations, walls of wood and clay, and their roofs supported on free-standing inner posts. They were presumably the substantial farmhouses of chieftains. A similar building has been identified at Ovre Dal, but this cannot be definitely dated to the Vikings. All these houses in the well-timbered country of eastern Norway can be presumed to have been wooden ones. Corner timbering, incidentally, although in a primitive form, is illustrated in the burial chamber in the Gokstad Ship (about 900).

Viking houses outside the Nordic homelands are much rarer in the east than the west. Some small corner-timbered buildings were found in Russia on the excavations at Old Ladoga (Aldeigjuborg); a farmhouse at Novgorod has signs of the same technique, and so have some burial chambers in the Ukraine. In the west we know about Viking houses on some of the Scottish islands, in the Faroe Islands, Iceland, and Greenland. In these areas the climate is wet and windy and there are no forests. The builders therefore had to use materials other than wood. Of these the first was stone. In the Orkneys and Shetlands they used flat stones or flags, admirably suited for dry walls. In the Hebrides the choice was field-stones, not a very good material. Basalt blocks were popular in the Faroes; in Iceland field-stones or blocks of lava; and in Greenland flagstones. The next material used in these regions was grass-sod or turf. The wide grazing lands of the Atlantic islands produce good turf, some of it solid, durable, and well stuffed with earth, and some thin and tough, rather like carpet. Timber does appear occasionally, for although the islands were treeless, the sea yielded a supply of driftwood heavy enough for building. It is seldom possible to find dateable sites of Viking building on the minor Atlantic islands; one can only draw inferences. It is generally believed that the Vikings must have taken with them to the islands their habit of building 'long houses'; a stone 'long house', probably Viking, has been dug out at Jarlshof in the Shetlands.

We are better informed about Iceland, where large sites have been located and dated to the later Viking period. Examples have been found at Hofstaðir, at Myvatn, in the north of the island, and the site Skallakot, not far from Hekla in the south. Hofstaðir was a big 'long house', over 110 ft long, built north-and-south with thick and slightly curved sod walls, and a fireplace in the middle. At its northern end was a small separate room, cut off from the hall, with a door to the outside; and the hall itself had a door at the northern end of the eastward wall. At Skallakot, too, there was a large long house, 80 ft long, with walls built entirely of earth to a width of more than 7 ft and again so curved that the house was almost oval in shape. Here too there was a hearth (the 'long-fire') in the middle of the floor. The excavator, Aage Roussell, points out that cattle had not been kept in this 'long house', so presumably here the Vikings had byres or cattle folds. He says: 'One long central room, the *skaalen*, served as living-room, cooking-room, and bedroom; the cooking was done at one end of it, perhaps behind a wooden partition.' In this long room were found two rows of stone-set holes in which had been sunk the posts which bore the roof. The floor in both side-aisles was somewhat higher and was divided by stone partitions into sleeping compartments. The central room, the *skaalen,* would accommodate a large number of people for feasts, but it was low and dark and full of smoke. This one-room dwelling does not correspond with the descriptions given in the sagas (which apparently apply to the Middle Ages), but it fits very well the conditions of the old-fashioned houses today in the Orkneys, Hebrides, and Shetlands. The truth must be, Roussell concludes (and rightly, I think) that in Iceland the notion soon developed of enlarging the plan of the 'long house' by adding rooms to the *skaalen* – lobby, kitchen (fire-house), dairy, and bath, thus evolving a new pattern altogether: the medieval 'long house' with annexes. It was not until later, in the fourteenth century, that the so-called 'passage house', a scheme with rooms built on either side of a corridor, came into existence.

Poul Nørlund's excavations in Greenland have unearthed housing-sites of the late Viking period and the Middle Ages; the actual house of the celebrated Erik the Red is one of his finds – at Brattahlid in Østerbygden. The house in Greenland proves to have been originally the 'long house' with one large room – the *skaalen;* later on various annexes appear. Apart from Brattahlid there is the *skaalen* at Hvalsey, also in Øster-bygden. Erik the Red's *skaalen* was some 49 ft long and 15 ft wide, with solid earth walls over 10 ft thick; a stone conduit carried water through from the back wall and out through the front. The Hvalsey '*skaalen*' was 43 ft by 12 ft. In Green-land, gradually, as in Iceland, various small outbuildings came to be added to the *skaalen,* and finally, in the Middle Ages, this pattern was superseded by the 'passage house' which afforded so much better protection against the cold. The passage house' may well have originated in Greenland, but in any case it did not arrive on the scene until the Viking period had given way to the Middle Ages. And from this house developed the latest type in Greenland: the large 'central house' with all its rooms concentrated into one big block. It is odd that most of our knowledge about Nordic houses in Viking times and the Middle Ages should be thus derived from distant Greenland.

One question may well occur to anyone who tries to visualize the Viking in his home: had he any windows to look through? We do not know for certain; neither archaeology nor literature provides any clues. It is generally assumed that windows did not appear in the Nordic countries until the Middle Ages, and that until glass was discovered pigs' bladders and foetus membranes served to let in the light. The north-west Scandinavian 'long houses' with their thick walls built of stone, earth, and turf had no windows of any kind, and even today there are on the Hebrides houses of the same sort, completely windowless. Windows no doubt began in wooden houses, and to start with were probably narrow peep-holes protected by inside shutters. It is possible that the Vikings had something of the sort in their wooden houses, but we have no evidence.

SOCIAL ORGANIZATION

Let us look next at the social organization of the Vikings: the importance of the family, the status of women, the powers of the king, the code of law. We may approach these matters from a famous Icelandic poem (influenced maybe by Celtic sources) called *Rigsthula* (the 'Rigmarole' about Rig). It recounts the origins of the social classes in a story with the threefold repetitions and strings of names usual in fairy tales. Rig is identical with the god Heimdal. He is wandering far and wide. First he comes to a cottage with a half-open door, and a fire on the floor where live a frail and ragged couple Oldefar (great-grandfather) and Oldemor (great-grandmother) who give him what food they can: 'unclean bread, lumpy and sticky and full of husks', but with a bowl of soup and boiled veal. He gives them advice and gets into bed with them, stays for three days, and nine months later Oldemor bears a son, Træl (serf), of whom it is said 'the skin on his hands was wrinkled, his knuckles were swollen, his nails short, his face ugly, his fingers coarse, his back bent and his heels long' – and he was a hard worker. Next there comes to the farm a girl called Tøs (wench): 'her legs were coarse, her arms sunburnt, her nose pendulous.' These two produce children, a whole flock of them, girls and boys, a family of slaves all of whose names are given. They do the hardest chores: tend the pigs and goats, manure the fields, build fences, dig peat.

Again Rig is wandering. He comes to a hall with its door closed, he enters; there is a fire on the floor where sit Bedstefar (grandfather) and Bedstemor (grandmother) both at work. He with combed fringe and well-cared-for beard, in a tight shirt, is busy cleverly making a loom; she with a coat on her shoulders, a ruff round her neck and a linen cloth on her hair, is moving the spindle and spinning the thread. Rig gives them advice and gets into bed with them and departs after three days. In nine months' time Bedstemor produces a child, a son called Bonde (peasant), red and fresh and bright-eyed. He loves his work: breaking in oxen, making ploughs and timber houses, raising barns, building carts, and turning the plough. Along comes a bride for him – 'with the keys of the house, wearing a goatskin jacket'. They have many children whose names are catalogued in the Rigmarole, and these become the peasant stock.

And again Rig is wandering. He comes to a hall facing south, its door, decorated with a ring, closed; he enters, and 'there sat a couple on a floor strewn with rushes, looking at each other, their fingers playing – Far (father) and Mor (mother). And the big farmer twisted a bow-string, bent an elm-bough, pointed a shaft; while the mistress looked at her arm, stroked her clothes, tightened her sleeves. On her breast was a brooch, her shift was blue, her cap straight, her cape long. Her breast was brighter, her brow lighter, and her neck whiter than new-fallen snow.' Rig gives them advice. 'Then Mor took a patterned cloth of bright flax and covered the table; then she took fine bread of bright wheat and covered the cloth. She carried in full bowls embellished with silver, put on the table pork and meat and game-birds. There was wine in the jug; the silver mug was heavy. They drank and talked; the day was waning.' Rig gets into bed with them, stays three days, and in nine months' time Mor produces a son 'Jarl' (earl) and wraps him in silks. 'Blond was his hair, his cheeks pale, his eyes piercing as a young serpent's.' Jarl grows up: makes bows, rides horses, hunts with hounds, is a fine swordsman and swimmer. Rig meets him, teaches him runes, and bids him take possession of the ancient estates. Immediately Jarl begins to make war; he manages horses, cuts with swords, breaks the peace, stains the land with blood, fells his enemies. He then owns eighteen farms, and gives rich gifts of gold and horses to his friends. He marries Erna, the daughter of Here, beautiful, white, and wise, her hands slender. They have children (whose names are duly given), the sons as doughty as their father, especially the youngest, Kon (King). He learns to read the runes and discusses the runic mysteries with his father. Soon he can blunt his enemies' weapons, calm the waves, save men, quell flames, dispel grief. He has the strength and capacity of eight men. He knows the language of the birds, and one day in the forest as he stands over a bird he has shot, a crow perched in a tree eggs him on to attempt greater deeds of daring and valour . . . and at this the *Rigsthula* breaks off. The rest is lost.

This colourful poem thus classifies the three social groups

of the Viking period – the serf, the peasant, the noble. The names given in the Rigmarole are entertaining: the serf boys, for instance, are Hæs and Fjøse, Kløds and Klumre, Kævle, Stygge, Drunte, Diger, Dvask, Graamand, Lunt, Ludrygget – Hoarse, Foolish, Clumsy, Awkward, Ugly, Clot, Fat, Torpid, Grey, Hunchback. The serf girls are Clot, Clumsy, Restless, Talkative, Ash-nose, Quarreller, Torn-Skirt, Crane-legs. The peasant's sons have more dignified names – Free, Warrior, Brave, Broad, Smith, Settler; and the girls: Quick, Bride, Wife, Woman, Weaver, Ornament, Modest. And finally, of the Earl's sons we are told that Byrd (Birth) was the eldest, and that the others were Child, Young, Noble, Heir, Boy, Lineage, Offspring, Son, Swain, Cnut; they practised sports; the youngest was Kon. And the Rigmarole finishes forgetting to give the names of the Earl's daughters!

In this vivid language, then, the three classes of the Viking community are described. In the highest class, the king, chosen by the chiefs, is *primus inter pares,* the first among his equals. We find the same thing in Tacitus's description of the Germanic peoples about A.D. 100. Here we learn that the power of the king was limited by the Thing or Parliament, that is to say by the will of the free people assembled for periodic deliberation; it was difficult, virtually impossible, for the king to take a decision in opposition to the Thing of chieftains, who were his equals in all but name. In early Viking times, when the North was divided into many loosely-associated clans, a chief became king simply by the nomination of a group of other chiefs. In later Viking times, when the monarchy had become a more powerful instrument, inheritance rather than nomination became the rule. Generally, however, the Vikings were certainly rather independent individuals. The answer given by Danish Vikings in the late tenth century to a messenger from the Franks is famous. The messenger, standing on the bank of the river Eure in France, hailed the Viking ships and demanded, 'What is the name of your master?' 'None', came the answer; 'we are all equals!'

The earls were landowners sufficiently wealthy to have a company of house-carles and several vessels. Of their life and status we have heard in the *Rigsthula*. Possessions passed by inheritance to the eldest son, and their pride of family is illustrated by the names given in the *Rigsthula* to the sons of earls: such as Birth, Noble, Heir, Lineage, Offspring.

The solid backbone of the Viking people was the peasant class – smallholders but, however modest their possessions, free men. In *Rigsthula* the first peasant of all is called 'Free', the next 'Warrior'; and only farther down the list come such names as 'Smith' or 'Settler'. In the two superior social classes, earls and peasants, women enjoyed high esteem and full freedom, as Nordic literature abundantly testifies.

Lastly the serfs, as their name implies, were the drudges of the community, but of the details of their conditions and obligations we know little. Killing a serf, however, was not considered a major crime.

Our knowledge of the legal system of Viking society is scanty, for the contemporary primary sources are almost entirely missing. Something may be inferred from what we learn from the legal texts and from the literature of the Nordic Middle Ages, but it must be accepted as little more than mere inference or probability. We have real knowledge only of Iceland. What can be positively asserted about all the Nordic countries, however, is that Viking law was based upon the proceedings of the institution called the *Thing* – the assembly of free men.

In Viking times Denmark was divided into a couple of hundred *Herreds* or districts, each with its own *Thing*. The *Thing* was the gathering of the free men of each district to resolve differences and disputes and to discuss matters of interest within the community. The laws and observances on which their judgements were based formed an oral code communicated from one generation to the next, and it was therefore the responsibility of the older members of the *Thing* to ensure that the complex tradition of justice was remembered and recited on these occasions in the customary alliterative formulae. The punishments for murder or acts of violence were graded on a scale of retribution (*mandebod*); the full penalty was exacted for killing a free man or for chopping off his nose; half for putting out an eye, a quarter for an ear, etc. Judgement was delivered by the members of the *Thing*, but the enforcement of the penalty was sometimes a difficult matter. In a feud between a strong family and a weaker one, for example, the injured member of the weaker side, although adjudged the victim of an aggression, might find it difficult to exact the penalty. This failure of *Thing*-law to secure the application of justice was its inherent and chronic weakness.

The word *Herred* should possibly be derived from *Hær* (army) and may point to military obligations – for example to furnish a quota of warriors and ships in wartime. The major decisions of the country – choice of king, declaration of war, or fundamental problems of justice – were reached at the great regional assemblies called the *Landsthings*. In Jutland they were held at Viborg, in Zeeland at Ringsted, in Skaane at Lund.

Complicated disputes were often decided by duels (*holmgang*) fought under elaborate traditional rules, or by *jernbyrd* (that is, ordeal by fire), an admission that the case was to be decided by the law of superior force or by the judgement of the Gods. Stealing was a dangerous crime to indulge in, for the penalty was hanging – not from any moral point of view but rather because of the assumption that the culprit evidently being (by the nature of his offence) a poor man, could pay his penalty only with his life. The most dreaded punishment was banishment, and those who refused to accept the decision of the local or *Herred Thing* and appealed to the higher Court of the *Landsthing* risked this dire fate. It was virtually impossible to exist as an outlaw from the community, and therefore anyone sentenced to banishment found himself making a choice between fleeing the country altogether, and death. The man who respected and obeyed the unwritten Viking traditions, and the laws laid down from the time of Arild, had nothing to fear. If he had 'good luck' he could enjoy a prosperous and varied life. In the summer an earl or chieftain could organize and lead a Viking raid, or join with others in a similar and profitable enterprise, returning in the winter laden with loot. Or he might apply his talents to a trading venture. When he was home he had his lands to attend to, to serve as a judge at the *Thing* and, as a priest, to make himself responsible for seeing that the forms of public worship were properly observed.

Conditions similar to those in Denmark prevailed also in Sweden: a closely integrated community governed by traditional laws and observances as laid down at the *Things*; joint responsibility for the provision of men and ships in war time; and a monarchical power subject always to the consent of the people. Of the latter principle Ansgar's biography tells us, indeed, that major issues were decided, in council at Birka, by the will of the people rather than by royal decree. We shall deal later with two fundamental concepts of Viking behaviour – luck and honour. It is from Sweden that we have some interesting information about duels as a method of resolving disputes of honour between individuals or families. The oldest existing fragment of written law we possess, a Swedish one, reveals the pride and touchiness of the Vikings, and their belief that might ought to prevail. This fragment declares that if anyone abuses his neighbour, saying 'You are not a man's equal nor have you a man's heart' or 'I am a better man than you', then the disputants must be summoned together at a place where three roads meet. If the man who has offered the insult turns up, but the other man does not, then the latter must be considered to deserve the epithets applied to him; his honour is tarnished, he is no longer allowed to take an oath or to bear witness. But if the aggrieved man turns up but not his accuser, then the former cries out three times the word *nidding* (knave) and makes a mark on the ground. The accuser loses face for not substantiating his charge. The two must now meet and fight it out. 'If the insulter falls, it is well: crime in words is the worst. The tongue killed first, and it gets its deserts.'

In Norway, again, the same pattern of social life existed: local *Things* for each *bygd* or district, and regional ones of higher status for coping with major problems under the guidance of chiefs and experienced old men; here, too, a community where the individual with the support of his family tried to get his rights through a graded scale of penalties (*mandebod*), and so on. In Norway, too, the primary sources of knowledge about social and political organization are missing, and we have to rely largely on inferences from what we know of the later practices in the Middle Ages as disclosed in the Frosta *Thing*-Law and the Gula *Thing*-Law, which, according to the sagas, were drawn up by Haakon the Good for the government, respectively, of the Trøndelag and Vestlandet. From these we may conclude that it was the duty in Norway, as in Denmark, of each district to raise levies of men and ships in times of national emergency for *leding,* that is for war. Furthermore, the power of the monarch was limited by the sovereign will of the people as expressed in the *Things*. It would be wrong, however, to underrate the royal status among the Vikings. The king's corps of house-carles, the *hird*, which had originally been little more than a private bodyguard, became in the course of time a powerful armed force capable of serving as the *élite* nucleus of a greater army.

Iceland had no king. Its social and constitutional pattern was, naturally, based on west Norwegian practice, on the rules and principles reflected in the medieval code of the Gula

Thing. The *Thing* constitution seems to have been adopted by the entire island from about 930. Every summer the common *Thing*, the *Alting*, was convened, the real power being exercised by the law-speaker and the pagan priesthood, the *goder*. Subsequently the island was divided into four provinces (*Herdinger*), three of them administered by three *Herred Things*, the other by four. As the chiefs were also the priests it would be proper to describe the Icelandic Free State as an oligarchy, a kingless union of chieftains.

VIKING ANTHROPOLOGY

There is some interesting anthropological evidence about the Vikings. The skeletons from graves which have been examined and measured do not provide very satisfactory data, partly because these remains are so scanty and partly because they are difficult to date. Most of the material comes from Denmark with remains of some fifty individuals from authentic Viking graves – Norway provides sixty, but no more than half of these are reliably dated. In Sweden the material is both scanty and scattered. The skeletons measured from the churchyard at Skeljastaðir, in Iceland, are without doubt partly from the Middle Ages. In the light of this limited availability of material the following conclusions may be offered.

The Danish skeletons, for the most part, have long (dolichocephalic) crania of the kind usually called Nordic: a slender, gracefully-shaped cranium, the face low and slightly slanting, low eye-sockets. The height of the men seems to have been around 5 ft 8 in. (170 cm.). An examination of material from Trelleborg discloses much wear on the crown of the teeth, but very little caries (less than one per cent). The Swedish material is too unsatisfactory to permit of any substantial conclusions, but it appears that the Swedish Vikings were taller than the west and Nordic ones – a feature which conforms to the comparision in modern times, and which also bears out what is said in Arabic commentaries of the Viking period about the exceptional height of the Rus folk. Of the Norwegian male skulls about three-quarters were long, a sixth medium, and very few (about one-fourteenth) were short ones. Of the female a half were long, one-third medium, and one-tenth short. On these proportions it seems that Norwegian Viking women showed less tendency to long skulls (dolichocephalic) and a greater tendency to short skulls (mesocephalic) than their men. Fanciful scholars might seek to explain this difference by the supposition that the Norwegians got many of their women from raids upon the Celtic countries, such as Ireland; but my conclusion is that the Norwegian material (the dating of which, in any case, is dubious) is far too small in quantity to afford statistical results of any worth. All one can say for certain of these fifty-five male and thirty female Norwegian crania is that they belong to the Nordic type.

The Icelandic material reveals a shorter cranium than the Danish and Norwegian, which the Icelandic scholar Jón Steffensen attributes to the influence of the Irish. (The part played by the Celts in the first colonization of Iceland seems to be estimated more highly by the Icelandic scholars than by the Norwegian.) According to the information in the *Landnámabók* 84 per cent of the Icelandic colonizers came from Norway, 3 per cent from Sweden, and about 12½ per cent from the British Isles. From these proportions one would expect a greater conformity between the Norwegian and Icelandic cranium material than there is, and Steffensen therefore is disposed to believe that the Irish element among Iceland's earliest inhabitants was much larger than the figures given by the *Landnámabók*. The Icelandic material, however, cannot wholly be assigned to the Viking period, some of it probably dating only from the Middle Ages, and it is surely too small to allow of any substantial or massive statistical use. On the basis of the available evidence the average height appears to have been 5 ft 8 in. for the Icelanders (170–1 cm.).

One curious deduction from the examination of the female shin-bones was that the Icelandic women must have sat a great deal in a squatting position. There are signs of tuberculosis, but the teeth, again, are sound and healthy, although the crowns are worn down – probably, according to Steffensen, by the grit in their dried fish and dried meat.

APPEARANCE

What did the Vikings look like? What would we not give for a contemporary portrait of Olav Tryggvason or Harald Bluetooth or Erik Sejrsæl? All we have are some free sculptures in wood and bone of heads which *could* be portraits. There are three heads on the Norwegian Oseberg cart (see Pl. 23A); a head forming the top of a bone stick from Sigtuma in Sweden (Pl. 23B); and a small head on a bronze pin from Denmark (Pl. 24A). Of course, many other engravings of human heads exist but these are either magic masks to ward off evil, or a theme in a piece of decoration, and can therefore scarcely be regarded as actual likenesses or portraits. Two of the Oseberg heads (the bearded ones) seem to me the conscious expression of an artistic purpose. They impress me as being more than naturalistic representations, and although the artist used models for his work – old chieftains in a benign mood – he seems to have wished to give something more than a mere likeness; that is to say these two Oseberg carvings seem to me a kind of expressionism. The third head on the Oseberg carriage is of a totally different kind, the realistic depiction of a greedy, savage, and ruthless man. The fourth head, that from Sigtuna, is equally realistic; but whereas the Oseberg Viking looks a rough plebeian, the Sigtuna portrait is that of a man of high birth, an earl with a finely shaped head, a short beard on his strong jutting chin, his hair well groomed, and his fine profile forming a unity with his conical helmet. Thus might Styrbjorn or Torkil Høje have looked. The fifth head, finally, the

Danish one, is half ornamental decoration, half humorous portraiture. These five heads can be said to reveal the presence of notable artistic talent among the Vikings; we can only regret that no more samples have survived.

BEHAVIOUR AND THE 'HÁVAMÁL'

Of Viking manners, behaviour, and habits of thought we know very little from contemporary sources, but some of the later literature, such as the Edda poems and the sagas, throws an oblique light upon their mentality. It is always a problem, of course, to determine how far this sort of testimony can safely be applied to a period two or three hundred years before the literature was written down; but where the sagas and poems are permeated with the pagan beliefs and attitudes they are surely admissible in this sense. This is the generally accepted view of the celebrated poem *Hávamál*, or 'The High One's Words' (that is, Odin's), which seems to embody the wisdom and experience of the later Vikings of Norway and Iceland. The *Hávamál* contains aphorisms, advice, and admonitions sometimes cynical, sometimes matter-of-fact, sometimes ironical or sarcastic, sometimes earnest, and warmly well-meaning – which, combined, unfold a daily life world which we may believe reflects the real Viking mentality Here are some samples of it:

Let the man who opens a door be on the look-out for an enemy hidden behind it.

When a guest arrives with limbs chilled from his journey through the mountains, he needs fire, food, and raiment.

A man must be imperturbable, wise, and ready for battle; cheerful and active until death.

A coward seeks to escape death by avoiding his enemies, but old age no man escapes even if he survive the spears.

A man must not outstay his welcome; he becomes odious if he bides too long in the house of his host.

A man should never be parted one step from his weapon; neither on the road nor on his field he never knows, when abroad, when he will need his sword.

To one's friends one must be a friend to him and to his friend; but to one's enemy's friend no man should be a friend.

Young I was long ago, I was wandering alone and lost my way, but I found wealth in a companion. In man is man's delight.

A man must be content with enough wisdom and never be too wise. Let our fates be hidden from all of us, then our minds will be most care-free.

A man who wishes to despoil others of their lives and goods must be up betimes. A loafing wolf never gets fat, a sleeping man never wins a battle.

Beer is not so good for man as it is said to be; the more a man drinks the less conscious is he of his spirit.

If you do not trust a man and yet want him to do you good, speak him fair; but think him false and give him treachery in return for his lies.

A lame man can ride a horse; a man without hands can be a shepherd; a deaf man can kill; it is better to be blind than to be burned on the funeral pyre. Nothing is any use to a dead man.

Cattle die, kinsmen die, I myself shall die. I know what does not die: the judgement of a dead man's life.

There is much of this robust and practical guidance in the poem. Take life as it comes: better alive than dead; cherish a friendship and do not practise deceit; do not bore or irritate a friend by trading upon his hospitality; outwit your enemy, if you can, with false words. The spoken word seems to have meant much to the Vikings; they were influenced by its potency and respected its continuing value. The last quotation above from the *Hávamál* is really an enjoinder that a man should do his best to deserve a good obituary notice. Some modern commentators have read an ethical meaning into this injunction, but to me it seems to be quite plainly a reminder that the spoken word can be either a tribute to a man's memory or a condemnation of it. The Vikings were susceptible to satirical verses (*Nidviser*) and there was a carefully worked-out system whereby the insults of such verses could be wiped out or rendered ineffective by duels.

The foregoing quotations from the *Hávamál* are all taken from the first, and most valuable, part of the poem. From the later portions come these fragments of wisdom based upon experience. The misogynist speaks:

Do not trust a woman's words, be she single or married; their hearts run on wheels, they are a prey to moods.

There are abundant injunctions against excess, in drink or in love, and pleas for the cultivation of friendship, reason, and moderation:

Be cautious but not over cautious; be most cautious with beer and with another man's wife. Beware, too, that thieves do not fool you.

No man is so good as to be free from all evil; nor so bad as to be worth nothing.

Never confide your troubles to a bad man: he will never respect your good intentions.

Never quarrel with a fool. A wise man will often refrain from fighting, whereas a fool will fight without cause or reason.

Do not break an alliance with a friend; your heart will grieve if you lose the friend in whom you can confide.

The *Hávamál* even goes into homely detail, such as advising men to get up in the night to relieve nature, or to make a good meal in the morning if they are setting out on a long journey across mountains and fiords.

FOOD

The Sagas have a good deal to say about food and drink; but their evidence belongs to the thirteenth and fourteenth centuries rather than to the Viking period. It is fair to surmise that the Viking's staple diet included wholemeal bread made of rye; oats and barley porridge; fish (especially herrings);

the flesh of sheep, lamb, goat, horse, ox, calf, and pig; cheese, butter, and cream; and for drink beer, mead, and (among the wealthy) wine. In Norway and Iceland whale-meat, seal-meat, and the flesh of the polar bear were popular foods. Boiled flesh seems to have been preferred to roast: the *Rigsthula* recounts that even in the modest hut of a serf Heimdal was offered boiled beef; and in Valhalla boiled pork was served. Broth made from the various meats must have been a familiar dish; and the Vikings were also practised in methods of drying meat and fish. Game-birds, too, were an item in Viking diet. The most common vegetables were cabbage and onions; and apples, berries, and nuts were abundant. Honey was much in use, largely as the basis for the manufacture of sweet fermented mead. The preservation of food was an important consideration for the Vikings, and for this purpose they learned to make use of ice, salt (from the sea or from burnt seaweed), and whey. In those countries remote from the sea, but well-wooded, much of the Viking sustenance came from hunting elk, deer, wild boar, and bear. Hares and geese, and chickens as well, were other popular items of diet and, in the far north, reindeer and bison. But in spite of these natural resources, many areas of the Nordic countries suffered shortages of food and, when crops failed, such conditions of famine could occur as to force the population to make shift with seaweed, bark, and lichen.

EATING HABITS

Viking houses were equipped with tables and chairs, table-cloths and plates; and for eating utensils there were spoons and knives – but not forks. (Sven Splitbeard, or Forkbeard, by the way, was named after a pitch-fork, not a table fork!) It seems to have been the Viking custom to eat twice a day, one meal called *davre* in the morning and one called *nadver* in the evening. King Harald Hardrade's habit of eating only once a day attracted attention because it was so unusual. Of this somewhat tyrannical monarch it is recounted, in the Flatø Book, that he was served first, as was right and proper, but that by the time the rest of the company was served he had just about eaten his fill and thereupon rapped sharply upon the table with his knife as the signal for the food to be cleared away. 'There were many,' is the rueful comment, 'who had by no means had enough to eat.'

PERSONAL CLEANLINESS

It has been much debated whether or not the Vikings were a clean people. The sagas give the Icelanders and Norwegians a clean bill in this respect. One of the earliest sentences in the *Hávamál* speaks of a guest being met at table by his host 'with a greeting and a towel'. Later on it says: 'Newly washed and well filled with food should every man ride off to the *Thing*, even though he may not possess fine raiment.' One of the days of the week, Saturday, was named as the day for washing. The Icelandic scholar Skuli Gudjonsson notes a reference in the *Landnámabók* to Thorolf Mostraskegg, who spoke of a holy mountain 'to which no one must turn an unwashed face'. A very different story is told of the Swedish Rus folk, who are described by the Arab Ibn Fadlan as notoriously dirty. On a visit to the Volga region, about 920, he found them (he declares) the most unclean of God's creatures: 'They are as lousy donkeys,' he adds. Other Arabic sources, however, are less critical. The Danes in England appear to have been more careful of their toilet, at least according to a chronicler, who says that they combed their hair, had a bath on Saturdays, and changed their linen frequently 'in order to overcome the chastity of the women and procure the daughters of noblemen as their mistresses'! All this evidence, such as it is, makes a poor basis for generalizations about the Vikings of Norway, Iceland, Sweden, and

Denmark. The probable truth is that cleanliness was not an uncommon habit of the Vikings but that they practised it as a rule on special occasions. Whether they had real soap is not known; but for washing their coarser clothes they probably – as people did later on in Iceland – stored up in buckets the urine of cows which contains that valuable cleansing element, ammonia.

MEDICINE

The science of medicine must have been in a primitive state, yet there is reason to believe that these warlike people had developed some skill in the treatment of severe wounds. Skuli Gudjonsson, the Icelandic scholar already mentioned, has called attention to Snorre's famous tale of the death of Thormod Kolbrunarskjald after the battle of Stiklestad in 1030, a tale which reveals some medical knowledge. (Thormod, it will be remembered, mortally wounded, plucks the arrow from his breast and, observing the bits of flesh adhering to the barb, says: 'I still have fat round the roots of my heart!') Snorre's saga gives some account of the way the wounded were treated, after this battle, in a barn. The women heated water (to sterilize?) and dressed the wounds; then they prepared a porridge made of onions and other herbs which the wounded man proceeded to eat. If a smell of onions subsequently came from the wound in a man's belly it proved that his intestines had been pierced and that he would die of peritonitis: in other words a test meal was used to make a diagnosis. When Thormod is offered this treatment he answers, 'I am not suffering from the porridge-illness': i.e. his wound is not in his belly but in his heart.

GAMES

Chess was a favourite game of the Vikings (the story of the game between Knud the Great and Earl Ulf is well known).

As early as A.D. 100 Tacitus had remarked upon the Germanic peoples' passion for gambling. Chess reached Europe, via the Arabs, from India and became widely popular in the north during late Viking times. Other board-games were also favoured, such as draughts and fox-and-geese, and there have been archaeological discoveries of boards and pieces. In the Gokstad Ship (*c.* 900) a board was found marked out for a different game on each of its sides; and during the American excavations at Ballinderry in Ireland, in 1932, there came to light a well-preserved board presumably for the fox-and-geese game, which is now in the National Museum at Dublin. It is decorated in a Norwegian Celtic pattern and is thought to have been made in the Isle of Man during the tenth century. Playing bricks have been found in many excavations of the Viking period and early Middle Ages.

FAMILY LIFE

The Viking in peacetime seems to have had a strong taste for family life. Marriages were arranged by the families, which were indeed powerful society units in every way. A man stuck to his family in all circumstances; it was from it that he drew assistance and support in all conditions of strife and trouble, and it was therefore his duty to give the family his full allegiance and devotion. To fail in this could prove fatal to a man and involve the worst thing of all: ostracism, outlawry. It was impossible to pursue a selfish individualistic course of behaviour, for there were duties and obligations to the family which a man must accept, however arduous and dangerous they might prove. A man had to follow and practise these communal obligations. This is the reason why the *Hávamál* urges men to be prudent and balanced, and to cultivate friendships – otherwise they will find themselves alone and without help when unforeseen dangers arise. A man without a friend is like 'a naked fir tree, without bark or foliage, lonely on a barren hill'. Therefore always be on your guard, avoid arrogance towards men less important than yourself, do not seek to penetrate fate, be guided by your experience. There is much emphasis on caution as the keynote: 'Not until evening shall the day be praised, the woman until she is burnt, the sword until it is tried, the maiden until she is married, the ice until it is crossed, the beer until it is drunk.' This pervasive prudence may indeed sometimes seem a stolid and negative virtue, but it was one which evidently sprang from the hazardous conditions of Viking life.

The Vikings possessed a lively appreciation of satire, and were also very susceptible when it was applied to their own behaviour. The *Hávamál* uses it frequently: e.g. when it comments on the thrifty hospitality which 'welcomes me as a guest only if I need nothing to eat or if two legs of mutton still hung from my host's roof after I had eaten one'! The Vikings had a vigilant eye for the oddities and frailties of their neighbours, a characteristic illustrated by their extreme fondness for epithets which were often embodied as nicknames, especially for notables: Harald Bluetooth, Sven Forkbeard, Harald Fairhair, Harald Hardrade ('the hard ruler'), Erik Sejrsæl, ('victorious'), Bue the Fat, Ragnar Lodbrog ('with fleecy trousers'), etc. Many of these appellations refer to some physical deformity: Sigurd Worm-in-the-Eye, Ivar the Boneless; as well as other nicknames such as 'cat-back', 'crooked foot'. One of the oddest of these is 'juice-head'. Whether this referred to eczema on the face and head or to a man who liked sucking the juices of vegetables (i.e. a vegetarian) is a speculation which cannot be settled. Nicknames, again, often developed from a memorable situation in which a man had been involved. There was frequently an element of satirical paradox in the nickname, as the philologist Finnur Jonsson has pointed out: thus Tord the Short was an exceptionally tall man, and another Viking who was worried about his very dark complexion was known as 'the White'.

THE VIKINGS ABROAD

The Vikings took with them their culture, skills, laws, and beliefs when they founded their foreign communities in the west and the east, among the Irish, Anglo-Saxons, Franks, and Slavs, and upon the remote Atlantic islands. On the Atlantic islands, of course, they had no rivalry or competition to meet, and could transplant their culture straight from their homeland to virgin soil. But it was a very different matter to assert their culture in well-established foreign communities which already had their own ways of life and, indeed, in most cases an equal or superior culture. In these circumstances did the Vikings make a deep impression on the foreign community, a permanent contribution, or an ephemeral one?

In Ireland

In Ireland the Norwegians encountered a community split into numerous small kingdoms, politically independent units which were unable to organize a consolidated military resistance. They encountered, too, a Christian church many centuries old, independent of Rome, fortified by its own separate traditions and practices, and concentrated in numerous monasteries. And, finally, they came up against a people of fanatical and uncompromising temperament who had no inclination for peaceful co-existence with strangers. The Norwegians, for their part, were a tough lot who preferred force to persuasion, and thus there was no prospect of any fusion of cultures between them and the Irish. It was not, indeed, until the Viking period was over, at the end of the twelfth century, that there seemed to occur any such integration of cultures, but then came the English – the Anglo-Saxon-Norman fusion – called in by the Irish themselves, to begin their command which was to last more than seven centuries.

But although the Norwegians achieved no real colonization

in Ireland, and did not succeed in the protracted occupation of substantial areas of the Irish interior, there is no doubt that their centuries of settlement along the coastal areas left a marked influence upon the country. They established a series of fortified harbours in the east, south, and west, at such places as Dublin, Wexford, Waterford, Cork, and Limerick, and round these prosperous trading-centres the country was occupied by Norwegian settlers. The reason why no such coastal towns were founded in northern Ireland – the direction from which the Norwegians came – must be that Ireland was not the main goal of their voyagings, and that they sought to press on to the coastal countries of western Europe. For these further trading ventures the southern tip of Ireland was, of course, a better spring-board than the northern end, which faced the grey and desolate Atlantic Ocean. These coastal towns throve as centres of trade; Dublin became a wealthy centre, and when in 968 the Irish captured the Norwegian town of Limerick they took a rich plunder of gold, silver, satins, and silks. The Norwegians taught the Irish a good deal about shipbuilding and navigation, and they managed to a certain extent to establish contacts between their coastal settlements and the Irish interior.

In England

A different situation developed in England, especially within the Danelaw, where protracted colonization left a distinct mark upon the native population. For one thing there was the administrative division of the country into 'hundreds' and 'wapentakes'. The hundreds must have been districts which represented a hundred of something or other: warriors, perhaps, or ploughs; the wapentakes refer to the *Things* themselves, the assemblies where decisions were confirmed by the brandishing of arms (*vapnatak*). From this the wapentake came to mean, in effect, the area covered by the members of the *Thing,* the district whence they came. The word 'hundred' seems to be an old Anglo-Saxon term, but wapentake is Danish, although the two had virtually the same meaning of administrative unit. Stenton notes that as late as the eleventh century Anglo-Saxon sources used either word for a district. Danish influences also left a mark upon legal codes and institutions. In the Danelaw, for example, the size of the fine imposed for a murder varied according to the status of the victim, while elsewhere in England it was assessed according to the staus of the victim's master, a difference which illustrates the Nordic conception of free men's equality. The swearing-in of juries, unknown in Anglo-Saxon rules of law, possibly originates with the Danes in the Danelaw, where twelve thanes in each wapentake were called to take their solemn oath not to accuse an innocent man or to protect a guilty one. Furthermore, these enactments in the Danelaw, preserved in the so-called code of Ethelred II, affirmed that the verdict of eight of the twelve thanes would be accepted – the first example in England, says Stenton, of the principle of a majority verdict on juries.

The backbone of these Danelaw communities was free but poor men. These *sokemen*, as they were called, owed certain obligations to the large estate owners, both in service and dues, but the soil they possessed was considered their real property. This fundamental condition of the Danelaw society has been described as a peasant aristocracy, and it is clearly reflected in the *Domesday Book* of William the Conqueror, where many Danish place-names (ending in 'by' and 'thorp' etc.) are to be found. The Danish place-names of the Danelaw preserve the memory of the Danish peasant population which settled there, just as the Norwegian place-names which survive in the north and north-west of England provide a similar testimony to the Norwegian settlements in those regions. The Viking came to England with sword in hand, but he came to stay and to wield the plough and till the ground. He doubtless dispossessed some of the native population, but he never sought to exterminate it. He brought his language with him, his laws and ways of life, and their effect was felt far into the Middle Ages; it was a long time before the Viking laws became assimilated with the feudal system. The one part of their inheritance which the Vikings abroad quickly abandoned was their pagan religion, despite such instances of the opposite as the behaviour in Ireland, around 840, of the pagan fanatic, Turgeis. The heathen faith must have been weak, or the religion it found abroad too strong, for in Ireland, England, France, and Russia the Vikings were not long in embracing Christianity, sometimes no doubt for political reasons, as when Rollo in Normandy accepted the new faith in 912.

In Normandy

Normandy, granted in 911 to Rollo at the head of a Nordic army, was for the next 200–300 years a mixed Nordic-Frankish dukedom. But its development was very different from that of the Danelaw in England. Its proximity to the Frankish and Germanic empires exposed it to the influence of their feudalism, a principle fundamentally different from the Nordic pattern of government, and the colonizers of Normandy had to accept the inevitable. Rollo seems to have discerned this necessity of compounding with an unfamiliar feudalism – and by this opportunism established himself as sole ruler, and future dukes of Normandy as absolute overlords. During the time of Rollo and his successors nothing is heard of *Things* or similar assemblies of free and equal men and very little of any of the standard Nordic practices of government. 'Hundreds' did not exist in Normandy. The duke and his notables retained full power in a centralized and militarized administration. There is a story characteristic of this state of things, which recounts how, about the year 1000, the peasants of Normandy summoned an assembly to demand their right to use the country's woods, lakes, and rivers. Duke

Rollo sent his uncle, Count Rudolf, to round up these peasant delegates, mutilate them all by chopping off a hand and a foot, and send them back to their villages to tell them who held sway over the woods and waters. It is not reported that these unfortunates were the original Frankish inhabitants. No; doubtless the Nordic inhabitants, too, were among the victims of this savage lesson about where the final power in Normandy really resided. The only assemblies permitted in the dukedom were gatherings of the civil and ecclesiastical members of the duke's court. Even if feudalism was not yet fully developed in Normandy during the tenth and eleventh centuries it was well on its way. If the warriors in the familiar story who cried 'We are all equals' were Rollo's men they were soon to learn a different motto.

In Normandy as in the Danelaw the Vikings left tokens of their presence in many place-names: such suffixes as *-bec, -bu, -digue, -tot* are pure Nordic ones (*Baek, By, Dige, Tofte*) and so are *-torp* and *-tved*; and prefixes to names with *-ville* and *-tot*. Most of these Nordic place-names in Normandy seem to be of Danish origin, but many are Norwegian. It is not certain whether Rollo himself was Danish or Norwegian. Later Nordic sources assert he was from Norway, but earlier sources (such as the Frankish Dudo, who was born around 960) say he was Danish. All things considered, the strong development of feudalism in Normandy does not quite obscure the impression made on the country by the Vikings.

In Russia

In considering the impact made by the Swedish Vikings in the east, we must bear in mind that their predominant motive was the expansion of trading interests. The Swedes did not penetrate Russia with the intention of conquest and settlement, as the Danes did in England and France; they set out to establish and maintain extensive trade-routes. These ventures somewhat resemble the Norwegian settlements in

Ireland, which, as we have seen, were trading-posts surrounded by a narrow tract of colonization; and whereas the Norwegians in Ireland established their posts on the coasts, Swedes in the east did this in the interior and on rivers. Thus at certain periods Novgorod, Smolensk, and Kiev were no doubt Slav towns under Swedish garrisons; the large burial-ground at Gnezdovo, near Smolensk (to which I shall return later), seems to indicate the presence of Swedish warriors and trading people at this flourishing and active military base. But there were not created in Russia – at least not on any significant scale – those permanent agrarian colonies which were developed in the Danelaw and Normandy. The trade routes were too long, the countries which would have had to be pacified were too vast. There was, too, the same difficulty as in Ireland concerning assimilation with a native population of different stock and language – there Celtic, here Slav – whereas in England the Anglo-Saxons were at least a Germanic stock related to the Viking invaders. By the end of the Viking period, it is fair to say, the long Swedish trade-routes from the motherland to the Byzantine world were abandoned, the areas of Kiev and western Russia resumed their wholly Slavic nature, and before long the Swedish penetration of these distant lands became simply a chapter of history. But in northern Russia (the Ladoga region), in Finland, and in the northern Baltic countries Swedish colonization continued throughout the twelfth and thirteenth centuries.

The degree of assimilation which occurred between the Vikings and the people with whom they came in contact seems slightly more evidenced in regard to Russia than to western Europe. There is archaeological testimony provided by the Nordic graves discovered in Russia, which reveal a mixture of Nordic, Slav, and oriental; and there is literary testimony provided by two Arabic writers of the tenth century, Idn Fadlan and Ibn Rustah, who tell us of the Swedish

Rus folk of respectively the Volga and presumably western Russia. Ibn Fadlan says:

I saw the Rus folk when they arrived on their trading-mission and settled at the river Atul (Volga). Never had I seen people of more perfect physique. They are tall as date-palms, and reddish in colour. They wear neither coat nor *kaftan*, but each man carried a cape which covers one half of his body, leaving one hand free. No one is ever parted from his axe, sword, and knife. Their swords are Frankish in design, broad, flat, and fluted. Each man has a number of trees, figures, and the like from the finger-nails to the neck. Each woman carries on her bosom a container made of iron, silver, copper, or gold – its size and substance depending on her man's wealth. Attached to the container is a ring carrying her knife which is also tied to her bosom. Round her neck she wears gold or silver rings: when a man collects 10,000 dirhams he gives his wife a neck-ring, when he has 20,000 he gives two rings, and so the wife gets a new ring for each 10,000 dirhams added to the husband's wealth. One woman often has many neck-rings. Their finest ornament is the green clay-pearl on the ships. To provide this they go to great trouble; they buy one pearl for a dirham and combine the pearls into necklaces for their women.

They are the filthiest of God's creatures. They do not wash after discharging their natural functions, neither do they wash their hands after meals. They are as lousy as donkeys. They arrive from their distant lands and lay their ships alongside the banks of the Atul, which is a great river, and there they build big houses on its shores. Ten or twenty of them may live together in one house, and each of them has a couch of his own where he sits and diverts himself with the pretty slave girls whom he has brought along for sale. He will make love with one of them while a comrade looks on; sometimes they indulge in a communal orgy, and, if a customer should turn up to buy a girl, the Rus man will not let her go till he has finished with her.

They wash their hands and faces every day in incredibly filthy water. Every morning the girl brings her master a large bowl of water in which he washes his hands and face and hair, then blows his nose into it and spits into it. When he has finished the girl takes the bowl to his neighbour – who repeats the performance. Thus the bowl goes the rounds of the entire household.

On beaching their vessels, each man goes ashore carrying bread, meat, onions, milk, and *nabid* (beer?) and these he takes to a large wooden post with a face like that of a human being, surrounded by smaller figures, and behind them there are high poles in the ground. Each man prostrates himself before the large post and recites: 'O Lord, I have come from distant parts with so many girls, so many sable furs (and whatever other commodities are in his catalogue). I now bring you this offering.' He then presents his gift, and continues. 'Please send me a merchant who has many dinars and dirhams and who will trade favourably with me without contradicting me'. If after this his business does not proceed quickly and well, he returns to the statue and presents further gifts. If results continue slow, he then presents gifts to the minor figures and begs their intercession. . . . If his pleas prevail, and trade picks up, he says, 'My Lord has requited my needs, and now it is my duty to repay him'; and, on this, he sacrifices goats or cattle, some of which he distributes as alms. The rest he lays before the statues, large and small, and the heads of the beasts he plants upon the pole. After dark, of course, the dogs come and devour the lot – and the successful trader says, 'My Lord is pleased with me, and has eaten my offerings.'

If one of the Rus folk falls sick they put him in a tent by himself and leave bread and water for him. They do not visit him, however, or speak to him, especially if he is a serf. Should he recover he rejoins the others; if he dies they burn him. But if he happens to be a serf they leave him for the dogs and vultures to devour. If they catch a robber they hang him to a tree until he is torn to shreds by wind and weather.

Now follows the description (p. 280) of a chieftain's funeral, and thereafter Ibn Fadlan continues, 'It is customary for the king of the Rus to have a bodyguard in his castle of 400 reliable men willing to die for him. Each of these has a slave girl to wait on him, wash him, and serve him, and another for his bed-fellow. These 400 sit below the royal throne, a large and jewelled platform which also accommodates the forty slave girls of his harem. The King frequently has public intercourse with one of these. He does not bother to leave his throne to make water, but has a basin brought to him for the purpose; and when he wants to go riding his horse is led up to him, and when he returns from the ride the horse is brought right up to the throne. A substitute warrior leads his armies in battle and holds the audiences with his subjects.'

This Ibn Fadlan was a member of a diplomatic delegation sent in 921-2 by the Baghdad Khalifate to Bulgar on the Volga. His account of his personal experiences creates the impression that the Rus folk of the Volga region, dealing in furs and slaves, were a pretty rough lot in both sexual and hygienic matters. Whether their women were Nordic or not we do not know; but what emerges from Ibn Fadlan's commentary is that, in general, these wandering Swedish Rus folk retained their Swedish manners and observances in such matters as weapons, punishments, ship-funerals, and religious sacrifices. They seem, on the other hand, to have come under foreign influence in matters exemplified by the overloading of their women with jewellery and the dead chief's costume (p. 282). Whether in other ways, such as their treatment of the sick and their tattooing (if it is tattooing), they were following Swedish or Slav practice we do not know. What seems, however, to indicate an assimilation (to the Turkish this time) is the description of the Rus king's crude and mixed-up household of earls (*hird*) and concubines (harem).

Ibn Rustah, astronomer and geographer, seems to have been writing twenty years later than Ibn Fadlan. About the Rus folk he says:

They keep to the island in the lake, an island covered with forest and brush, which it takes three days to walk round and which is marshy and unhealthy. They have a prince called Hagan-Rus. They sail in their ships to ravage as-Saqaliba (i.e. the surrounding Slavs) and bring back captives whom they sell at Hazaran and Bulgar (both towns on the Volga). They have no cultivated fields but depend for their supplies on what they can get from as-Saqaliba's land. When a son is born the father advances on the baby, sword in hand, and flings it down, saying, 'I shall not leave you any property: you have only what you can provide with this weapon!' They have no estates, villages, or fields; their only business is to trade in sable and squirrel fur, and the money they take in these transactions they stow in their belts. Their clothes are clean and the men decorate themselves with gold armlets. They treat their slaves well, and they wear exquisite clothes because of their eager trading activity. They have many towns. They are sturdy to each other, they honour their guests and are hospitable and friendly to strangers who take refuge with them and to all those who usually visit them. They do not allow anybody to molest their guests or do them any harm, and if somebody dares insult them or do them injustice they help and defend them. They use Sulaiman swords. If a group of them is challenged, they band together as one man until they secure victory. If two men quarrel, their case is considered by the Prince, in whose presence they plead, both of them, and if they agree about his ruling his decision stands; but if they do not agree he tells them to settle the dispute with their swords – and let the sharpest sword win! The fight takes place in the company of the combatants' friends who stand sword in hand, and the man who gets the better of the contest also gets the decision about the matter under dispute.

There are *atibba,* or medicine men, who wield great power. They tell people exactly what offerings to make of women, men, and cattle, and when the sacrifices have been thus selected the medicine man takes the victim, human or animal, and hangs it from a pole until it expires, saying 'this is a sacrifice to God.' – They are courageous in battle and when they attack a neighbourhood they persist until they have destroyed it thoroughly. They take the women prisoners and make the men serfs. They are well built and good looking and daring, but their bravery does not appear on land. They always make their attacks and expeditions from ships. They wear very full trousers (ab. 200 feet of fabric a pair), with baggy knees, and when they want to relieve themselves they go out in groups of four, with their weapons, so as to protect each other. There is little security among them, and much deceit, and even a man's brother or comrade is not above plundering him if he can.

Ibn Rustah's account of the Rus folk concludes with the short remark on the funerals of their notables, given later (p. 284).

There is no evidence that Ibn Rustah was an eye-witness of what he narrates, but although his stories are doubtless based on other sources they have a stamp of reliability. The island on which he says the Rus folk established themselves is thought by many scholars to have been Novgorod (the Nordic Holmegaard), although it cannot be proved. There is special significance in his assertion that the Rus folk were not an agrarian people, that they had no fields nor villages but many towns, that is to say they concentrated in fortified garrisons of which the remains have been found in great numbers, for instance, in the province of Smolensk. He mentions specifically the principal commodities they dealt in, slaves – taken in the surrounding lands and brought to the Volga – and furs. He does not suggest any pronounced non-Nordic characteristics among them, except the oriental swords and baggy trousers. They seem in the main to have retained their Nordic manners in such matters as hospitality, courage, settling disputes, human and animal sacrifices, handling of ships, and burial customs. We get no impression of a solidly established government: that came later, but in the middle of the tenth century the organization was more or less equivalent to that of a trading company. Their position and activities were compared, indeed, to those of the Jews – by Ibn Horradadbeh who wrote, in 840, the earliest account of the Swedes in Russia. It must have taken these Swedish Viking merchants a century or more to lay even the foundation of a solid political state.

CHAPTER 14

RELIGIOUS BELIEFS AND BURIAL CUSTOMS

ICELANDIC literature – i.e. the Volve's prophecy of the Elder Edda, a pagan poem, and *Gylfe's Infatuation,* in which the Christian author Snorre Sturluson gathers together from many sources a picture of the beliefs of his pagan forbears – gives us a magnificent and colourful 'Theatrum', a grandiose stage-set of the old Nordic religion. Snorre's story, compounded as it is of myths and legends of different periods and origins, offers an extensive and vivid rendering of Viking religious concepts, whereas the Edda poem, that ambitious highly emotional work, is permeated by a single emotional flood. We are told, through these sources, about the creation and the ultimate end of the world, the battles of the gods and the giants, and the pantheon of the two categories of the gods, the 'Aser' and the 'Vaner'. In the middle lies the home of the gods, Asgaard, within which is Valhalla with its 640 gates: the palace of the mighty Odin and his warriors, the abode from which Odin on his high throne Lidskjalv surveys all creation. This heaven of the gods is separated from the earth by the bridge Bifrost the trembling rainbow; the disc of the earth is surrounded by the great ocean, home of the Midgaard serpent and on its farthest shore lie the mountains of the giants, Jotunheim, in which stands their castle Udgaard. Beneath the disc of the earth lies Hel, the land of the dead.

What we learn about the great ash-tree Ygdrasil, itself a world of good and evil, of joy and sorrow, sounds like a song from a completely different world. Ygdrasil is gigantic. Its crown reaches the sky, its branches cover the earth, its three

roots stretch out to Hel and to Jotunheim and beneath Midgaard, the home of mortals. At the base of Ygdrasil are two
wells, one belonging to Mimer, god of wisdom, the other to
Urd, goddess of destiny. In the branches of the tree sits the
eagle, and between its eyes perches a hawk, bleached by wind
and weather. A serpent gnaws at the root of the tree, and
between it and the eagle a chattering squirrel runs to and fro
conveying words of evil. Four deer nibble away at the young
shoots of the tree, and one side of the tree is peeling away.
'The ash tree Ygdrasil suffers and endures more than mankind can imagine!' But the Norns give solace and renewal
at the well of Urd, from which they pour water daily on
Ygdrasil so that it shall not wither. The bees feed happily on
Ygdrasil's honey-dew. At a shrine by Urd's well the gods
meet for their *Thing*, and here live the three highest of the
Norns, the goddesses of Past, Present, and Future: Urd,
Verdandi, and Skuld.

In the centre of the world above the humans are the abodes
of the gods, where live the two races of gods, the Aser and
the Vaner. We shall return later to this Nordic pantheon;
meanwhile let us look briefly at the Nordic conception of
the end of the world – Ragnarok.

Nothing lasts for ever, and when the gods have fulfilled
their destiny the end of all things will arrive. This is the event
so graphically narrated in the Volve's prophecy and in
Snorre's tale. The first sign of the approaching end will be
the coming of horrible events and desperate desires – 'sword-
time', 'Wolf-time', fratricide, and incest. The cocks will crow
in Odin's halls, in Hel, and in the sacrificial groves. Horror
and eeriness grow. It is the time of giant monsters. The Hound
of Hel, Garm, will howl, the wolf Fenris will wander un-
chained, its jaws stretching from earth to heaven. The Midgaard serpent will whip the ocean into foam and spew its
venom upon the earth. The giant Hrym will cross the seas
in his ship Nagelfar, built from dead men's nails, and the

sons of Muspel will sail forth with Loke as their leader. The tree Ygdrasil will tremble, the sky split asunder, the rocks roll down; in Jotunheim there will be rumbling, the dwarfs will scream. Odin will watch, Heimdal will blow his horn, the bridge Bifrost will crash, and the giant Surt will break loose, spouting fire. Then will come the final battle between gods and beasts. The wolf Fenris devours Odin, but is then slain by his son, Vidar, who smashes the brute's jaws with his heavy boot. Thor kills the Midgaard serpent, but after walking nine paces falls dead, poisoned by its venom. Tyr and the Hound Garm kill each other, so do Heimdal and Loke. Surt kills Frej and burns up everything with his belching flames. The sun turns black; the stars go out. Yet hope survives. The earth rises again from the ocean. The two guiltless Aser gods, Balder and Høder, return and on the golden *Gimle* the sinless live on. The eagle flies again above the thundering waterfall, the sun shines once more upon a new world. Although nothing is said about the coming of Christianity, the tale implies the emergence of a new triumphant faith for a newly created humanity. It is a drama of extinction and resurrection.

THE GODS

Like the Egyptian, the Greek, and the Roman, Nordic religion was polytheistic. There were numerous gods, each governing a particular human need or action. In this hierarchy the gods varied considerably in power and status: some were in the prime of their potency, others apparently were old and half-forgotten; some assumed a high rank of precedence, others were secondary figures. Let us look here at the principal Nordic deities in Asgaard.

Odin

Supreme among them is Odin: a magnificent, dominating, demonic and sadistic figure. He is consumed by his passion for wisdom; for its sake he sacrifices an eye, even hangs himself. Uncharitable, moody, and ruthless, he is the god of battle and of the fallen warriors. He owns the spear Gungner, the self-renewing gold ring Drøpner, the fabulous and fleet eight-footed horse Sleipner. He is guarded by his two wolves and is brought news from everywhere by his two ravens. He communes with the head of the wise decapitated Mimer, he finds the runes and knows their secret power. He hunts by night, with his retinue, through mountains and woods; he appears to the doomed on the battlefield as a tall one-eyed shape clad in a long cape and wearing a broad-brimmed hat. Odin is the god of minstrels as well: he governs the mystic ecstasy, the great pathos, the passion of the soul. He knows witchcraft and sorcery; he can fathom the soul's subtleties. He is the god of the great ones, an aristocrat, a dangerous god. He is called sometimes Great Father, and justly, in so far as he takes the chair among the deities; but we must not take the words 'Great Father' as denoting paternal tendencies and sympathy; with this meaning they do not apply to Odin. His human clientèle consists of kings, earls, chiefs, magicians, and poets. The warriors who die in battle for him are borne by the Valkyries to Valhalla, where they are enrolled in his immense host, the *Einheriers*, the army of the resurrection which will be at Odin's back on Ragnarok, the Last Day. To achieve his domination of knowledge and wisdom and mystery Odin stops at nothing in the way of deceit and cunning and treachery, and if he is hard to others so also is he to himself. His characteristics cover a wide range: from cold cynicism to Dionysiac enthusiasm, from ferocity to ecstasy.

Thor

Between Odin, greatest and most profound of the Nordic deities, and the next Aser god, the great red-bearded Thor with the goat-carriage and the mighty hammer, there is a considerable gap. Odin is the god of the great, while Thor is the god of the common man, and he is amply endowed with that sense of humour which Odin so sadly lacks.

Numerous legends and anecdotes are recounted of Thor, the strong and faithful protector of the peasant, and the superb fighter, too, who finds no lack of targets for his hammer among the giants. When he races across the clouds with his he-goats, the thunder rumbles, and when he goes forth with his hammer, Mjølner, in his hand, he is irresistible. He is unpractised in cunning and stratagems, but although he is often outwitted by the tricks of the giants he always wins in the end. The Northerners invented many vivid stories of his deeds: he wrests the great beer cauldron from the giants, he wins back the stolen hammer, fishes for the Midgaard serpent; encounters strange adventures with Udgaardsloke, king of the giants, whom he visits accompanied by the clever, but in this case rather unhelpful, Loke.

Thor was quick-tempered, but quick also to recover himself. The Viking peasant understood and appreciated him. He was not merely an amiable companion round the fire in the evening; he was the helpful deity who made the crops grow, the god of agriculture (except perhaps in Norway). For this reason, because he was so involved in the daily life of the people, he seemed more real and important to the peasants than Odin himself. This is illustrated by the fact, related by Adam of Bremen, that it was Thor's idol, not Odin's, which stood in the central position in the temple at Uppsala where the three principal gods, Odin, Thor, and Frey, were worshipped. Thor was also called upon at weddings to bless the bride with fertility, and it is he and not Odin who is invoked on the runestones to consecrate the runes. When a symbol was needed to resist the potency of the Cross the Vikings chose the hammer of Thor, not the spear of Odin. Thor was, finally, a more universal and popular deity than Odin – his favour was sought not only by the farmer but by the blacksmith, the fisherman, the sailor; he was closer to the ordinary man than was the complex, unapproachable, and violent Odin.

Tyr

Tyr was a deity less clearly defined than the other two. We hear that he is brave and virtuous, that he loses a hand in overpowering the Fenris wolf, and that during Ragnarok he fights with Garm, the Hound of Hel. He seems, in Viking days, to have been an ancient half-forgotten and superseded King of Heaven.

These three major gods, Odin, Thor, and Tyr, are by no means newcomers to the Germanic pantheon. All of them are mentioned, under Roman names, in Tacitus's famous book about the Germans, written around A.D. 100, where Mercury, Hercules, and Mars correspond respectively, no doubt, to Odin, Thor, and Tyr and where Mercury is said to be the principal Germanic god, and the only one to whom human sacrifices are made. Mercury (and the Greek Hermes as well) has it in common with Odin to be guide of the dead, to wear a mantle and a broad hat and to carry a stick (or spear). Beyond this, however, there is not very much resemblance between them; in Mercury there is none of that savagery so characteristic of Odin – an attribute derived by some scholars from the proximity of the eastern Germanic peoples to those wild Asiatic hordes which poured into Europe during the migration. It has been suggested that this image of Odin, coloured by Mongolian passions (Shamanism), was transmitted first to Sweden, and from there to the other Nordic lands, through the cultural Gothic impulses that ran north and south from the Black Sea to the Baltic. The equivalence of Thor with Hercules is acceptable enough, but does not account for the thunder or the hammer; Thor must have been an ancient god of agriculture and a thunder god as well. Tyr, again, is only the partial counterpart of

Mars; his Nordic name, Tyr or Tir or Ti, is linked with the Roman Jupiter, the Greek Zeus, and the Indian Dyaus. How old, in Tacitus's time, this trinity was among the Germanic peoples it is not possible to say (perhaps not very old; Caesar, as is well known, observed that the Germanic races worshipped powers of Nature exclusively – fire, the sun, and the moon). The Germanic peoples called their days after these gods: Tuesday (Tyr), Wednesday (Wodan, Odin), Thursday (Thor).

Balder

A special place within the circle of the gods is taken by Balder the son of Odin and Frigg. Snorre's account of him is a celebrated story: how this genial and friendly god met with a tragic death from the arrow shot by his blind and innocent brother, how he was laid on the funeral pyre amid the lamentations of the elements, how the gods tried to liberate him from Hel and the machinations of the wicked Loke. The figure of Balder is a unique phenomenon in Nordic mythology and an enigma which scholars have not yet solved. Some of them discern a resemblance between Balder's story and legends of the Middle Ages; others observe similarities to Oriental myths of the god of growth, for whose death Nature weeps and laments. But these comparisons fail to account for the fact that in the Balder myth, unlike the others, the theme of resurrection is totally absent. The Danish Saxo Grammaticus, of the Middle Ages, also tells of Balder, but his version is quite different from Snorre's and is not of great interest. Compared with the trinity of Odin, Thor, and Tyr, Balder is a young deity.

Viking art owes one of its motifs to the Balder myth – the theme of how the gods, trying to push the heavy funeral ship into the sea, have to send to Jotunheim for the witch Hyrrokkin, who comes riding on a wolf, with an adder for a bridle, and pushes the funeral ship into the water with a violence which shakes the earth and angers Thor. This event is depicted on a picture-stone dated about 1000 from Hunnestad in Skaane. It shows the riding giantess, wearing a shift and a pointed hat, her snake-tongue hanging out, the adder used as a bridle for her magnificent wolf which gallops along with fangs open, ears pointed, and a tasselled long tail. That vivid picture can be no one but Hyrrokkin.

Heimdal

Heimdal is the god with the war-horn which sounds for Ragnarok. He is vigilant and alert, the watchman of the gods and the guardian of the bridge of Bifrost. 'Volve's Prophecy' calls human beings 'Heimdal's sons', and Heimdal is the wandering god who, in the *Rigsthula,* creates the three classes of society. He and Loke, old enemies apparently, kill each other during Ragnarok. Apart from that Heimdal is not very well defined in the circle of the Nordic gods.

Ull

The god of hunting is Ull, who excels at shooting (with bow and arrows) and at ski-ing. His status in the hierarchy is even more sketchy than Heimdal's; there are no myths about him, and in late Viking times he remains very much in the background. His identity is preserved in certain Nordic place-names, and on that evidence he must have been particularly known and worshipped in southern Norway and central Sweden. In Denmark there is no trace of him. The general conclusion is that by Viking times Ull was a superannuated deity well on the way to oblivion.

The Vaner Gods

Among the gods were three who did not belong to the leading family of Gods, the Aser, but to a different and apparently older dynasty of deities called Vaner, representatives of a religion which in the Viking period was losing ground to that of the Aser gods. These three were Njord, Frey, and Freya. According to Snorre the two families of gods came to terms after a battle and gave each other hostages. The three Vaner hostages who went to live in Asgaard were those just named, and all three were deities of growth, conception fertility, sexual life. In other words, old gods of fertility whom the Aser gods did not succeed in replacing.

Njord was the eldest of the three; in fact by his sister he begot Frey and Freya. In the myths he is married to Skade, a giantess who inhabits the mountains, whereas Njord prefers the beaches, for he is ruler of the winds and the bountiful god of sea-faring; he gives wealth. Njord philologically is the Nerthus whom Tacitus names, about A.D. 100, as a north-west Germanic goddess (not god) of fertility; but this confusion of sexes is no rarity in the history of religion. There is no doubt some connexion between Njord and Nerthus, and it is worthy of note, in passing, that (as Wessen has pointed out) Swedish place-names embodying '*njard*' are female. Tacitus calls Nerthus 'Mother Earth'; she dwells in a virgin grove 'on an island in the ocean'. Each spring she is driven by her priest round the island, with great ceremony, in a consecrated covered carriage drawn by oxen, and is everywhere received with the greatest delight. Weapons are laid aside and feasting is universal. Returned after the ceremonial visit her carriage and the linen too are washed in a secret lake by serfs who, their task finished, are summarily drowned. Archaeologists are inclined to think, as we shall see again later, that this goddess of the Roman age, this earth-god promoting fertility, existed in much earlier times in the Nordic countries, probably as far back as the Bronze Age.

The strongest and most celebrated of the three Vaner gods in Asgaard was Njord's son, Frey, the god of sexual intercourse, whose statue in the temple at Uppsala was distinguished by a gigantic phallus. He appears to have inspired particular devotion in Sweden, as evidenced by erotic statuettes (Pl. 24B) and amulets, and by the tradition of carriage processions in the style of Nerthus. He was apparently popular also in Iceland, in the Trøndelag of Norway, and in Denmark. This god of fecundity and growth is attended by a sacred pig, the celebrated pig Gyldenbørste in Asgaard. There is a famous myth of Frey's passionate love for Gerd of the White Arms. The worship of Frey may have reached Norway and Iceland from Sweden via Jæmtland, in the central lake of which, called Storsjøn, lie the islands of Norderøn and Frøsøn (Njord's island and Frøj's island). In Iceland Frey is sometimes called 'the Swedish god'.

The third of the Vaner gods is Freya, Frey's sister and in every way his female counterpart. His name means 'master'; hers 'mistress'. A goddess of love and fertility, she has the reputation of being generous with her favours, and in the Eddas she is accused by Loke of being the willing paramour of any of the gods and of having bought her magnificent jewellery from four dwarfs at a disreputable price. She, too, possesses a carriage, but hers is drawn by cats (cf. the lion-drawn carriage of Cybele). Barren women invoked her blessing, and she was the Death Goddess not only of all women but also of half the warriors slain in battle where she was present.

These three deities of the Vaner family seem to be very ancient gods: older than Odin and Thor, older even than Tyr. The question arises – what gods did they dispossess when, possibly during the last few centuries B.C., they penetrated the Germanic peoples? The latter doubtless had their Nature Powers, as Caesar noted, and they worshipped too, it may be supposed, their old gods from the Bronze Age. We know from archaeological finds of the Bronze Age, as well as from rock carvings, that they worshipped a god with large hands and bristling fingers, sometimes armed with an axe, who appears to have been the god of thunder; that they wor-shipped also a naked goddess adorned with a necklace, and a goddess seated in a carriage. The latter seems to appear in Early Iron Age discoveries – e.g. the carriage with women's belongings in it found at Dejbjerg in west Jutland. This car-driving goddess is possibly the same as Nerthus who, if the supposition is correct, must have derived from the Bronze Age. It is reasonable to surmise, in that case, that the naked goddess was a forerunner of Freya. This cannot be accepted as certain, but it encourages the conclusion that the Vaner family, partly superseded in Viking times by the rival Aser, originated back in the Bronze Age at least 500 years B.C.

Loke

The last of the Aser in Asgaard is Loke, half god and half devil, next to Odin the most singular and strange. He is the offspring of a giant 'Fotte' and in many ways a split personality. A giant's son himself he is married to a giantess, Angerbode, by whom he has three fearful monsters, the Midgaard serpent, the Fenris Wolf, and Hel. He haunts the doors of the Aser and is, indeed, foster-brother to Odin whose complex personality in many ways matches his own. Loke relishes satire but has no sense of humour; he is cunning and deceitful, and lacks all capacity for friendship; his stinging words can touch and hurt and strike; the tricks he plays on the gods and goddesses are invariably vicious and cruel, and he is always animated by self-interest. Both Edda and Snorre harp upon his unpleasant character and his perpetual malice. He is a sexual freak, too, capable of begetting such oddities as Odin's eight-footed horse, Sleiper. Of his many misdeeds the most notorious is his share in the murder of Balder, the crime which finally determines his fate. He seeks to escape by changing himself into a salmon, but the Aser capture him and fetter him to a rock underneath a serpent dripping poison. His second wife, Sigyn, manages to catch the venom, and whenever she misses a drop his trembling makes the earth quake. In this plight he survives until Ragnarok when, joining forces with the enemies of the Aser, he and Heimdal kill each other. In modern jargon Loke would be reckoned the psychopath among gods; on the basis of his feud with the gods, he has been likened to Prometheus and to Satan. But he has none of the splendid defiance of the first named, and none of the fallen Lucifer's secret longings. He loves evil for its own sake. has a sharp eye for the vulnerable qualities of his enemies, and so nourishes his evil nature as to develop in himself every hue and aspect of sin. His weakness is his passion to see how deeply he can commit himself to evil without paying the price – and at last he goes too far and brings down catastrophe upon himself. In the Viking nature there must have been characteristics which account for the pleasure they took in the personality of this bizarre deity. Nations get the gods they deserve. Loke has features in common with the Mephistopheles of the Middle Ages – thus far one can point out a Christian influence. Loke is not as old a figure as Odin, Thor, and Tyr, nor as ancient as the Vaner. He is not truly a god at all, in the sense of being a figure which men are impelled to worship. Rather is he a product of mythological speculation.

Gods and Place Names

Nordic place-names provide clues to the identity of the gods who were worshipped in various localities. Place-names embodying the name of Odin are found nearly everywhere (except Iceland), a factor which implies that he was extensively worshipped. (Incidentally, Swedish place-names ending in 'tuna' are never found in combination with the name of Odin.) The name of Thor occurs abundantly in all Nordic place-names, including those of Iceland. In Norway and Sweden the name of Thor frequently occurs in combination with such suffixes as -hof (temple) but in Denmark his name is associated not with -hof but with -lund (grove). In Norway Thor's name is never linked with agrarian associations such as -akr (field) or -vin (meadow), which suggests that in Norway he was not such an agrarian deity as in Denmark and Sweden; nor in Iceland is Thor's name to be found combined with agrarian elements. Tyr or Ti seldom appear in Norwegian or Swedish place-names, but they do so frequently in Denmark. Balder's name turns up sporadically in all the Nordic countries; and Heimdal's so infrequently as to lead to the conclusion that he enjoyed no cult at all. Ull is incorporated in many place-names in Norway and eastern Sweden, but not in Denmark. The names of the three Vaner gods, Njord, Frey, and Freya, recur considerably. In Norway all three are abundant, and in eastern Sweden as well, and as far north as Jæmtland. In Denmark Njord appears in place-names on Zeeland and Fyn; Frey and Freya appear on those two islands and also in south Jutland. Loke, like Heimdal, to judge by the place-names, seems to have enjoyed virtually no cult; Loke names are extremely few. In many place-names the word 'god' or 'holy' is used instead of any individual god.

The place-names often include an indication of the object which is consecrated to the god and therefore belongs to him. Endings such as -hov or -hof show that he had a house or temple; -harg or -tuna signifies his place of sacrifice; -hylde the base of an idol; -vi the god's fenced-in sanctuary; -ager his cultivated field. Or the god's name may be linked with some natural object associated with him – a grove, a hill, a rock, a lake, a spring, a bay, an island, etc.

FORMS OF WORSHIP

Little is known about the forms of worship of these deities, or about their temples, although both archaeology and literary sources disclose a few impressions. There is Adam of Bremen's famous description of the most renowned temple of the north, at Gamla Uppsala, still flourishing, when he wrote around 1070, as the centre of paganism and strong resistance to Christianity. Here is his account of it:

These people have a celebrated sanctuary called Uppsala, not very far from Sigtuna and Birka. In this temple, entirely covered with gold, are three idols which the people worship: Thor, as the mightiest god, has his throne in the middle of the hall and Odin and Frey theirs on each side of him. Their fields of action are the following: Thor, it is said, rules the elements of wind and weather – thunder, lightning, storm, rain, fine weather – and is guardian of the crops. The second, Odin, i.e. Fury, is the god of war who inspires men with courage to fight their enemies. The third is Frey who gives to mankind peace and sensuous pleasures. His idol, therefore, they endow with a mighty phallus. Odin is armed in the fashion of Mars, the sceptre of Thor resembles that of Jupiter. Sometimes these people elevate men also to the status of deities and worship them as a tribute to some great achievement they have accomplished – the reward, according to St Ansgar's biography, which was bestowed upon King Erik.

Attached to the gods are priests who arrange the people's sacrifices. If sickness or famine threaten they sacrifice to Thor; if war, to Odin, and if a wedding is to be celebrated they sacrifice to Frey. There is also a festival at Uppsala every nine years common to all the lands of Sweden. Attendance at this event is compulsory and it is the universal practice for kings and peoples and everyone to send offerings to Uppsala and – a cruel thing – those who have become Christians may secure exemption, but only on payment of a fine. The sacrifice on this occasion consists of the slaughter of nine males whose bodies are hung in a grove near the temple, a sanctuary so holy that each tree is regarded as itself a deity, in consequence of the death and decay of the victims. Dogs and horses hang there beside human beings, and a Christian has told me that he has seen as many as seventy-two carcasses hanging there side by side. By the way, it is told that the songs sung during the ceremony are numerous and obscene so that it is better to say nothing about them.

Some later additions to this account run thus:

Near this temple stands a huge tree, which stretches out green branches in summer and winter alike; of what species nobody knows. There is also a spring there at which the pagans' sacrifices take place. A man is lowered into it alive, and if he does not manage to reappear it is a sign that the people's wishes will be fulfilled.

And farther on:

A chain of gold surrounds the temple hanging over the roof and greeting visitors from afar with its brightness, for the temple lies in a plain, as an amphitheatre encircled by mountains.

An older literary source, the German Tietmar of Merseburg (*c.* 1000), describes a sacrificial feast held every nine years in January at Lejre on Zeeland. Here, says Tietmar, in the public eye, ninety-nine human beings and ninety-nine horses were sacrificed to the gods, to say nothing of dogs and cocks, in order to protect the people against evil powers and atone for its sins. It is not clear whether this feast occurred during the time of the Vikings, or before.

A pagan holy sacrificial feast was called a *blót*. Snorre describes those held at Lade, in Trøndelag: all the peasants had to attend, bringing beer and horsemeat. The walls of the temple, outside and in, were daubed with the blood of the horses, and the flesh was cooked in fires built upon the floor of the temple and dedicated to Odin, Njord, Frey, and to Brage too before it was eaten. The story is famous how the Trønder peasants forced the Christian king Haakon the Good to take part in such a feast.

Not only the major gods but also the lesser deities, the 'Diser' and 'Alfer' were celebrated with sacrifices. The Diser were mysterious female beings related, possibly, to the 'Fylgjer' and the 'Valkyries', and perhaps connected with Freya in her capacity as the goddess of the dead. It was wise to keep in with the Diser, and to remember them with sacrificial gifts, for they could foretell death and had also certain protective powers over houses and crops. The Diser were not always friendly powers, and it was important to treat them with a certain awe and respect, rather as one would respect the dead. In Viking times the Diser were celebrated at Uppsala during a large winter feast held in February at full moon. The Alfer, or elves, were low-grade deities, not strictly gods at all but figures who were worshipped within the home for their protective powers. Sigvat, a Christian, who was minstrel to St Olav, describes in his poem *Østerfareviser* how he went to heathen Sweden and at night reached a shuttered house. From inside they answered his knocking by crying out that they were engaged in holy practices. 'Come no nearer, you miserable fellow,' explained a woman. 'I fear Odin's wrath, we worship the ancient gods.' 'This wicked woman,' Sigvat writes, 'who would drive me away like a wolf, said she was preparing for *alfeblót*.' On such an occasion there was no scope for traditional Nordic hospitality.

Another species of invisible beings who frequented human habitations, and with whom it was well to be on good terms, were the 'Vætter', and on a lower level still, trolls and goblins (*Nisser*). But these beings were not actually worshipped.

An example of a curious primitive cult is related in the Edda poem called *Volsapáttr*. The scene is described as a lonely farm in northern Norway inhabited by the farmer and his wife, their son and daughter and their serf and his wife. *Volse* is the name given to the sex-organ they have cut from a horse and which is carefully preserved in herbs by the wife and kept wrapped in a linen cloth. Every night the six of them pass this object from hand to hand, addressing it in short verses the while. This ceremony becomes their nightly habit until the Saint-King Olav and some travelling companions unexpectedly arrive on the scene, fling the pagan phallus to the dog, and teach Christianity to the benighted family. Such a medley of sexuality and magic was no doubt far from exceptional among the primitive Nordic peasants.

PLACES OF WORSHIP

There are references in literature to heathen temples, sanctuaries, and sacrificial groves, beside the accounts already quoted: Snorre's of the Norwegian *blót*, Adam of Bremen's of the temple of Gamla Uppsala, and Tietmar's of sacrifices at Lejre. The latter, incidentally, can be compared with the story in *Beowulf* of King Roar's hall, called 'Hjort', in Lejre, and both are, no doubt, somewhat older than the Vikings. But what evidence can archaeology offer about temples, sanctuaries, or enclosed holy places? It is scanty evidence, it must be admitted, and certainly not sufficient to enable reconstructions to be made. Ejnar Dyggve's excavations under the choir of the Romanesque church at Jelling, in south Jutland, have yielded traces – this is, of course, the same Jelling where, as previously described, two great barrows and two royal runic stones are standing. Here Dyggve found the remains of a wooden church (stave church) with a rectangular apse in the east, four great roof-supporting beams forming a square in the middle of the church, and at the western end an open space enclosed by stones. He also found traces of a still older wooden building, namely the remains of a floor made of clay through which a great supporting beam had been embedded.

The first of these two finds is thought to be the church which King Harald Bluetooth built after his conversion to Christianity, while the older wooden building is generally considered the remains of the heathen temple of his father Gorm. Sune Lindqvist similarly found traces of a temple below the stone church at Old Uppsala, though insufficient to justify the reconstruction he has made. The discovery is yet to be made of remains which can be so definitely interpreted as to provide us with the shape and plan of a heathen temple. Why are they sought for under the stone churches of the Middle Ages? The reason is that these are often found to have been built over older wooden ones which, in their turn, may be presumed to have been put up on top of demolished heathen temples. In Iceland, as was noted earlier, certain long-houses with special end-sections (? for idols) have been interpreted as temples, but with no certainty. At Jelling about ten years ago Dyggve identified a large triangular area, which had been surrounded by upright stones, a holy place, no doubt – what is called a *vi* (from Danish *vie* = consecrated). Similar enclosed triangular areas have been located by him elsewhere in Denmark. We shall return later in some detail to the difficult problem of interpreting the Jelling finds – barrows, *vi*, temple, stave church, and runic stones.

IDEAS OF DEATH AND BURIAL CUSTOMS

The Viking attitude to death is to some degree disclosed by grave discoveries. Hundreds of Viking graves have been found, fewer in Denmark than in the other Nordic countries, but, far from presenting a uniform impression of the Viking idea of the after-life, they reveal a great complexity and variety of practice and belief. Both earth-burial and cremation occur. Burials occurred sometimes in large wooden chambers, sometimes in modest coffins; in a big long-ship or in a little boat, or sometimes in a symbolical boat made of stone, or in a carriage. There are graves under barrows and graves under flat fields; the funerary objects are sometimes rich, at other times poor, and sometimes completely absent. There are two main reasons for such wide variation of practice. The first is that in pre-Viking times, in Merovingian days, burial habits between the three northern countries varied, and this variation was continued in the Viking period. The second reason is that the Viking religion was very indeterminate in its doctrine about life after death. These two reasons deserve closer examination.

Variations in Burial Habits

In Denmark in Merovingian times a good deal of symbolic practice was observed, both in sacrificial offerings and in funerary objects. Fragments of objects were often used instead

of whole ones. In Norway and Sweden on the other hand
this tendency was much rarer, and it was a frequent custom
to deposit rich and precious objects with the dead. Another
difference was that in Merovingian times in Norway and
Sweden it was common to bury the dead man in his boat –
but this was practically unknown in Denmark. In Sweden and
Norway there are many traces of seventh and eighth century
boat-burials; even when the boat has burned or rotted
away there are the tell-tale rivets to confirm the fact. Differences of this kind in Merovingian days persisted in Viking
times.

In one respect the Danish fashion for symbols in burials
recurs in Sweden and Norway – in boat-burials. A boat could
not be spared, perhaps, and so the dead man was put into a
symbolic boat made of stone. The impact of Christianity was
a further factor in creating this complexity of Viking habit,
for Christianity forbade the practice of cremation, and required a simple earth or wooden grave facing east and west,
and devoid of presents for the dead. This effect of Christianity
is more apparent in Denmark and Norway than in Sweden,
which was about a hundred years behind the other two
countries in adopting the Christian faith (after 1100). As
regards cremation, this was much commoner in Sweden and
Norway than in Denmark; but just as cremation was not
entirely unknown in Denmark, so earth burials were by no
means unknown in Sweden and Norway. In Norway there
are many Merovingian graves and Viking ship-graves which
reveal that the corpses were buried and not burned. It would
be untrue, therefore, to assume that cremation in itself denotes
a particular religion. There are no hard and fast rules about
Nordic funeral practices; numerous factors determined the
methods adopted – such as local custom, social status, and the
relative supremacy of Christian or pagan tradition.

Pagan traditions themselves, moreover, were by no means
definite and unanimous in this matter. What was the Aser

religious teaching about life after death? and what the old family traditions? Many unsolved problems, indeed, turned up for the Viking. The mythology recorded by Edda and Snorre asserts that warriors who fell in battle went either to Odin's Valhalla or to Freya's fastness. To the latter also went the women who died. The criminals, outlaws, and cowards presumably all went to Hel. How much did the Vikings accept all this? It is customary among people who accept polytheism for the individual to select one god from the pantheon and entrust his fate entirely to the chosen deity. Then there was the strong family unity which had to be taken into account. The family unit was indispensable in death as well as in life. It was the family which built and preserved the last resting-place for the dead, and here the dead – burned or unburned – in a sense belonged even if they visited Valhalla or Heaven in between. Or they could be met with in the holy rock, or the holy hill, near the home farm. The dead were always near the family, and for that reason it was a family obligation always to maintain the grave or the burial mound in good order so that the departed would never feel so forsaken as to be obliged to become a vengeful ghost. If he were to become such a malignant spirit, then the only course open to the relatives was to break open his grave and kill him again. A. W. Brøgger believes that the numerous grave-breakings the archaeologists have noted may be partly explained on this principle: they were not always mere robberies. The phenomena associated with Viking burials are so complex and, indeed, contradictory, that no single explanation or theory can cover them.

Consider, for example, the ship-burials of the well-born Vikings. The king, or chieftain, after death is enthroned in his vessel. What determines the next step? Is he to be cremated? Is the ship to be burned? Should a burial chamber be constructed within the ship? The answer to such questions must evidently have been conditioned by what was considered to be the purpose of the burial. Is it to enable the departed to arrive in the beyond in his own vessel? Or is the main object to inter him in a suitable burial chamber, and to regard the ship as merely a burial present for the dead? The latter, evidently, was the purpose of putting the boat, bottom upwards, on top of the deep burial chamber of one chieftain's grave at Hedeby. On the other hand, the only known Danish ship-burial at Ladby on Fyn implies that the dead nobleman buried in it was going to sail his vessel towards the south and the sun, to Valhalla, for the ship's anchor was stowed in the bows ready to be dropped when he reached his destination. Yet a third conception of death and burial is revealed in the example of the Norwegian Oseberg ship, the bows of which were moored to the land, so that the dead was regarded as safely in harbour until some distant day of departure to another world. Of these Viking ship-graves there are, besides the ones mentioned, others at Tune and Gokstad in Norway.

The second method of interment for Nordic nobles was the burial chamber, sometimes (like the grave-ships) covered with a mound of earth, sometimes laid under a flat field. The corpses were not cremated, and were often laid in the chambers accompanied by their horses, dogs, weapons, and tools.

The common Danish and (partly) Norwegian type of grave for the ordinary Viking is the simple one in which the warrior is buried unburned with his weapons, and the woman with her jewellery. Corresponding to them in Sweden and Norway are cremation graves with or without a boat and with or without a low barrow; symbolic stone figures (boat-shaped or oval or triangular) in the surface over the graves are very common. One interesting variant, from the Fyrkat camp in Jutland, is that of a woman lying in the body of a carriage inside the earthen grave: a ritual which seems to suggest that she was conceived as riding in death to her final destination.

Major Burial Places

Three major burial places have been located in the Nordic countries: at Birka, Hedeby, and Lindholm. At Birka in eastern Sweden about 2,500 graves have been identified, and a thousand or so of these were examined by the archaeologist Stolpe between 1870 and 1880. The graves reveal a wide variety: there are unburned burials and cremation graves as well, some evidently of rich men and some of poor. In the large burial chambers where the dead were not cremated the corpses are usually men, and they were laid their with their weapons, riding-gear, food and drink, horse and dog – and sometimes with a woman as well, a wife or a serf. The greatest living specialist on Birka, Holger Arbman, has noted a peculiar burial chamber in which lay two women, one richly attired and the other lying in a twisted position. He infers that the dead mistress was buried with a live serf who died of suffocation in the burial chamber, and he cites Ibn Rustah's evidence, to be quoted presently. Most of the women in Birka, with this exception, were buried in simple wooden coffins. There are many cremation graves at Birka, and these often reveal that a boat was put into the grave of the cremated man as a burial present. Christian influence is also extensive at Birka, evidenced partly by the absence of funerary presents in the graves, and partly by the presence in the graves of small crosses corresponding to the pagan hammers of Thor. With that tolerance which seems so characteristic of the Vikings the Christian cross and the hammer of Thor are not infrequently found in the same grave, as though these ancient people wished to secure the favour of both gods, disregarding the rivalry between them.

At Hedeby, in south Slesvig, the graves are mainly found inside the city wall, not outside as at Birka. There were two cemeteries, both in the south-west part of the city. The more northerly of these contained a large number of wooden coffins lying east and west; the southerly cemetery, on the other hand, contained rather few graves, all of them burial chambers. There were no signs of cremation at either, and both contained men's bodies and women's. In the coffin cemetery there were no grave presents with most of the bodies, but some of the men had their weapons with them and quite a lot of the women were buried with their possessions. The burial chambers were more richly furnished: the men sometimes with shields, spears, a wooden bucket or a bronze bowl, and the only woman there with her ornaments, knives, and keys. The coffin cemetery at Hedeby, which dates from the early ninth to the mid eleventh century, contains about 3,000 graves, of which 350 have been examined. It was the main burial place of the town. The other cemetery was small (only 10 graves examined). It dates from c. 900 and was probably established by the Swedish conquerors of the city; its graves bear a close relation to the chamber graves at Birka, although they are not so richly furnished.

Christian influence is difficult to observe in the Hedeby graves; even in the coffin cemetery the oldest graves (which face east-west) are thought to be older than the first arrival of Christianity in south Slesvig. Moreover, unburnt burials and scanty grave presents are phenomena which already occurred in Denmark in the eighth century, long before the advent of Christianity in the north.

The third large Viking cemetery is at Lindholm Høje in north Jutland, north-west of Aalborg's sister-town of Nørresundby. Here on a large hill partly covered with shifting sand have been found (a) a settlement dating from 400 to 800; (b) a burial place, south of the settlement, partly covered by the sand, and dating from between 750 and 1000; (c) a village, dating from 1000 to 1100, built partly on top of the sand-buried cemetery. Archaeologists have excavated large areas of the cemetery and found there nearly 700 graves, most of them cremation graves. The leader of this dig, Th. Ramskou, describes the cemetery thus:

The cremation graves are all alike, whether surrounded by stones or not. The burning of the bodies had evidently not taken place in the actual graveyard, but elsewhere, and the funeral presents – such as ornaments, glass beads, knives, spindles, whetstones, wooden boxes, men for playing boards, a dog, a sheep, and (more rarely) a horse or a cow – had been burned with the bodies. The debris from the funeral pyre was taken to the cemetery, spread on the ground at an area about a yard wide (a 'cremation spot'), and covered with a thin layer of earth. A sacrificial vessel might be placed on top of this cremation grave.

Many of these graves were surrounded by stone fences of various shapes – oval, round, square, or triangular. Most interesting of these are the pointed oval shapes, the so-called 'ship shapes'. The notion behind this was evidently to provide the dead with a symbolic vessel, a representation of the ship instead of the ship itself, too precious to be spared from practical use. For this reason it seems unlikely that a real ship was burned on the funeral pyre. Ramskou has concluded, from his examinations of the Lindholm graves, that these stone-fenced graves were treated with scant piety by the community, and that the stones were usually removed to be used for another burial. It was only at the burial that these symbolic stones assumed any significance; once their symbolic purpose was served, and the spirit of the dead had begun its journey, the stones were of no further importance. A considerable number of ordinary unburned burials has also been found at Lindholm. Seldom are weapons found within them (or in the cremation graves), and there is no sign of Christian influence. One interesting feature of this site is that the eleventh-century village partly built on top of the graveyard had contained rectangular as well as elliptical houses, as at Trelleborg; more important still, it disclosed, for the first time in the history of Danish village-building, an example of the four-winged farm. Finally, at Lindholm, an unusual field-system was excavated resembling parallel rows of long beds separated by deep furrows.

Last, but not least, there are the Viking graves at Jelling, in south Jutland. In the tenth century this was the seat of the powerful Danish dynasty from which came Gorm and Harald Bluetooth, Sven Forkbeard, and Knud the Great. In Jelling there is a whole complex of archaeological monuments: (a) two large earth mounds; (b) two runic stones, one raised by the pagan Gorm for his queen Tyre, and one set up by the Christian Harald for his parents, Gorm and Tyre; (c) the remains of two wooden buildings beneath the choir of the present Romanesque church, one of them probably Harald's church and beneath it Gorm's heathen temple; (d) remains of a large triangular enclosure of erect stones (*bautas*), a *vi* or sanctuary. Excavation of the two earth mounds has revealed, in the northern one, a large wooden double burial chamber which had been broken into and pillaged of almost everything, including the skeletons. The southern one was found to be a cenotaph, i.e. a memorial without a grave, which, however, contained a curious symbolic pattern of frail branches, and on top of which were the remains of what seems to have been a watch-tower. This mound overlapped the southern end of the above-mentioned *vi* or sanctuary.

The chronological order of these Jelling remains and of the events connected with them can be assigned with some confidence. First came Gorm's *vi*, and associated with it the northern mound, the heathen temple, and the runic stone set up to Queen Tyre. The next stratum, so to speak, is Harald Bluetooth's contribution including the introduction of Christianity and the demolition of heathen memorials: his stave church is built on the site of the heathen temple, a new mound (the southern one) is built on top of the demolished pagan *vi*; the remains of Gorm and Tyre are taken from the northern grave-chamber to the Christian church (*translatio*), and

Harald's great Christian runic stone is erected to his parents between the two mounds. The third transformation at the site is the building of the now standing Romanesque stone church, so constructed that the square choir stands on the spot formerly occupied by the temple and thereafter by the stave church. We owe this disentanglement to the Danish archaeologist Ejnar Dyggve, who discovered among other things the triangular *vi*, examples of which he has also found elsewhere in Denmark. Certain obscurities, however, about this Jelling site remain. Why, for example, did the Christian king Harald build such a heathen memorial as a mound (the southern one), and whom does it commemorate? Another puzzle is the symbolic pattern of branches inside both mounds. Cenotaphs are not unknown in the Viking period: there is for example, in Norway, the greatest mound known in that country, called the Raknehaug, which also proved to contain no grave. Jelling has Denmark's greatest burial monument from Viking times. And King Harald's runic stone is memorable for the last words of the inscription – 'and made the Danes Christians': this is – as has been said – the Kingdom's certificate of baptism.

Graves Outside Scandinavia

It is reasonable to ask whether Viking graves have been found outside the northern countries. They have: in Russia, where large burial places have been excavated; and in western Europe where Norwegian investigations, led by Haakon Shetelig, were conducted thirty years ago in various museums which might provide at least provisional evidence. In Scotland and the Scottish islands thirty Norwegian Viking graves were found, none of them cremation graves, and most of them women's. Among these thirty a couple were boat-graves. The Hebrides and the Orkneys furnished about the same number of this kind, again mostly women's. One boat-burial had been found in the Orkneys. The Shetlands produced a couple of women's graves, neither of them cremations. In Ireland the main location of Viking graves is on a large destroyed site near Dublin (Kilmainham and Islandbridge). Here have been found 40 swords, 35 spearheads, 25 shield-buckles, a few axes and arrow-heads, and such women's articles as ornaments, spindles, and keys. Other finds in Dublin produced 8 swords, 7 spearheads, and a few shield-buckles and arrow-heads. At localities outside Dublin two men's graves and two women's have been found – all of them without a trace of cremation. The Isle of Man has produced 10 non-cremation graves, all of men; England 13 similar graves, and 3 of women.

On the western European continent only a few graves are known: a man's (unburnt) at Groningen in Holland; a women's (unburnt) at Pitres, in Normandy; and a cremated ship-burial in the Cruguel mound on the Île de Croix off southern Brittany, opposite Lorient. This is the only known Viking cremation grave in western Europe. The race and sex of those who were buried in these graves can be determined by the debris discovered in the graves: they were Nordic, people – not Scottish, Irish, Anglo-Saxon, or Frankish. It is not possible, however, to differentiate in the same way between Norwegian, Danish, and Swedish graves abroad, because the weapons, tools, and ornaments are so much alike. To a certain degree, however, the nationality can be determined according to the known spheres of interest of the Viking countries: thus the Viking graves in Scotland, Ireland, the Isle of Man, and north-west England are likely to be Norwegian; those in the Danelaw and in eastern and southern England, Danish; those in northern England and France either Norwegian or Danish. This does not exclude the possibility that some of the graves may have been Swedish: but proof is impossible.

In eastern Europe it can similarly be assumed that Viking graves are predominantly Swedish. In contrast to the west, the Viking graves in Russia usually show signs of cremation.

To the south and south-east of Ladoga are several large mounds (of the 'Volkhov' type) covering cremation graves, and besides these there are hundreds of smaller mounds ('Finnish' type) some containing unburned graves and others cremation graves. Most of these belong no doubt to Swedish Vikings. Farther south in Russia, at Yaroslav, north-east of Moscow, there are two large mound-cemeteries containing graves of both types, the contents of which have strong Nordic characteristics. In the province of Vladimir, east of Moscow, there are very large cemeteries also, but here the Nordic elements in the graves are much less specific and indicate no more than a modest Swedish influence upon a Slav environment. Novgorod, in western Russia, seems to have been essentially a Slav town, and there are few Nordic finds there; but the situation is different farther south at Smolensk, Chernigov, and Kiev. West of Smolensk, at Gnezdovo, is Russia's largest prehistoric burial-place, containing over 3,000 mounds. Several hundred of these were examined by Russian archaeologists between 1870 and 1880, and a further forty in 1949. These investigations showed that cremation was the most frequent burial custom, and that the objects buried with the dead vary a great deal in quantity. The Russian scholar Ardusin regards this burial place as partly, maybe mainly, Slavic, but with numerous Swedish elements. The Swedish archaeologist, Holger Arbman, on the other hand, deduces from the fact that most of the contents of the graves are Swedish that it was the tenth-century cemetery of a large Swedish colony of warriors and merchants. His verdict seems the right one; and the presence of Slav elements is not surprising in a colony set in the middle of Slav territory.

In and around Shernigov, north-east of Kiev, are many more mounds. The largest, about 30 ft by 120 ft, called 'Chernaja Mogila', was excavated in the 1870s and proved to contain in its centre an unburned wooden burial-house, in which were the skeletons of two men and a woman, surrounded by a quantity of objects, some Swedish (including a sword) but mainly Slav and Persian. The clothes, too, and a conical iron helmet, were Slav. Another large mound on this site, dated to the tenth century, proved to contain a similar unburned burial. Such graves as these may very well have been made for Swedish noblemen who had become partly assimilated with their Slav environment, for the clothing (as Arbman points out) bears a close resemblance to that described below by Ibn Fadlan as being used in the burial of a certain chieftain, who was Swedish. The Swedish Rus folk, then, appear to have become more and more influenced by Slav dress and equipment the farther south they went. Finally a number of tenth- and eleventh-century graves, men's and women's, have come to light at Kiev, mostly unburned burials, and again indicating in the funeral objects a degree of assimilation between Swede and Slav.

In Poland, too, there are some traces of Slav-influenced, Swedish Vikings. Near Lodz, at Lutomiersk, under a Jewish cemetery, were found 125 graves, mainly unburned, and consisting as a rule of deep wooden chambers, some of them containing rich funeral objects (such as riding gear) of mixed Scandinavian Slav and Dnieper-Swedish origin. As a rule this furniture dates from the early past of the eleventh century.

What the archaeologists have found out about the Nordic graves and burial customs in eastern Europe reinforces our general impression of the Vikings' shifting and loose beliefs about death and the after-life. Literary sources from the same region also exist. There is a contemporary eye-witness account of a Swedish ship-funeral, by burning, which took place on the river Volga in 922. The narrator is, again, the Arab diplomatic courier, Ibn Fadlan, and his famous account goes thus:

I was always told that when their chiefs died cremation was the least part of what they undertook and I was, therefore, very much interested to find out more about this. One day I heard that one of their great men had died. They laid him forthwith in a grave which they covered up for ten days till they had finished cutting out and sewing his costume. If the dead man is poor they make a little ship, put him in it, and conduct a cremation. But if he is wealthy they split his property and goods into three parts: one for his family, one to pay for his costume, and one to make *nabid* (probably a Nordic beer) which they drink on the day when the slave woman of the dead man kills herself and is burned together with her lord. They are deeply addicted to *nabid*, drinking it night and day. Often one of them has died with a beaker in his hand. When a chief among them had died his family demands of his slave women and servants: 'Which of you wishes to die with him?' Then one of them says: 'I do' and having said that the person concerned is forced to do so and no drawing back is possible. Even if he wished to he would not be allowed to. Those who are willing are mostly the slave women.

So when this man died they said to his slave women 'Which of you wants to die with him?' One of them answered, 'I do.' From that moment she was put in the constant care of two other women servants who took care of her even to the extent of washing her feet with their own hands. Then they began to get things ready for the dead man, to cut his costume and so on, while every day the doomed woman drank and sang as though in anticipation of a joyous event.

When the day arrived on which he and his slave woman were going to be burnt, I went to the river where his ship lay. It had been dragged ashore and four posts were made for it of birch and other wood. Furthermore there was arranged around it what resembled a big store of wood. Then the ship was dragged near and laid on the wood. And people began to walk about talking in a language I could not understand, and the corpse still lay in the grave, they had not taken it away. They then produced a wooden bench, placed it on the ship, and covered it with carpets of Byzantine dibag (painted silk) and with cushions of Byzantine dibag. Then came an old woman whom they call 'the Angel of Death', and spread the said cushions out over the bench. She was in charge of the whole business of dressing the corpse, and her function included that of killing the slave woman. I saw that she was an old giant-woman, a massive and grim figure. When they came to his grave they removed the earth from the wooden frame and they also took the frame away. Then they divested the corpse of the clothes in which he had died. The body, I noticed, had turned black because of the intense frost. When they had first put him in the grave, they had furnished him with beer, fruit, and a lute, all of which they now removed. Strangely enough the corpse did not smell, nor had anything about him changed save the colour of his flesh. They now dressed him in hose, and trousers, boots, coat, and mantle of dibag adorned with gold buttons, put on his head a hood of dibag and sable fur, and carried him to the tent on to the ship where they put him on the carpet and supported him with the cushions. Then they produced *nabid*, fruit, and aromatic plants and put these around the body; and they also brought bread, meat, and onions which they flung before him. Next they took a dog, cut it in half, and flung the pieces into the ship, and after this they took all his weapons and placed them beside him. Next they brought two horses and ran them about until they were in a sweat, after which they cut them to pieces with swords and flung their meat into the ship. They took two cows as well. These also they cut into pieces and threw them into the ship. Then they produced a cock and a hen, killed them, and threw them in. Meanwhile the slave woman who wished to be killed walked up and down, going into one tent after the other, and the owner of each tent had sexual intercourse with her, saying: 'Tell your master: I did this out of love for him.'

On the Friday afternoon they took the slave woman away to something which they had made resembling a door-frame. Then she placed her legs on the palms of the men and reached high enough to overlook the frame, and she said something in some language. Then they took her down. And they lifted her again and she did the same as the first time. Then they took her down and lifted her a third time and she did the same as the first and the second times. Then they gave her a chicken and she cut its head off and threw it away; they took the hen and threw it into the ship. Then I asked the interpreter what she had done. He answered: 'The first time they lifted her she said: "look! I see my father and mother." The second time she said: "look! I see all my dead relatives sitting around." The third time she said: "look! I see my master sitting in Paradise, and Paradise is beautiful and green and together with him are men and young boys. He calls on me. Let me join him then!"'

They now led her towards the ship. Then she took off two bracelets she was wearing and gave them to the old woman, 'the Angel of Death', the one who was going to kill her. She next took off two anklets she was wearing and gave them to daughters of that woman known by the name 'the Angel of Death'. They then led her to the ship but did not allow her inside the tent. Then a number of men carrying wooden shields and wooden sticks arrived, and gave her a beaker with a *nabid*. She sang over it and emptied it. The interpreter then said to me: 'Now with that she is bidding farewell to all her women friends.' Then she was given another beaker. She took it and sang a lengthy song; but the old woman told her to hurry, to drink up and enter the tent where her master was. Then I regarded her and she looked completely bewildered. She wanted to enter the tent and she put her head between it and the ship. There the woman took her head and managed to get it inside the tent, and the woman herself followed. Then the men began to beat the shields with the wooden sticks, to deaden her shrieks, so that the other girls would not become afraid and shrink from dying with their masters. Six men now entered the tent and all of them had intercourse with the girl. Thereafter they laid her by the side of her dead master. Two held her hands and two her feet. And the woman called the Angel of Death put a cord round the girl's neck, the ends twisted to both sides, and gave it to two men to pull. Then she advanced holding a small dagger with a broad blade and began to plunge it between the girl's ribs to and fro while the two men choked her with the cord till she died.

The dead man's nearest kinsman now appeared. He took a piece of wood and ignited it. Then he walked backwards, his back towards the ship his face towards the crowd, holding in one hand the wooden piece while the other lay on his behind; and he was naked. In this way the wood was ignited which they had placed under the ship after they had laid the slave woman, whom they had killed, beside her master. Then people came with branches and wood; each brought a burning brand and threw it on the pyre, so that the fire took hold of the wood, then the ship, then the tent and the man and the slave woman and all. Thereafter a strong and terrible wind rose so that the flame stirred and the fire blazed still more.

I heard one of the Rus folk, standing by, say something to my interpreter, and on inquiring what he had said my interpreter answered: 'He said: "You Arabs are foolish". "Why?" I asked. – "Well, because you throw those you love and honour into the ground where the earth and the beasts and the fields devour them, whereas we on the other hand burn them up quickly and they go to Paradise that very moment." The man burst out laughing, and on being asked why, he said: "His Lord, out of love for him, has sent this wind to take him away within the hour!"' And so it proved, for within that time the ship and the pyre, the girl and the corpse had all become ashes and then dust. On the spot where the ship stood after having been dragged ashore they built something like a round mound. In the middle of that they raised a large post of birch-wood. Thereon they wrote the names of the dead man and of the king of the Rus folk. On this they broke up.

Ibn Fadlan was a sharp observer and a good narrator who gives the impression of not being addicted to wild stories. I see no reason to disbelieve his eye-witness account or the interpretations he put on what he witnessed. One significant piece of information he provides is that the Vikings built a memorial mound, a cenotaph, and inscribed runic names on wood, suitable stones evidently not being available in the vicinity. It was apparently thought right that the dead man, although in Paradise, should have a haunt on earth. Similar empty memorial mounds are known, as we have seen, in the Viking homelands also.

Some time after Ibn Fadlan, about the middle of the tenth century, another Arabic writer, Ibn Rustah, has this to say about the Rus folk: 'When one of their notables dies, they make a grave like a large house and put him inside it. With him they put his clothes and the gold armlets he wore and, moreover, an abundance of food, drinking bowls, and coins. They also put his favourite wife in with him, still alive. Then the grave-door is closed and she dies there.' This comment confirms such archaeological evidence as that mentioned above of the grave-mound at Chernigov.

THE COMING OF CHRISTIANITY

The various burial rites of the Vikings reveal how vague and imprecise were their religious beliefs. In due course those beliefs were destined to be supplanted by the clarity of the Christian faith. A religion which offers the common man vague and contradictory concepts of the after-life is not a potent one. Nor is polytheism potent or strong. The Nordic system with its many gods was doubtless tolerant of foreign influences, and if one more god was offered the Vikings, such as 'the White Christ', they saw no reason why they should not, so to speak, give him a trial along with the others. When St Olav ordered the Viking Gaukator to adopt Christianity the man philosophically replied, 'If I must believe in a god it is no worse to believe in the White Christ than any other . . .', a remark which may, however, merely mean that Gaukator was an atheist! A better example, therefore, is Helge the Lean. In the Icelandic *Landnámabók* it is said of him that 'he was very mixed in his faith; he believed in Christ, but when he was at sea and in severe trouble he called upon Thor'. The traditional Aser religion was an aristocratic one and had little to give the ordinary man by way of an after-life. And so in the end he turned to the purposeful monotheism of Christianity with its hope and help for all. So, Christianity became triumphant.

Yet this new faith did not effect a rapid conquest. When the Viking period began, around 800, the whole of the North was pagan. It took 150 years to bring Denmark to Christianity, 200 for Norway and Iceland, and more than 300 years for Sweden. Why did it take so long for the well-organized Roman Church – with its powerful missionary motive and its tactical wisdom in seeking always to convert first of all the upper ranks of society – to supplant the easy-going dynasty of the Nordic gods? The answer probably is that the real

strength of the old religion resided in such traditional elements
as the fertility rites and practices. A change of gods at the
summit of society might occur easily enough; but lower down
the scale there was a natural resistance to any new religion
which sought to interfere with antique religious habits and
observances based on experience of life's needs and the whole
of existence dating back thousands of years. Any changes at
this level of society took a long time; and indeed the acceptance of Christianity in the North, as in the rest of Europe, only
began to make real progress as and when Christianity took
over old superstitions and usages and allowed them to live on
under a new guise.

Christianity in Denmark

In Denmark the development of Christianity began when,
in 823, Archbishop Ebo of Rheims was charged by the
emperor and the Pope to penetrate the heathen land of
Denmark. An effort was supported in 826 by the Jutish pretender to the throne, Harald, newly converted by the emperor
Ludwig the Holy, and by the Frankish monk Ansgar, but it
came to nothing, and both Harald and Ansgar were banished.
It was not until several years later, in 849, when Ansgar was
Archbishop of Hamburg, with his seat at Bremen, that real
progress began, in the reign of Haarik the Elder at Hedeby
and his successor, Haarik the Younger. Ansgar was permitted
to build a church at Hedeby (the remains have not yet been
found) and after a brief interlude of anti-Christian sentiment
around 854, during which the heathen Earl Hove, after
Haarik the Elder's death, closed the church, Christianity
revived and made good progress under Haarik the Younger.
Many people were baptized; many others accepted the 'first
sign' of the cross, as a temporary introduction to baptism,
and another church was built, this time at Ribe.

The kings themselves held back. Neither of the Haariks
was baptized, despite an urgent appeal from the Pope (sent

on Ansgar's initiative in 864) in such terms as: 'Desist from worshipping false gods and serving the Devil, for your gods are made with human hands and are deaf, dumb, and blind. What salvation can they bring you, they who being senseless cannot save themselves?' These exhortations were frequent. In 723 the German missionary Boniface was told by Bishop Daniel of Winchester to use the following argument in reasoning with the heathen: The old pagan gods are themselves born and created, but who created the world before they came into existence? – and the monk Hucbald (*c*. 900) used an exhortation of which the purport was: 'God has created us, not we ourselves; but the idols you revere are made of gold, silver, copper, stone, or wood; they do not truly live, nor move, nor feel, because they are made by mankind and cannot help others or themselves.'

Ansgar died in 865; and apart from the forcible conversion of the Swedish king Gnupa, at Hedeby, by German conquerors, little is heard of the progress of Christianity in Denmark for a century. But in 960 occurred the episode – recounted by a contemporary, the Saxon Widukind – of the priest Poppo whose gallant bearing converted Harald Bluetooth to Christianity. The Danes admitted, says Widukind, that Christ was a god, but asserted that other gods were greater, their signs and wonders mightier. No, said Poppo; God the Father, the Son, and the Holy Ghost were the one God: the rest were merely idols. King Harald ('keen to listen but slow to utter') asked Poppo if he would subject this bold assertion to God's own judgement. Poppo immediately agreed, and next day the king had a bar of iron made red-hot and told Poppo to hold it as a token of his faith. Poppo took the glowing bar and carried it about as long a time as the king wanted, whereafter he showed his undamaged hand and convinced all the bystanders. The king was converted and determined from now on to acknowledge Christ as his only god. The large Jelling runic stone bears an inscription which shows that Harald regarded himself as responsible for introducing Christianity into Denmark. His son, Sven Forkbeard, conqueror of England, proved an indifferent Christian, but Sven's son, Knud the Great, was ardent in the new faith. By the eleventh century Christianity had taken firm root in Denmark, and King Sven Estridson (1047–76) devoted his long reign to trying to liberate the young Danish church from the domination of the German bishopric at Bremen, an accomplishment which did not, in fact, occur until later. In general it may be asserted that Christianity was established in Denmark with effective assistance from the monarchy but not by royal compulsion.

Christianity in Norway

In Norway the first Christian king was Haakon the Good, son of Harald Fairhair. He died in 960 about the same time as Poppo achieved his spectacular miracle. But Haakon's conversion by no means implied Norway's adherence to the faith. He had been educated by the Anglo-Saxon king Athelstan, and he brought the new religion to Norway from England. The people protested and rejected Haakon's missionaries, and the king was unable to persuade his people to adopt the new message. When he died, indeed, he was given a heathen funeral. His successor, his nephew Harald Graafeld, laboured diligently (according to Snorre) for Christianity, but without notable effect, and Norway's next great monarch, Haakon of Lade (975–95) was a convinced heathen and a devotee of Thor. Norway's conversion was brought about finally by the two Olavs, Olav Tryggvason (995–1000) and St Olav (1014–30), whose persuasive efforts were violent and cruel. It is characteristic that Olav Tryggvason, before the battle of Svold (where he met his death), wanting to abuse the Swedes, derided their heathen condition and advised them to stay at home and lick their sacrificial bowls! In the fifteen years after his death, when western Norway had been converted to

Christianity by his terrorist methods, the rulers were Haakon of Lade's two sons, Erik and Sven. Both were Christians, but they were tolerant enough to allow others to go their own heathen way. It was not until St Olav assumed power that toleration vanished. Under his hard hand the whole of Norway was christianized and Olav became the Saint that the young Norwegian church so earnestly desired.

In Iceland christianization was rapid. Missionary activity began seriously in 981, with Thorvald Vidførle and the German Bishop Frederik, and in the year 1000 the Alting made Christianity the legal faith of the country.

Christianity in Sweden

In Sweden Ansgar led the first Christian mission to Birka in 829 after a perilous journey in which he was nearly killed by pirates. He was well received by King Bjørn at Birka, and permitted to build a church there. After he had worked two years there, during which period the young Swedish church was incorporated into the Roman ecclesiastical system, he became Bishop of Hamburg, with rights of jurisdiction over the Birka community. Such rights, however, were nothing but formalities; the Birka 'church' was weak and no serious impact was made, not even when Ansgar revisited the place in the middle of the century. The pagan religion remained intact. Later on, in the 930s, a further mission was sent, again from Hamburg, under Archbishop Anni, but this, also, was only an interlude. Thus in the middle of the eleventh century, when Denmark and Norway had gradually accepted Christianity, Sweden was still a completely heathen country. The battle to christianize Sweden now developed in earnest, and during the next hundred years its many Christian neighbours made strenuous efforts to make Sweden Christian. One of these neighbours was the north German Church at Hamburg and Bremen; another was the English Church; and similar influences were applied from Norway, Denmark,

France, and even from the Eastern Orthodox Church in Russia. Swedish paganism, however, proved a powerful enemy, and the battle swayed back and forth during the eleventh century. Adam of Bremen, in the 1070s, painted a gloomy picture of persistent paganism. The great heathen temple at Uppsala, described by him, was still the citadel of the traditional Nordic religion and indeed a base from which strong counter-attacks were launched upon Christianity. Yet several Swedish kings supported the Christians: Olav Skotking, Anund Jacob, Emund, Stenkil, and under the first of these a bishopric was established from Hamburg-Bremen at Skara in Västergötland. Christian inscriptions on runic stones reveal the slow penetration of Christianity, and in 1060 a special drive was planned by two bishops – Egino of Skaane and Adalward the Younger of Sigtuna – including the proposal to demolish by force the heathen temple at Uppsala. King Stenkil sympathized, but would not permit this forcible evangelism, and when he died in 1066 the heathens retaliated by driving out the bishop of Sigtuna. The bishopric of Skara was vacant, and heathenism remained strongly entrenched not only in Uppland but also in Götaland and Småland. By the end of the century we hear of the banishment of the Christian king Inge and the domination of the pagan Blót-Sven – although this position was subsequently reversed. Conditions in Sweden at the beginning of the twelfth century were described by the Anglo-Danish monk, Aelnoth of Canterbury, in these words: 'As long as things go luckily and well Svear and Göter seem willing to honour Christianity. A pure formality; for when things go wrong – bad harvests, drought, tempests, and heavy weather, enemy attacks or outbreaks of fire – they persecute the worship which they seem nominally to honour, and they do this not only in words but also in deeds; then they revenge themselves on the Christians and seek to chase them completely out of their country.'

This picture characterizes the closing chapter of the religious war in Sweden. The temple of Uppsala probably disappeared early in the twelfth century. At the same time the Swedish Christian church came under the authority of the Danish archbishop of Lund, in Skaane, and thus passed from the control of the German bishops. It is surprising that christianization took so long, for it was a foregone conclusion that the dynamic and purposeful monotheism from the south would prevail over the stagnant polytheism of the north. Yet the long time it took to prevail serves to remind us not to minimize the power of this ancient polytheism which remained capable of, at least, sporadic recovery and reassertion. There is much weight in the conclusion some scholars emphasize – namely, that it would be relatively easy for Christianity to prevail over Nordic religious beliefs; but far more difficult to overcome the complex culture beneath that religion, a culture so rooted in ancient magic; and even more difficult to substitute an ethical formula about loving your neighbours for the Nordic concepts of honour and family.

CHAPTER 15

POETRY AND THE VIKING SPIRIT

THE Vikings had their ideas of the perfect man. There is one such picture provided in the *Rigsthula*: the young Viking chief in all his glory, the blond earl with the flashing eyes, the fearless rider and hunter, skilled with all warlike weapons, the leader who wins men and conquers land and whose sons become kings. This fiction of a didactic poem is perhaps a little cheap and flashy. A better impression of Viking ideals is to be found among the stories told in the sagas, as well as among the actual figures of Viking history. Some of these figures have their roots in Nordic soil, some in south Germanic, but whatever their origin they were real and vital figures in the Viking imagination. Such figures were Bjarke and Hjalte, faithful unto death by the side of their slain king, Rolf; Starkad, the ruthless scourge of timidity; the wise Hamlet; the shrewd Ragnar Lodbrog; the proud and fated lovers Hagbard-Signe and Helge Hundingsbane-Sigrun whose loves endure beyond death. There is, again, the great tragic *Volsung* poem which narrates the fatal triangle of relationships between Sigurd, Brynhild, and Gudrun. How powerfully this Sigurd Fafnesbane caught the Nordic imagination is shown by the many representations of this saga-cycle, depicted in stone and wood, which have been found in Sweden, Norway, and the Isle of Man. And let us not forget among the heroes Vølund the Great Avenger. From Nordic history itself there can be no doubt that Knud the Great, Olav Tryggvason, St Olav, Harald Hardrade, and others were in their day invested with all the glory of popular heroes. These, then, are the figures, whether of legend or history, which display those attributes the Vikings most revered and sought to emulate – courage, bravery, daring, abandonment to love, contempt for death, munificence, strength of mind, fidelity; and, on the other side of the balance, ruthlessness, vengeance, derision, hate, and cunning. These are the ingredients by which the Icelandic sagas of the Middle Ages with their great traditions recreate the heroes of the vanished Viking times.

The Norwegian and Icelandic skaldic poetry is a complex and elaborate literary form, equipped with alliterations and with internal rhyme within the verse-line. It is full of verbal stratagems, too, of deliberate circumlocutions, and governed by stringent rules of prosody. Minstrelsy was a difficult art, but one profoundly appreciated by the men of the North. They loved the riddles concealed within the circumlocutions, especially when these were not merely an ingenious play on words but enshrined some wise motto of experience; and they relished fine, flamboyant epithets. Here are a few examples. The earliest known Norwegian bard, the ninth-century Brage the Old, describes the row of shields on the sides of the long-ships as 'leaves on the trees in the sea-king's field'. Battle scenes are embellished with such phrases as 'Odin's roaring storm', 'the Valkyr's magic song', and 'the shout of the spear'. The ship is called 'the steed of the waves', the sword 'the battle-storm's fish', the arrow 'the wounding bee'. The greatest of all known Norse bards, the Icelander Egil Skalla-grimson, calls the surf along Norway's rocky coast 'the island-studded belt round Norway', and to describe how his friends inside this belt gave him silver bracelets he employs such flowery images as 'they let the snow of the crucible [that is, the silver] fall upon the hawk's high mountain [his arm].'

In late Viking times, it appears, nearly all the bards were Icelanders. The last considerable Norwegian skald is Eyvind Skaldaspiller, whereas the later bards are Icelandic – the love-poet Kormak, and St Olav's two minstrels, Sigvat and

Tormod. The latter was the man who coined the *bon mot* as he plucked an arrow from his heart at the battle of Stiklestad. Egil Skallagrimson has an impeccable technique, and a wide range of feeling capable of expressing passion, terror, vengeance, and happiness; after the death of his sons he wrote the poem, 'The Loss of the Sons' in which initial hate and bitterness is compounded with a final calm and equanimity.

It is a tempting though dangerous exercise to compare Viking poetry with Viking decorative art. The unnaturalistic animal ornamentation of the early period, around 800, was superseded (a) in the ninth century by a naturalistic animal style ('the gripping beast'), (b) in the tenth by the Jelling ribbon-pattern, and (c) in the eleventh by the 'large animal' motive. What correspondence can be found with Viking poetry from the ninth to the eleventh centuries? The Norwegian scholar, Hallvard Lie, has attempted to trace a comparable development of metrical style, but the establishment of such parallels seems to me extremely difficult.

The greatest Icelandic poem to survive is the *Völuspá* – Volve's Prophecy: a cosmic view of the world and its final end, written with great prophetic force and compassion. The Aser gods are represented as deities above whom there is a greater power. The middle part of the poem describes Ragnarok, the end of the world, in a series of visions or revelations. All is consumed by fire, but when the fires are burnt out a new sun will dawn and life will be renewed. Volve's Prophecy proves that the religion based on the Aser gods had lost its spiritual potency. The poem is looking to a religious change and it discloses the conviction that, when Ragnarok is over, there will be one God, *the* Mighty. Is this to be taken as foretelling – in a whisper – the coming Christian god? Manifestly, the creator of *Völuspá* was a profound seer and a great poet.

The Viking spirit, however, involves more than the inspired

expression of poets, and to understand its full meaning we must now come down from poetic heights and see how that spirit was expressed in the everyday habit and behaviour of the Vikings. We might look again, for instance, at a poem mentioned earlier called the *Hávamál*, i.e. 'High Odin's Words', though Odin, truth to tell, is not so very high! The poem deals with ordinary people in their ordinary context. We are not heroes or princes, all of us. It gives us valuable clues to Viking conduct on the daily level. Here the accent is not upon legendary valour but on common sense; not upon princely generosity but on economic housekeeping; not on romantic passion but on abstinence and respect for the neighbour's wife. The *Hávamál* is cool and sober – a primer of practical behaviour.

From that great part of Norwegian–Icelandic literature which presumably gives a true reflection of Viking life scholars have tried to depict the Nordic Viking's own view of human existence, of the conditions of man and his surroundings. The Danish scholar Vilhelm Grønbech emphasizes, from these sources, two outstanding characteristics of the Viking: first, his concern for honour, his own and his family's; and his belief in luck in a man's life and undertakings. The Viking took nothing more seriously than his family. It is a continuing institution, even though the individuals within it die off. It is the man's master, it can do without him, but not he without it. The members of it are bound to assist and, if need be, avenge each other, and the honour of the family is supreme. If a man commits a crime which involves expulsion from the family he has condemned himself to the worst of fates: to be an outcast; for no man can be an entity to himself, he is part of the fabric of a family. To belong to a family of high degree is a rare blessing, but to belong to some family is a human necessity. Not to belong is to be the lowest of the species, the serf, the man who can scarcely be said to have a soul.

If a man had luck his honour would flourish the better: honour signifying not fame or fortune but, rather, esteem and security. In all things the honour of the individual was that of the family also; hence the importance of collective revenge for an injury done to one member of a family. The vengeance could mean either a killing or the performance of a penance by the guilty party. If penance had to be exacted it was important to strike a balance: the penance must not be so severe as to inflict shame upon the family of whom it was required, nor, on the other hand, so slight as to make the injured family feel aggrieved. Abundant diplomatic skill was needed to strike a balance of this sort, and the resort to such pledges as that, had the case been reversed, the parties would still find the proposed penance equitable. This fundamental principle of family responsibility and family obligation must have engendered a stubborn trait in the Viking character, as well as a check upon any individuals' disposition to forgive an affront or a wrong. For there was no escape from the family.

The Viking maintained his status in the community not only by his acceptance of the family tie but also by acquiring a wide circle of friends. The *Hávamál* ceaselessly praises the virtues of friendship. Loneliness was a dire fate, but to move among one's friends and receive their praise for one's actions was indeed a blessing. Acclaim was to the Viking like rain upon a parched meadow. When a bard sang the praises of an earl, everyone heard it, and when the earl rewarded him with the gold ring, everyone saw it: mutual appreciation! Both were delighted – the earl by the fame of his deeds, the skald by the celebrity of his bardship. When Egil's furrowed brow was cleared by the gift of a gold ring at the English court, it was not only the gold which pleased him but the public recognition of his bardic prowess. This kind of thing, however, had a reverse side: it led to an exaggerated dependence on what people said about one, and also to an excessive regard for satirical comment. The Viking was desperately sensitive to satire, derision, and malicious gossip: afraid for himself yet ready to inflict these barbs upon others; keen to discover the faults of others, to listen to cutting sarcasm. He was vulnerable to the malice he liked to bestow.

The Vikings were complex people. Their roots lay in an ancient, non-feudal tradition of freedom, and for a long time they had been cut off in their remote Northern lands from contacts with the rest of Europe. They were self-conscious and naturally intelligent; more responsive to an opportunity for quick action than for long-term perseverance; and endowed with a passion for daring ventures. The impact of the Vikings, then, was widespread but not deep nor lasting. No doubt, they brought new impulses and ferments to Europe, but they effected no fundamental political transformations there. Finally, they were a people of marked artistic talent. Of that they have left ample evidence in the discoveries of archaeology and in the great treasures of Icelandic literature.

EPILOGUE

THE Viking raids were not migrations. Although they have been described as such, and even vaguely associated with the great European migrations of the fifth century, these Nordic raids were not movements of people under pressure. That is just the point. During the entire period between 800 and 1100 there was no pressure which could have created a migration; this element was not present in the voyages from Denmark to England and Normandy, from Norway to Scotland and Ireland, from Sweden to Russia. The political impact which sent Norwegians to Iceland was purely local and partial. In short, the causes of the Viking raids were entirely different from those which accounted for the movements in fifth-century Europe, and there is no connexion between these two historical phenomena.

It is one thing for Scandinavia to call the period between 800 and 1100 a period or epoch of history, but how are these words justified in the perspective of European history? Scandinavia is a small part of the continent: have the Viking raids and feats of colonization an importance which can entitle them to be regarded as an epoch in Europe's history?

In western Europe the Vikings exerted at least some lasting influence. England was invaded from the continent on several occasions between 500 B.C. and A.D. 1100: by Celts, Romans, Anglo-Saxons, Danes, Normans; and these invasions produced the racial amalgam of which the English people were created. Two of the five invasions occurred in the time of the Vikings: the fourth was a directly Nordic one, the fifth was indirectly Nordic, and both were of substantial dimensions. This influence upon England is indeed a matter of European significance. In the east, the results of the Viking impact upon Russia cannot be regarded as so vital or permanent, because the proportion of the Viking newcomers to the native inhabitants was far less than in the west. Yet the Swedish infiltration was a not unimportant episode in the history of Russia. Upon central

Europe, evidently, there was no Viking impact, mainly for mercantile reasons. The Viking continental trade routes lay to the east, over Russia's immense plains and along her wide rivers, directly to the Byzantine and Arab markets; there were no impassable Alps to face, no powerful empires to cross. In the history of central Europe the phrase 'Viking period' has no meaning. Nor was southern Europe any more affected by the Vikings, although some of the small Normannic south Italian states reached some importance, after Viking times, during the Crusades; but their relationship with the Vikings is a trivial one. Although Byzantines and Arabs encountered the presence and influence of the Vikings it cannot finally be maintained that the Volgar trade of the Rus folk or the Nordic bodyguard of the Byzantine emperor could claim the name of a period within the history of those two great empires. As an epoch in European history, therefore, the 'Viking period' can only be taken in a limited sense and in a variable degree. It is a term which, on balance, must mean more to Scandinavians than to Europeans.

What did the Vikings give Europe? What did they get from Europe? To begin with they dealt out the *dona Danaorum*: destruction, rape, plunder, and murder; and later they expended their energy and blood on colonization. Otherwise, the Vikings could teach Europe nothing. On the other hand they derived much from Europe, although it took a long time for them to do so. It took them 300 years – strange to say – to learn to build in stone and brick instead of wood and clay. It took 300 years, too, for the new religion to penetrate all three Nordic countries. But when at last these transformations were complete – the material and the spiritual ones – there began in Denmark, in the twelfth century, a remarkable period of church building during which the new technique and the new faith worked together. And similar Christian impulses went to Norway and Sweden. When at last the Viking age faded into history, the Vikings had received from Europe more than they had given, and the North that they left after them, animated by these European influences, had not been weakened; but it had been changed by being led into a new cultural life.

SELECT BIBLIOGRAPHY

CHAPTER 1

A. DOPSCH. *Wirtschaftliche und soziale Grundlagen der europäischen Kulturentwicklung aus der Zeit von Cäsar bis auf Karl den Grossen,* I and II. Vienna, 1923–4.

H. PIRENNE. *Mahomet et Charlemagne.* Brussels, 1935. German translation: *Geburt des Abendlandes.* Leipzig, 1939.

H. PIRENNE. 'Un contraste économique: Mérovingiens et Carolingiens.' *Revue belge de philologue et d'historie,* 1922–3.

W. VOGEL. *Die Normannen und das fränkische Reich bis zur Gründung der Normandie.* Heidelberg, 1906.

R. H. HODGKIN. *A History of the Anglo-Saxons,* II. Oxford, 1939.

B. NERMAN. *Grobin-Seeburg, Ausgrabungen und Funde.* Uppsala, 1958.

JOHANNES STEENSTRUP. *Normannerne,* I. Copenhagen, 1876. pp. 218 ff.

CHAPTER 2

JOHANNES STEENSTRUP. *Normannerne,* I–IV. Copenhagen, 1876–82.

A. BUGGE. *Vikingerne,* I and II. Christiania [Oslo], 1904–6.

E. WADSTEIN. *Norden och Västeuropa i gammal tid.* Göteborg, 1925.

T. D. KENDRICK. *A History of the Vikings.* London, 1930.

FRITZ ASKEBERG. *Norden och kontinenten i gammal tid.* Uppsala, 1944. (See espec. about the word 'Viking', pp. 115 ff.)

H. ARBMAN & M. STENBERGER. *Vikingar i Västerled.* Stockholm, 1935.

H. ARBMAN. *Svear i Österviking.* Stockholm, 1955.

H. SWEET. 'King Alfred's Orosius.' *Early English Text Society,* 1883.

ALEXANDER SEIPPEL. *Rerum Normannicarum fontes Arabici.* Oslo, I: 1876; II: 1928.

G. JACOB. 'Arabische Berichte von Gesandten an germanische Fürstenhöfe aus dem 9. und 10. Jahrhundert.' *Quellen zur deutschen Volkskunde,* I. Berlin–Leipzig, 1927.

H. BIRKELAND. 'Nordens historie i middelalderen efter arabiske kilder.' *Norske Videnskaps-Akademis skrifter.* Oslo, 1954.

A. ZEKI VALIDI TOGAN. 'Ibn Fadlān's Reisebericht.' *Abhandlungen für die Kunde des Morgenlandes*, Vol. XXIV 3. Leipzig, 1939.

ADAM BREMENSIS, magister. *Gesta Hammaburgensis ecclesiae pontificum.* ed. H. B. Schmeidler. Hanover-Leipzig, 1917.

CHAPTERS 3 and 5

J. H. HOLWERDA. *Dorestad en onze vroegste middeleeuwen.* Leiden, 1929.

F. M. STENTON. *Anglo-Saxon England.* Oxford, 1947.

VILHELM THOMSEN. *The Relations between Ancient Russia and Scandinavia and the Origin of the Russian State.* Oxford, 1877. Revised edition in Danish in the author's *Samlede Skrifter* I. Copenhagen, 1919.

W. J. RAUDONIKAS. *Die Normannen der Wikingerzeit und das Ladogagebiet.* Stockholm, 1930.

H. PASZKIEWICZ. *The Origin of Russia.* London, 1954.

A. STENDER-PETERSEN. *Varangica.* Aarhus, 1953.

A. STENDER-PETERSEN. 'Das Problem der ältesten Byzantinisch-Russisch-Nordischen Beziehungen.' *Relazioni*, Vol. III: *Storia del Medioevo*, pp. 165 ff., ed. *Comitato internaz. di scienze storiche, X congresso internaz.* Rome, 1955.

JOHANNES STEENSTRUP. 'Normandiets Historie under de syv første Hertuger 911–1066' (with a summary in French). *Det. kgl. danske Vidensk. Selsk. Skrifter*, 7. Række. Copenhagen, 1925.

JEAN ADIGARD DES GAUTRIES. *Les noms de personnes scandinaves en Normandie de 911 à 1066.* Lund, 1954.

EJNAR DYGGVE. 'The Royal Barrows at Jelling.' *Antiquity* 88. December 1948, pp. 190 ff.

EJNAR DYGGVE. 'Gorm's Temple and Harald's Stave-Church at Jelling'. *Acta Archaeologica,* Vol. XXV. 1954, pp. 221 ff.

H. SHETELIG. 'An Introduction to the Viking History of Western Europe.' *Viking Antiquities in Great Britain and Ireland.* ed. by H. Shetelig. Part I, Oslo, 1940.

P. DU CHATELLIER & L. LE PONTOIS. 'La sépulture scandinave à barque de l'Île de Groix.' *Bulletin de la Soc. Arch. du Finistère,* Vol. XXXV. Quimper, 1908.

J. STEFANSSON. 'Vikings in Spain.' *Saga-Book of the Viking Club,* VI, 1909.

K. GJERSET. *History of Iceland.* London, 1924.

P. NØRLUND & M. STENBERGER. 'Brattahlid. Researches into Norse Culture in Greenland.' *Meddelelser om Grønland,* Vol. 88: 1. Copenhagen, 1934.

LIS JACOBSEN. *Svenskevældets fald.* Copenhagen, 1929.

T. J. ARNE. 'Le Voyage d'ibn Fadlan à Bulgar.' *Fornvännen.* Stockholm, 1941.

T. J. ARNE. 'Die Varägerfrage und die sovjetische Forschung.' *Acta Archaeologica* XXIII. Copenhagen, 1952.

W. HOVGAARD. *The Voyages of the Norsemen to America.* New York, 1915.

H. HERMANSSON. 'The Problem of Wineland.' *Islandica,* Vol. 25. 1936.

J. BRØNDSTED. 'Norsemen in North America before Columbus.' *Smithsonian Institution, Annual Report* 1953. Washington, 1954, pp. 367 ff.

CHAPTER 6 and 7

JAN PETERSEN. 'De norske vikingesverd. En typologisk-kronologisk studie over vikingetidens vaaben.' *Videnskaps-selskapets skrifter* II. Hist.-filos. klasse no. 1. Oslo, 1919.

JAN PETERSEN. *Vikingetidens smykker.* Stavanger, 1928.

JAN PETERSEN. 'Vikingetidens redskaper' (with a summary in English). *Skrifter utgitt av Det norske Videnskaps-Akademi i Oslo* II Hist.-filos. klasse no. 4. Oslo, 1951.

C. A. NORDMAN. 'Vapnen i Nordens forntid.' *Nordisk Kultur,* Vol. XIIB, *Vaaben,* pp. 46 ff. Stockholm-Oslo-Copenhagen, 1943.

ADA BRUHN HOFFMEYER. *Middelalderens tveæggede sværd* I-II. Copenhagen, 1954 (with a summary in English).

P. PAULSEN. *Axt und Kreuz bei den Nordgermanen.* Berlin, 1939.

D. SELLING. *Wikingerzeitliche und frühmittelalterliche Keramik in Schweden.* Stockholm, 1955.

BJØRN HOUGEN. 'Osebergfunnets billedvev.' *Viking,* Vol. IV. Oslo, 1940.

AGNES GEIJER. 'Die Textilfunde aus den Gräbern.' *Birka, Untersuchungen und Studien,* Vol. III. Uppsala, 1938.

SUNE LINDQVIST. *Gotlands Bildsteine,* I-II. Stockholm, 1941-2.

K. FRIIS JOHANSEN. 'Le trésor d'argenterie de Terslev.' *Mémoires de la soc. royale des antiquaires du Nord.* 1908–13, pp. 329 f.

R. SKOVMAND. 'Les trésors danois provenant de l'époque des vikings et Moyen Âge le plus ancien jusqu'aux environs de 1150.' *Aarbøger for nordisk Oldkyndighed og Historie,* 1942, pp. 1 ff.

S. GRIEG. 'Vikingetidens skattefund.' *Universitetets oldsaksamlings skrifter,* Vol. II. Oslo, 1929.

M. STENBERGER. *Die Schatzfunde Gotlands der Wikingerzeit.* Vol. II *Fundbeschreibung und Tafeln,* Lund, 1947; Vol. I *Text,* Stockholm, 1958.

<h2 style="text-align:center">CHAPTER 8</h2>

H. SHETELIG. 'Tuneskipet.' *Norske Oldfunn.* Vol. II. Christiania [Oslo], 1917.

N. NICOLAYSEN. *Langskibet fra Gokstad ved Sandefjord.* Christiania [Oslo], 1882.

A. W. BRØGGER, HJ. FALK, S. GRIEG, & H. SHETELIG. *Oseberg funnet.* Utgitt av Den norske stat, Vols. I–IV. Christiania [Oslo], 1917–1928.

A. W. BRØGGER & H. SHETELIG. *Vikingeskipene. Deres forgjengere og etterfølgere.* Oslo, 1950.

THORLEIF SJØVOLD. *Osbergfunnet og de andre vikingskipsfunn.* Oslo, 1957.

H. MÖTEFINDT. 'Der Wagen im nordischen Kulturkreise zur vorund frühgeschichtlichen Zeit.' *Festschrift Eduard Hahn,* 1917, pp. 209 ff.

GÖSTA BERG. 'Sledges and Wheeled Vehicles.' *Nordiska Museets Handlingar,* no. 4. Stockholm, 1935, pp. 65 and 155 f.

SUNE LINDQVIST. 'Färdesätt och färdemedel.' Quoted in the author's book: *Svenskt forntidsliv.* Stockholm, 1944, pp. 248 ff.

<h2 style="text-align:center">CHAPTER 9</h2>

SOPH. MÜLLER & C. NEERGAARD. 'Danevirke, archæologisk undersøgt, beskrevet og tydet.' *Nordiske Fortidsminder* I, Copenhagen, 1903.

H. JANKUHN. *Die Wehranlagen der Wikingerzeit zwischen Schlei und Treene.* Neumünster, 1937.

H. JANKUHN. *Die Ausgrabungen in Haithabu* (1937–9). Berlin, 1943.

H. JANKUHN. *Haithabu, ein Handelsplatz der Wikingerzeit.* Neumünster, 1956.

H. JANKUHN. 'Die Frühgeschichte vom Ausgang der Völkerwanderung bis zum Ende der Wikingerzeit.' *Geschichte Schleswig-Holsteins*, Vol III. Neumünster, 1955–7.

H. JANKUHN. 'Die frühmittelalterlichen Seehandelsplätze im Nordund Ostseeraum.' *Vorträge und Forschungen*, Vol. IV, Lindau, 1958.

VILH. LA COUR. *Danevirkestudier. En arkæologisk-historisk Undersøgelse.* Copenhagen, 1951.

OTTO KUNKEL & K. A. WILDE. *Jumne, 'Vineta', Jomsburg, Julin: Wollin.* Stettin, 1941.

B. EHRLICH. 'Der preussisch-wikingische Handelsplatz Truso.' I. *Balt. histor. Kongress.* Riga, 1938.

H. ARBMAN. *Birka, Sveriges äldsta handelsstad.* Stockholm, 1939.

H. ARBMAN. *Birka, Untersuchungen und Studien*, Vol. I. Stockholm, 1943.

H. ARBMAN. in *Situne Dei, Sigtuna fornhems årsbok*, Sigtuna, 1942.

H. ARBMAN. 'Hague-Dike. Les fouilles en 1951 et 1952.' *Meddelanden från Lunds Univ.'s hist. museum.* Lund, 1953.

POUL NØRLUND. 'Trelleborg.' *Nordiske Fortidsminder* IV 1. Copenhagen, 1948 (with a summary in English).

C. G. SCHULTZ. 'Vikingetidshuset paa Trelleborg.' *Fra Nationalmuseets Arbejdsmark*, 1942, pp. 17 ff.

PALLE LAURING & A. HOFF-MØLLER. 'Trelleborghusets rekonstruktion.' *Aarbøger for nordisk Oldkyndighed og Historie*, 1952, pp. 108 ff. (with a summary in English).

J. LARSEN. 'Rekonstruktion af Trelleborg.' *Aarbøger for nordisk Oldkyndighed og Historie*, 1957 pp. 56 ff. (with a summary in English).

C. G. SCHULTZ. 'Aggersborg. Vikingelejren ved Limfjorden.' *Fra Nationalmuseets Arbejdsmark*, 1949, pp. 91 ff.

H. P. L'ORANGE. 'Trelleborg–Aggersborg og de kongelige byer i Østen.' *Viking*, Vol. XVI, 1952, pp. 307 ff.

CHAPTERS 10—12

Nordisk Kultur Vol. XXIX, Mønt. Denmark: G. Galster pp. 141 ff.; Sweden: B. Thordeman pp. 7 ff.; Norway: Hans Holst pp. 95 ff. Stockholm–Oslo–Copenhagen, 1936.

A. W. BRØGGER. 'Ertog og øre. Den gamle norske vegt.' *Videnskapsselskapets skrifter*, Vol. II. Hist.-filos. klasse no. 3, Christiania [Oslo], 1921.

T. J. ARNE. 'La Suède et l'Orient.' *Archives d'études orientales publiées par J. A. Lundell*, Vol. VIII. Uppsala, 1914.

Nordisk Kultur, Vol. VI, *Runerne*, pp. 83 ff. (Magnus Olsen, J. Brøndum-Nielsen, Otto v. Friesen). Stockholm-Oslo-Copenhagen, 1933.

LIS JACOBSEN & E. MOLTKE. *Danmarks Runeindskrifter*. Copenhagen, 1942.

Norges innskrifter med de yngre runer, Vol. I ff., ed. Magnus Olsen. Oslo, 1944 ff.

Sveriges runinskrifter, Vol. I ff., ed. Søderburg, Brate, Wessén, Kinander, Jungner. Uppsala, 1900 ff.

A. BÆKSTED. *Målruner og troldruner. Runemagiske studier* (with a summary in English). Copenhagen, 1952.

E. WESSÉN. 'Om vikingatiden runor.' *Filologiskt Arkiv* VI (with a summary in German). Stockholm, 1957.

E. WESSEN. 'Runstenen vid Röks kyrka.' *Kungl. Vitt. Hist. och Antikvitets Akademiens Handlingar*, filol.-filosof. serien. Stockholm, 1958.

P. KERMODE. *Manx Crosses*. London, 1907.

H. SHETELIG. 'Stil- og tidsbestemmelser i de nordiske korsene paa øen Man.' in *Opuscula archaeologica Oscari Montelio dicata*. Stockholm, 1918.

The Guildhall-runestone: *Vict. Hist. Co.* I, London, pp. 167 f.

The Berezanj-runestone: H. Arbman. *Svear i Østerviking*. Stockholm, 1955, p. 153, cf. p. 159.

SOPHUS MÜLLER. *Die Thier-Ornamentik im Norden*. Hamburg, 1881.

H. SHETELIG. *Osebergfunnet*, Vol. III, Christiania [Oslo], 1920.

JOHANNES BRØNDSTED. *Early English Ornament*. London, 1924.

Nordisk Kultur, Vol. XXVII, *Kunst*, pp. 124 ff. (Jan Petersen, Sune Lindqvist, C. A. Nordman). Stockholm-Oslo-Copenhagen, 1931.

H. ARBMAN. *Schweden und das karolingische Reich*. Stockholm, 1937.

H. ARBMAN. 'The Skabersjö Brooch and some Danish Mounts.' *Meddelanden från Lunds Univ. Hist. Mus.* 1956, pp. 93 ff.

N. ÅBERG. 'Keltiska och orientaliska stilinflytelser i vikingatidens nordiska konst.' *Kungl. Vitt. Hist. Antikv. Handlingar*, Stockholm, 1941 (with a summary in English).

G. ARWIDSSON. *Vendelstile, Email und Glas*. Uppsala, 1942.

J.-E. FORSSANDER. 'Irland–Oseberg.' *Meddelanden från Lunds Univ. Hist. Mus.* 1943, pp. 294 ff.

SUNE LINDQVIST. 'Osebergmästarna.' *Tor*, Uppsala, 1948.

T. D. KENDRICK. *Late Saxon and Viking Art*. London, 1949.

H. SHETELIG. 'The Norse Style of Ornamentation in the Viking Settlements.' *Acta Archaeologica*, 1948.

H. SHETELIG. *Classical Impulses in Scandinavian Art from the Migration Period to the Viking Age*. Oslo, 1949.

H. SHETELIG. 'Religionshistoriske drag fra vikingetidens stilhistorie.' *Viking*, 1950.

W. HOLMQVIST. 'Germanic Art During the First Millennium A.D.' *Kungl. Vitt. Hist. och Antikv. Handlingar*. Stockholm, 1955.

SUNE LINDQVIST. *Gotlands Bildsteine*, Vol. I–II. Stockholm, 1941–2.

H. SHETELIG. 'Billedfremstillinger i jernalderens kunst.' *Nordisk Kultur*, Vol. XXVII, *Kunst*, pp. 214 ff.

CHAPTERS 13—15

ADAM BREMENSIS, magister, see above under Chapter 2.

P. V. GLOB. *Ard og plov i Nordens oldtid*. Aarhus, 1951 (with a summary in English).

BJØRN HOUGEN. *Fra seter til gård. Studier i norsk bosetning-historie*. Oslo, 1947.

Nordisk Kultur, Vol. XVII, *Bygningskultur*: Sweden pp. 31 ff., Norway pp. 59 ff. (M. Stenberger); North-Atlantic islands pp. 108 ff. (Aa. Roussell). Stockholm–Oslo–Copenhagen, 1953.

AA. ROUSSELL. *Norse Building Customs in the Scottish Isles*. Copenhagen–London, 1934.

Forntida gårdar i Island. ed. M. Stenberger. Copenhagen, 1943 (with a summary in English).

P. NØRLUND. *Meddelelser om Grønland*, Vol. 76, 1930; Vol. 88, 1934 (Gardar, Herjolfsnes, Brattahlid).

R. MEISSNER. *Beiträge zur Geschichte der deutschen Sprache und Literatur*, Vol. 57, 1933 (ab. *Rigsthula*).

JEAN I. YOUNG. *Arkiv för nordisk filologi*, Vol. 49, 1933 (ab. *Rigsthula*).

K. V. AMIRA. 'Recht.' Paul, *Grundriss der germanischen Philologie*, 1913.

CL. V. SCHWERIN. *Germanische Rechtsgeschichte*. 1936.

V. GRØNBECH. *The Culture of the Teutons,* Vol. I–II. London–Copenhagen, 1931.

Anthropology. Denmark: *Acta Archaeologica,* Vol. VII, 1936, pp. 224 ff.; P. Nørlund, *Trelleborg,* 1948, pp. 112 ff.; Norway: K. E. Schreiner, *Crania Norvegica,* Oslo, 1946; Iceland: *Forntida gårdar i Island,* ed. M. Stenberger (pp. 227 ff., by Jón Steffensen). Copenhagen, 1943.

SK. V. GUDJONSSON. *Folkekost og Sunhedsforhold i gamle Dage.* Copenhagen, 1941.

A. BUGGE. *Vesterlandenes indflydelse paa nordboernes og særlig nordmændenes ydre kultur, levesæt og samfundsforhold,* Christiania [Oslo], 1905.

A. WALSH. *Scandinavian Relations with Ireland during the Viking Period.* Dublin, 1922.

F. M. STENTON. *Anglo-Saxon England.* Oxford, 1947 (pp. 495 ff., 'The Danelaw').

JOHANNES STEENSTRUP. See above under Chapters 3–5.

H. BIRKELAND. See above under Chapter 2.

JAN DE VRIES. *Altnordische Literaturgeschichte,* Vols. I–II. Berlin, 1941–2.

F. JÓNSSON. *Den oldnorske og oldislandske litteraturs historie,* Vols. I & III. Copenhagen, 1920–4.

G. VIGFUSSON & F. YORK POWELL. *Corpus Poeticum Boreale, the Poetry of the Old Northern Tongue from the Earliest Times to the Thirteenth Century,* edited, classified, and translated with Introduction, Excursus, and Notes, Vols. I & II. Oxford, 1883.

A. HEUSLER. *Die altgermanische Dichtung.* Potsdam, 1941.

G. NECKEL. *Die altnordische Literatur.* Leipzig, 1923.

JAN DE VRIES. *Altgermanische Religionsgeschichte,* Vols. I & II. Berlin, 1956–7.

FR. VON DER LEYEN. *Die Götter der Germanen.* Munich, 1938.

G. DUMÉZIL. *Loki. (Les Dieux et les hommes,* Vol. I.) Paris, 1948.

M. OLSEN. *Farms and Fanes of Ancient Norway. The Place-Names of a Country Discussed in their Bearings on Social and Religious History.* Oslo, 1928.

Nordisk Kultur, Vol. V, *Stednavne.* Stockholm-Oslo-Copenhagen, 1939.

S. K. AMTOFT. *Nordiske Gudeskikkelser i bebyggelseshistorisk Belysning.* Copenhagen, 1948.

NILS LID. 'Scandinavian Heathen Cult Places.' *Folk-Liv*, Vols. XXI & XXII. Stockholm, 1957–8.

F. STRÖM. 'Diser, norner, valkyrjor. Fruktbarhetskult och sakralt kungadöme i Norden.' *Kungl. Vitt. Hist. Antikv. Akad. Handlingar*, filolog.-filosof. serien 1 (with a summary in German). Stockholm, 1954.

E. DYGGVE in *Acta Archaeologica*, 1954, and in *Antiquity*, 1948; see above under Chapter 3.

A. W. BRØGGER & H. SHETELIG. *Vikingeskipene*. Oslo, 1950, pp. 92 ff.

J. BRØNDSTED. 'Danish Inhumation Graves of the Viking Age.' *Acta Archaeologica*, Vol. VII, 1936.

TH. RAMSKOU. 'Viking Age Cremation Graves in Denmark.' *Acta Archaeologica*, Vol. XXI, 1950.

H. ARBMAN. *Birka, Untersuchungen und Studien*, Vols. I & II, *Die Gräber*. Stockholm, 1943.

H. JANKUHN. *Haithabu, ein Handelsplatz der Wikingerzeit*. Neumünster, 1956, pp. 104 ff.

TH. RAMSKOU. 'Lindholm, Preliminary Report.' *Acta Archaeologica*, Vol. XXIV, 1953. Ibid. 1955 and 1957.

Viking Antiquities in Great Britain and Ireland, ed. H. Shetelig. Oslo, 1940.

O. ALMGREN. 'Vikingatidens gravskik i verkligheten och i den fornnordiska litteraturen.' *Nordiska studier tillägnade Adolf Noreen*. Uppsala, 1904.

H. ARBMAN. *Svear i Österviking*. Stockholm, 1955, pp. 81 ff. (Gnezdovo).

H. LJUNGBERG. *Den nordiska religionen och kristendomen. Studier över det nordiska religionsskiftet under vikingatiden*. Uppsala, 1938.

INDEX